ADVANCE PRAISE FOR
Mountain of Paradise

Praise for the first edition:
" ... [this] brilliant essay points to the future of California studies better than any comparable statement I have ever read."
—Kevin Starr, late University Professor and Professor of History, University of Southern California, author of *Americans and the California Dream* series

Praise for the new edition:
"The best and most defining writing about California has always been visionary. In *Mountain of Paradise* Josef Chytry joins a visionary company of historians, explorers, travelers, wayfarers, and natives who know how to summon a spirit of place. As a philosophical history, *Mountain of Paradise* is remarkable for its vivacity of style, its prodigious learning in many languages, its range in time and space. A decade ago, Chytry proposed "Greater California" as that realm was defined during Spain's long dominion as a world civilization. This 2025 reissue raises the question of whether California, which has a geopolitical heft exceeding that of all but five or six nation-states, might be deserving of sovereignty, a question that current events make more urgent by the day. This eloquent and searching book is equal to the hour we are living."
—David Reid, Editor of the Berkeley magazine *Dispatches*

"Fit with sharp interdisciplinary acumen, Josef Chytry has offered one of the richest accounts of California's vigorous culture and life. Capturing key features of California's dynamic identity with its social and political consequences for understanding the history and future course of the world, the re-release of *Mountain of Paradise* at this important moment underscores the unique role California continues to play with ever-increasing relevance to world civilization."
—Jason S. Sexton, UCLA Department of Sociology and Institute of the Environment and Sustainability, editor of *Redemptive Dreams: Engaging Kevin Starr's California*

Mountain of Paradise

Josef Chytry

Mountain of Paradise

Reflections on the Emergence of Greater California as a World Civilization

PETERLANG
New York - Berlin - Bruxelles - Chennai - Lausanne - Oxford

Library of Congress Control Number: 2025008314

Bibliographic information published by the Deutsche Nationalbibliothek.
The German National Library lists this publication in the German
National Bibliography; detailed bibliographic data is available
on the Internet at http://dnb.d-nb.de.

This book is a second revised edition of *Mountain of Paradise* by the same author, published by Peter Lang Publishing Inc. in 2013 (ISBN 978-1-4331-2322-1).

Cover design by Peter Lang Group AG
Cover artwork and photograph by Olivia Wise.

ISBN 978-3-0343-5857-6 (paperback)
ISBN 978-3-0343-5858-3 (ebook)
ISBN 978-3-0343-5859-0 (epub)
DOI 10.3726/b22888

© 2025 Peter Lang Group AG, Lausanne
Published by Peter Lang Publishing Inc., New York, USA
info@peterlang.com - www.peterlang.com

All rights reserved.
All parts of this publication are protected by copyright.
Any utilization outside the strict limits of the copyright law, without the permission of the publisher, is forbidden and liable to prosecution.
This applies in particular to reproductions, translations, microfilming, and storage and processing in electronic retrieval systems.

This publication has been peer reviewed.

Die Zeiten ändern sich und mit ihnen die
Anforderungen. So ändern sich die Jahreszeiten
im Lauf des Jahres. So gibt es auch in Weltenjahr
Frühling und Herbst der Völker und Nationen, die
gesellschaftliche Umgestaltungen erfordern.
      "Die Umwälzung (Die Mauserung)"

"The times change and with them the demands.
Thus the seasons change in the course of the
year. Thus also in the world cycles there are
spring and fall of peoples and nations, which
demand social transformations."
      "Revolution (Molting)," *I Ching*
      (Richard Wilhelm translation)

est locus, Hesperiam Grai cognomine dicunt,
terra antiqua, potens armis atque ubere glaebae; ...
hae nobis propriae sedes,

"There is a place called 'Hesperia' by the Greeks,
an ancient land, powerful, warlike rich; ...
Here is our rightful home,"
      Virgil, *The Aeneid*, iii, 163–164, 167

"What America is to Europe, what Western America is to Eastern,
that California is to the other Western states. It has more than any other
the character of a great country, capable of standing alone in the world."
      Lord Bryce, *The American Commonwealth*

To my son Gabriel and daughter Sophia,
native-born Californians

Acknowledgments

This inquiry began thanks to the initiation of Michael Bielicky in arranging an invitation for me to lecture on California civilization at the Center for Theoretical Study at Charles University, Prague, Czech Republic, in 2003. Subsequently Peter Murphy generously agreed to publish a developed version of the lecture as "California Civilization" in a special issue of *Thesis Eleven*. Chapter 1 is a further version of the lecture and article.

Once launched on the theme, I was grateful to be invited to present a paper at the annual conference of the Western Humanities Alliance at the University of Arizona in 2005 which was then published in a special issue of the *Western Humanities Review* as "Bordering the Civilization of Greater California: An Inquiry into Genealogy, Treaty-Making and Influence." Chapter 2 is a fuller account of my paper and article.

Particularly with its inclusion of Franz Werfel, Chapter 3 is a larger version of the article "California Civilization and European Speculative Thought: An Evolving Relationship" published in *California History* in 2008, for which I am particularly grateful for the illustrations provided for the publication version by Shelly Kale.

Chapter 4 is largely based on my article "California Irredenta" published in *History and Theory* in 2011 thanks to Brian Fay.

Finally, Chapter 5 stems from my participation in a Max Planck Institute workshop on "emotional styles – communities and spaces" that was held in Berlin, Germany, in 2010. Thanks to Benno Gammerl, it was published as "Walt Disney and Emotional Environments: Interpreting Walt Disney's Oeuvre from the Disney Studios to Disneyland, CalArts, and the Experimental Prototype Community of Tomorrow (EPCOT)" in a special issue of *Rethinking History* in 2012, while thanks to Stuart Kendall a somewhat different and shorter version was published as "Disney's Design: Imagineering Main Street" in a special issue of *Boom: A Journal of California* in 2012.

As primarily a European intellectual historian I would never have ventured on this project without the inspiring guidance of the oeuvre of Kevin Starr, particularly his monumental *Americans and the California Dream* series.

I am particularly grateful to the many inputs from students attending my course "California civilization" given at the California College of the Arts over the past decade as well as the consistent financial support provided by Faculty Development Grants of the College.

As ever, I could always count on my daughter Sophia and son Gabriel: "home-grown" Californians.

Contents

Introduction: Ruminations on the Prospects of a Civilization of Greater Califonia – *After* 2024 xiii

Introduction 1

1. Beyond the United States of America? California as a World Civilization 5

2. Bordering the Civilization of Greater California: An Inquiry into Genealogy, Treaty-Making and Influence 33

3. The Coming of European Speculative Thought: Three Stages 69

4. A Golden Age? The California Fifties as Watershed 107

5. California Political Economy: The Emotional Environments of Walt Disney 125

6. Metaglobal California: California Irredenta 149

Epilogue: California and the *Paradiso* 173

Bibliography 181

Introduction:
Ruminations on the Prospects of a Civilization of Greater Califonia – *After* 2024[1]

January 2025

The historic turning point marked by the Presidential election of 2024 raises the following striking question:

How ready – *or* willing – is California to join the collection of independent Sovereign States in the world today?

My book *Mountain of Paradise*[2] first coined the term "the Civilization of Greater California" to encompass, beyond the familiar rubric "California civilization," lands subsumed under the former Hispanic *California* or *Las Californias*. Within a modern context the term was intended to cover the massive U.S. state of California clout over those same territories. Granted its recent and present status (as of 2024) as possibly the fourth or fifth largest economy in the world, it was speculated that problems would continue to arise that "might well be inevitable in principle once California had surpassed a certain index of global economic and cultural power without acquiring full sovereign control over its resources, and such fallout may be the price that a politically constricted, albeit 'mega-state' *may have to be prepared to pay into the indefinite future.*"[3]

That was 2013. In 2020, the year of the Great Covid Pandemic, Gregory Treverton and Karen Treverton[4] -- the former a highly respected University of Southern California academic and previous member of important U.S. national security institutions -- opined, on the basis of the increasing acrimonies between blue and red U.S. states, that "the American union will not hold." Pinpointing the impact of that thought on such U.S. states as Florida, Texas, and California, the authors quote California Governor Gavin Newsom's classification of California as already a "nation-state" -- something incidentally touted much earlier by

---

1   My thanks to David Reid for originally suggesting an updated essay along such lines on California civilization. I am also deeply indebted to Gregory Treverton and David Teece for their reading of an earlier draft and for very helpful suggestions.
2   Josef Chytry, *Mountain of Paradise: Reflections on the Emergence of Greater California as a World Civilization* (New York, NY: Peter Lang, 2013).
3   Chytry [2013], 134 (emphasis added).
4   Gregory F. Treverton & Karen Treverton, "Is California nearing its 'Boston Tea Party Moment'?," *The Hill* (3 May 2020).

xiii

former California Governor Arnold Schwarzenegger around 2005 (probably following the lead of California state historian Kevin Starr).[5]

Covid and its Discontents have also brought an added characteristic of present-day California into the mix. As Dan Waters, writing for the *East Bay Times*,[6] pointed out by drawing on newer California Department of Finance and State Population Reports, these days the California population is flattening out at "just under 40 million." Such a disclosure is worth noting, granted its contrast to the meteoric growth of the California population during the entire twentieth century, and was signaled when, for its share of the pie of 435 House of Representatives seats, California added only one seat from the 2000 census, nothing from the 2010 census, and lost one seat in the 2020 census. Listing Covid's probably constricting effects over certainly the 2021–2023 economic landscape, an overall long-term decline in the "Anglo" population, and net emigration to other U.S. states, Waters concluded that it may even turn out this same population could actually decline (at present it stands at 38.97 million [2023 estimate]).

Add a third feature and the preconditions for a distinctly sovereign California take on further intriguing ramifications. That feature concerns the percentile distributions among California's present ethnic populations, a far cry from the "Anglo-Saxon" combine predominating during much of the twentieth century when the state advanced to its present preeminence demographically, economically, and even ideologically, although it does hark back to a much older Hispanic California launched long ago on the third of May 1535, when that paradigmatic *conquistador* Hernán Cortés presumably baptized the Bay of La Paz as "California." With the Latino population leaping past the Anglo at around 39% (and rising), the Asian advancing to 14–15%, and the African-American dropping to 5.7% (compared to a general 12–13% for the United States as a whole), shares of claims on California wealth and identity might easily take on new contestatory contortions. All this incidentally, quite apart from the simultaneously widening gap between general wealth and poverty/destitution.

Context requires historical guidance of a sort. Kevin Starr's original magisterial "California Dream" series came to include Starr's later exhaustive volume on the 1990–2003 period,[7] as well as his concise rendering of an overall California History that added allusions to the missing decades.[8] Indeed, Starr's

---

5 See the references in Chytry [2013], 132.
6 Dan Waters, *East Bay Times* (21 May 2020).
7 Notwithstanding his modest disclaimer that "it is merely a collection of snapshots and sketches." Kevin Starr, *Coast of Dreams: California on the Edge, 1990–2003* (New York, NY: Alfred A. Knopf, 2004), xii.
8 Kevin Starr, *California: A History* (New York, NY: The Modern Library, 2005).

closing assessment, shortly before his death in 2017, claimed that "the Golden Age of California is *now*," thanks to more equity, diversification, and indeed globalization. To drive home these points, Starr simultaneously endorsed a "global California" propounded by his colleague Abraham Lowenthal;[9] nor was Starr anything less than enthusiastic about his "great hope" for the growth of a new more Latino California urged by David Hayes-Bautista.[10]

To the cynic such apparent exhortations must smack of special pleading, particularly in light of the range of policies that have proved an environmental train wreck on much of the land through frequently unreflective growth projects. Yet Starr himself was being perfectly sincere in his outspoken vision of a "Mediterranean" California – what his friend Forrest G. Robinson once described as Starr's "best possible California – a Mediterranean Catholic California."[11] -- of which he may have hoped to be the "high priest." If the option of a continued "Wilderness" California was never much in the cards, there were singular moments when Starr's California still faced a choice between a world of irrigated farmlands owned by Jeffersonian yeomen farmers and a universe of cities and suburbs.[12] To be sure, California did after all go for the "big cities" and Starr himself seems to have been partly seduced by the striking results of Los Angeles as "possessed…of a city-state identity second only to the national allegiance." Nor was he less than impressed by the subsequent expansion of this economic behemoth and its growth policies after the second world war: "the California moment" as he put it.[13] Only subsequently did Starr ruefully acknowledge and trace out the environmental wreckage that derived, at least partly, from an extensive range of

---

9   "California is Free, Vibrant and Diverse: Interview with Kevin Starr," 28 July, *Los Angeles Times* (2009), emphasis added. "Foreword" to Abraham F. Lowentahl, *Global California: Rising to the Cosmopolitan Challenge* (Stanford, CA: Stanford University Press), ix-xi.
10 See Starr's praise on the cover of David E. Hayes-Bautista, *La Nueva California: Latinos in the Golden State* (Berkeley, CA: University of California Press, 2004). Hayes-Bautista pointedly mentions "the Yankee-Latin society discerned by Kevin Starr, which flourished from the 1830s to the 1880s" (206).
11 Albeit one which, Robinson quickly adds, "never had a chance." Forrest G. Robinson, "Spiritual Radiance, Expressive Delight: The Baroque Historiography of Kevin Starr," *California History* (Winter 1999–2000), 280.
12 As formulated by Starr himself. Kevin Starr, *Material Dreams: Southern California through the 1920s* (New York, NY: Oxford University Press, 1990), 61. Starr's later articulation of the options was: "the family farm versus agribusiness, a civilized yeomanry living on the land versus corporate ownership farming vast acreages with advanced machinery and hired help." Kevin Starr, *Golden Dreams: California in an Age of Abundance, 1950–1963* (New York, NY: Oxford University Press, 2009), 276.
13 Kevin Starr, *Embattled Dreams: California in War and Peace, 1940–1950* (New York, NY: Oxford University Press, 2002), 266.

practices making at least some of that growth possible: after all, "the entire civilization of California rested on arrogant assumptions of water appropriation."[14]

All the same it does seem that Starr would have been unwilling to entirely renounce the accompanying affluence attached to the status of postwar California as "the very model of the social democratic experience."[15] In fairness to Starr, it should be added that Starr himself consistently pinned the culprit responsible for this larger turn of events to the early control of Californian land by "a few individuals or corporations" sustaining a land monopoly "that thwarted Jeffersonian hopes for a yeoman life on the land,"[16] and it was Starr who made sure to also single out the many efforts, utopian, communal, and collectivist, already at U.S. California's origins to keep that dream alive. Notwithstanding recurrent disasters, the "California Dream," such as it is, may not be fully disengageable from persisting visions of California as an ongoing "Paradise" (in the strict ancient Persian sense of a "walled garden"), thanks to its undeniable fecundity for further natural and human evolution while protected by the soaring ramparts of the Sierras. After all, one of the most prominent candidates for the etymological origins to "California" remains: *Karī-ī-fern*: "the Mountain of Paradise," a theory that has been rated "the most interestingly plausible."[17]

*

Is this enough to justify political sovereignty to California as, in the pointed phrasing of Carey McWilliams, "*the Great Exception*" – even, perhaps, of trumping an overarching American "Exceptionalism"?[18] In comparison candidates for state-sovereignty have often called upon far less ideological buttressing than such empyrean aspirations on California's behalf. With his carefully crafted summary of a bevy of past political states that have succeeded in dividing, Gregory Treverton helps lay out where in effect any such Californian option might possibly fit.[19]

---

14 Starr [2004], 487–588, 506. But see also David Vogel, *California Greenin': How the Golden State Became an Environmental Leader* (Princeton, NJ: Princeton University Press, 2018). The paradox is perhaps best captured by Starr [2005]: "A society that had consumed nature so wantonly, so ferociously, was paradoxically nature's most ardent advocate" (xiii).
15 Kevin Starr, *Endangered Dreams: The Great Depression in California* (New York, NY: Oxford University Press, 1996), 222.
16 Kevin Starr, *Inventing the Dream: California through the Progressive Era* (New York NY: Oxford University Press, 1985), 164.
17 Dora Beale Polk, *The Island of California: A History of the Myth* (Lincoln, NE: University of Nebraska Press, 1991), 131.
18 Carey McWilliams, *California: The Great Exception* (Westport, CT: Greenwood, 1949).
19 Gregory F. Treverton, *Dividing Divided States* (Philadelphia, PA: University of Pennsylvania Press, 2014).

As Treverton recounts from studying a host of examples, it goes without saying that amicable relations and trust should obtain from the very start between the contesting parties – obviously conditions of hostility or war can be fatal for negotiations and "good" divorces. Such negotiations should start early, avoid different timetables and "drop-dead" deadlines, and agree on an initial framing with subsequent sequencing. Where relevant, the status of the "continuing" state – the one retaining the original state identity – should be quickly agreed upon. As to specific matters: assessments of possible refugees and returnees in any exchange of populations should be clarified as quickly as possible, currency issues should be handled early and transparently, and water demands should be based on needs rather than history; as to border and security arrangements, these do not appear to throw up serious blocks to negotiations, although critical differences might arise relating to offshore claims. All in all, vision is needed on both sides by leaderships owning their responsibilities and even showing willingness to call on third parties where and when necessary. For California negotiators one might add the encouraging, if delicate, observation that, as Treverton's compendious secessionist list highlights ever since those obtrusive Panamanians broke away from Colombia in 1903, secession is not all that unique, and the "richer" side often comes out the winner.

Of course, the general challenge of secession is itself highly convoluted. To take one recent prominent example, although the Scottish independence referendum of 2014 went against leaving the United Kingdom, new pressures following Brexit encouraged the ruling Scottish National Party to push for a new referendum, partly on the grounds that conditions had radically changed, given that British withdrawal from the United Kingdom was presumably anathema to a majority of Remain-oriented Scots. In the interim a new movement calling itself the Alliance4Unity briefly fielded candidates for the Scottish Parliament in order to undermine such efforts; ironically at one time it even touted as one of its leading candidates Alan Sked, himself the Father of Brexit for launching the British UK Independence Party (UKIP) in 1993.[20] At present the secession idea seems dormant, perhaps thanks to Covid teaching the Scots the benefits of accessing the resources of London.

In any case, Californians have been more vocal about *intra*-state successions. Separation into North and South – not to mention the occasional flurry of support in the very north for a State of Jefferson – may turn out to be the more prime "secessionist" concern for at least some Californian voters. If that is so, it would arguably scotch or at least interfere with any program committed to a comprehensive gesture of sovereignty. Already floated as early as 1851, an 1859

---

20   Alan Sked, electronic communication, 24 July 2020.

state legislative bill called for the separation of North and South California; it was passed and sent to Congress, but stopped by the outbreak of the Civil War.[21] Such measures have come and gone over the succeeding centuries. The most recent actually called for a split into *three* states (the third capturing the middle agricultural counties); primed for a referendum vote, it was however thrown out by the courts for violating a right reserved solely for the U.S. Congress.[22]

Granted such preliminary matters of potential dispute, a more practical initiative may be to entertain the holding of a California State Constitutional Convention, something which might help clear the air on a host of questions about voters' aims, including the secessionist option, for a future California. In itself the justification for such convening rests on a number of factors. At a minimum California's antiquated 1879 constitution is riddled with shortcomings attached to its size: it has been calculated that only the constitutions of the sovereign state of India and the U.S. state of Louisiana are longer. Matters that should be kept separate have been thrown into its basic principles, violating the Rousseauist distinction between fundamental laws and practical implementations and specifications. In this light the U.S. constitution remains a beacon of commendable brevity and transparency (although it too of course modestly expands with each added amendment).[23]

More substantial is the criticism that since 1879 California has grown into an entirely different muscular beast, for which fundamental rethinking on its present and future course would seem necessary to help propagate an increasingly prosperous and just polity. To be sure, the stakes at play could substantially shift to political realms undreamt of at present, as witness the dramatic prelude to the French revolution when confident aristocrats embarked in 1788 on a regaining of former privileges against the monarchy only to be trumped by more democratic and middle-class pamphleteers surging to domination of a National Assembly that helped set off the global Revolution of 1789. Still, granted that calls for a California Constitutional Convention have surfaced more than once, and although it must be expected that such a gathering would release a Pandora's Box of the most diversifying and disputative of voices especially in this Age of Social Media, these are challenges that any relatively open political process may finally need to risk.

**

---

21   Starr [1985], 19.
22   https://sf.curbed.com/2018/7/19/17590594/california-supreme-court-three-californias-cal3-split-divide
23   *California Constitution 2018 Edition* (Sacramento, CA: California Legislature, 2018).

These thoughts are simply intended to widen discussion on a variety of topics and concerns that necessarily accompany any project or vision for a future Californian civilization contemplating possible membership in the world of sovereign states. Perhaps a charitable approach for any such separation from the United States of America may draw on President Thomas Jefferson's letter of 29 January 1804, soon after he executed the Louisiana Purchase of 1803:

> "Whether we remain in one confederacy, or form into Atlantic and Mississippi confederacies, I believe not important to the happiness of either part. Those of the western confederacy will be as much our children & descendants as those of the eastern, and I feel myself as much identified with that country, in future time, as with this; and did I now foresee a separation at some future day, yet I should feel the duty & the desire to promote the western interests as zealously as the eastern, doing all the good for both portions of our future family which should fall within my power."[24]

For historian Gordon S. Wood such utterances were symptomatic of Jefferson's "strange ideas of the American nation," which was not so much a matter of "a precisely bounded territory" as of an overall "ideology" underscoring the American identity.[25]

Bearing such thoughts in mind on California, divided states, and secessions, one is left with important questions following the President election of 2024. In light of the overall victory of the Republican Party and its candidate, convicted felon and former president Donald J. Trump, it is worth noting that the four Pacific states (not counting Alaska) of California, Oregon, Washington, and Hawaii collectively voted 56–39% in favor of Trump's opponent, Vice-President Kamala Harris of California. Assuming major political adjustments and upheavals to follow in the second Trump Administration, issues of secession and, at least, states' rights would seem to take on new prominence.

One might then do well finally to mull over what turns out to be the Trevertons' closing admonition -- *and* shot: "The complexity of the divorce is reason to think about it *sooner rather than later,* and soberly."[26]

---

24 Thomas Jefferson, *Writings* (New York, NY: The Library of America, 1984), 1142–1143.
25 Gordon S. Wood, *Empire of Liberty: A History of the Early Republic, 1789–1815* (Oxford, UK: Oxford University Press, 2009), 371.
26 Treverton & Treverton [2020] (emphasis added).

Introduction

The following volume on the civilization of California and of Greater California advances a theme developed in a body of published articles over the last half-decade through which I have clarified my reading of California as a world civilization in the making (see Map 1).

The title of the volume is inspired by California historian Carey McWilliams' suggestion that the word *California* was "probably borrowed from the Persian, *Kari-i-farn*, 'the mountain of paradise'."[1] McWilliams' source was a 1922 essay by the French orientalist A. Carnoy which argued the case with considerable eloquence.[2] Fascinated as I was by this suggestion, I have never been able to find clear confirmation of McWilliams' hypothesis despite informative discussions with experts on the variants of the Persian language – ancient Avestan, Pahlavi, as well as Farsi, the language generally used today by Iranians. In the meantime, other, perhaps more plausible, alternatives for the origin of the word California have been essayed.[3]

Nonetheless, I could not lightly give up on such a genial connection between the possible origins to "California" and the mountains of the Alburz Range – including the commanding Mount Demavand – circling the north of Tehran, Iran, where I happened to be born. Legends regarding this immense range had permeated ancient Persian myths of a magical Mount Qaf or the Emerald Mountain sustaining innumerable Sufi tales that recounted the canonical pilgrim's quest toward metaphysical and spiritual Truth. So even if McWilliams' conjecture cannot be in all probability philologically sustained, "Mountain of Paradise" still conveniently serves to capture my own sense of the greatness to its signified: the realms alternatively known as *California* and *las Californias*.

Indeed, what land has been more often associated with the evocative term "Paradise" than California – whatever the justification for that claimed conjunction? And what "Paradise" is more indebted to a range of mountains for its life-sustaining powers than California with the towering peaks of its Sierra Nevada, justly celebrated by California's naturalist chronicler John Muir's paeans to its "Range of Light" and its renowned *omphalos*, the Yosemite Valley?[4]

---

1 McWilliams [1949], 3. Polk [1991] calls this theory "the most interestingly plausible" (131).
2 Carnoy [1922].
3 See Chapter 2 below for more details on the varied candidates.
4 And apparently still rising. See San Francisco Chronicle [2012].

Map 1

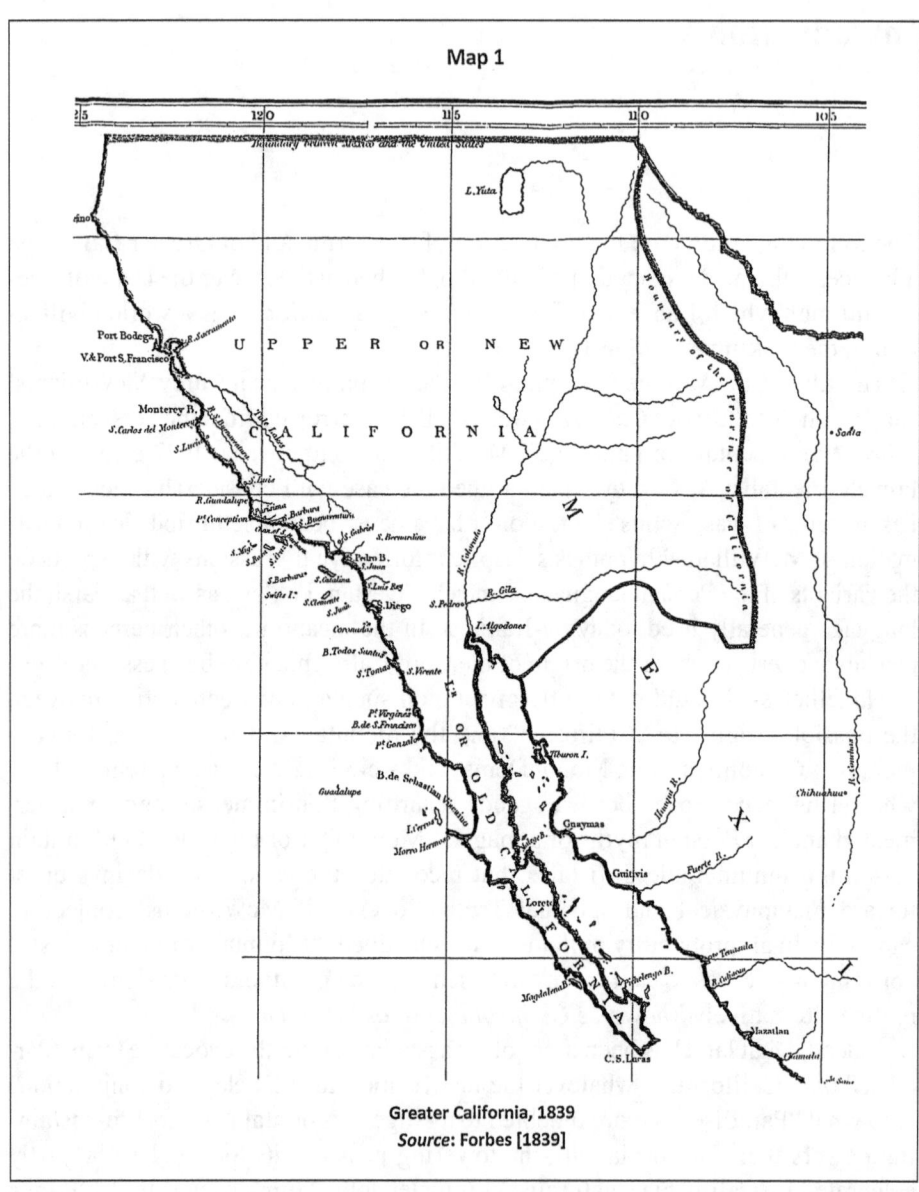

Greater California, 1839
Source: Forbes [1839]

One of the more regrettable aspects of contemporary discursivities regarding this California, this Mountain of Paradise, is the commonplace failure to recognize the deep mythical origins to the phenomenon of California which, once attached to its unprecedented growth and flowering as a global economic power – notwithstanding stern challenges of the moment –, should raise the general question: how is it that of all the global economies on the planet today, California stands out as the only one lacking sovereign political status? This volume may not directly answer that question – and the gravity of its implications, but it does push it to the forefront. To that extent its intentions differ from even the many highly researched and glowing celebrations of California.

*

Given that the original California named by the Spanish and later by the Mexicans was far more extensive than the present U.S. state of California, I have adopted the following terminology for the distinction: in the text "California" will refer to the U.S. state of California and its boundaries, while – in the spirit of irredentist nomenclatures – "Greater California" will refer to that larger realm, which once included Nevada, Utah, much of Arizona, slivers of Colorado and Wyoming, and Mexican Baja California.[5]

Finally, italicized references to *California* or *Las Californias* should be generally understood as referring to Spanish and Mexican California.

---

5   This is the sense in which the term "Greater California" is generally used in this volume. In the literature "Greater California" is sometimes applied in a different manner. For Abbott [1993], 160 (map), "Greater California" means the "domination" of economic and social patterns by the "metropolitan complexes" of California over (besides California itself) Oregon, a western sliver of Idaho, and the population centers of western Nevada and of southwestern Arizona. Pomeroy [2008] meanwhile uses it to refer to the common population growth patterns for California, western Nevada, southwestern Arizona, and Oregon (Figure 12.3, 390). See Chapter 6 below.

Chapter 1
Beyond the United States of America? California as a World Civilization[1]

Around the turn of the millennium an economic fact occurred that is worth recording. Passing the Republic of France, the U.S. state of California became the fifth economic power in the world. Admittedly, as of the date of this chapter, that same Californian economy has undergone more challenging convolutions that only recently have shown signs of letup, and the most recent estimates place California somewhere between the eighth and ninth ranks (see Table 1). Still, granted that Britain, France and Italy remain within range, and that Germany is not all that significantly ahead, nor that Japan is entirely beyond reach, a few more great surges of the Californian economy, comparable to the last burst of the dotcom 1990s, could conceivably lift California right back into the top five.

Naturally it could be argued that such surges, quite apart from the usual controversy over the validity of the indices used, whether GNP, GDP, GSP, or PPP, are ephemeral. However, excepting the steady advance of another new economic power, China, into the Valhalla of economic preeminence, it is difficult to imagine future expansion by California's immediate rivals on a scale that would match California's own constantly increasing wealth, crucial Pacific location, strategic position in all the distinctly postmodern economic sectors from high tech and media to agribusiness, university research, and green technology, possibly important new sources of oil, not to speak of the growth of a multiethnic population that, were it to advance from the present 37 million to 50 million in the next quarter-century, a not unlikely probability, would fuel further qualitative advances that could easily raise California to permanent status as anywhere between the third and fifth most powerful economy in the world.

At the same time, California has never been granted its deserved autonomy as a force to be reckoned with in world history. This myopia is often supported by such pejorative references to Californian civilization as "Lalaland," "Dream-

---

[1] An early version of this chapter was published as "California Civilization: Beyond the United States of America?," *Thesis Eleven*, 85 (May 2006), 8–36. It was originally presented as an invited lecture at the Center for Theoretical Study, Czech Academy of Sciences and Charles University, Prague, Czech Republic, on 6 August 2003. I am grateful to the Center and its Co-directors Dr. Ivan Havel and Dr. Ivan Chvatík for giving me the rare opportunity to discuss the role of California civilization with a primarily European audience and to Michael Bielicky for arranging the process of collaboration.

Table 1
World Economic Powers 2000–2010
GDP & GSP (Millions of US $)

	2000	2001	2008	2009	2010
1. United States	9,837	10,171	14,204	14,119	14,582
2. China	1,080	1,159	4,306	4,985	5,879
3. Japan	4,313	4,842	4,909	5,068	5,498
4. Germany	1,873	1,874	3,652	3,330	3,310
5. France	1,294	1,303	2,853	2,649	2,560
6. United Kingdom	1,415	1,406	2,645	2,174	2,246
7. Italy	1,074	1,091	2,293	2,112	2,051
8. Brazil	644	554	1,650	1,622	2,088
9. **CALIFORNIA**	**1,344 (5)**	**1,359 (5)**	**1,846 (8)**	**1,891 (8)**	**1,936 (9)**

GREATER CALIFORNIA (2010)

California	1,936
Arizona	261
Nevada	127
Utah	117
Baja California	28
Baja California Sur	4
Total	**2,473 (6)**

Ranking of California for given year in parentheses

Sources: World Bank; Bureau of Economic Analysis, U.S. Department of Commerce

land," "the Land of Oz," even where these same references often enough carry the underlying concern that perhaps the power of California is really here to stay – with, no doubt, deleterious effects on the rest of innocent humankind. Moreover, even in cases of more favorable classifications, the best that such boosterism is able to articulate is the status of California as a "regional civilization" rather than a civilization in itself.[2]

It is incumbent on contemporary students of global or world history to question such provincial readings. This chapter – which is primarily directed to such students – claims, first, the fact of a distinctly Californian civilization sufficiently different from (and, in time, possibly superior to) the United States of Amer-

---

[2] In the California History Sequiscentennial Series edited by Richard J. Orsi, the general preface launching the series by Michael McCone and Richard J. Orsi does state that "it is incumbent on Californians to take stock of their civilization." Gutiérrez and Orsi [1998], ix. In his mammoth and crafted study of California up to 1963 (as well as 1990–2003 as of the date of this chapter), a work that I largely follow, Kevin Starr generally speaks of California as a "regional civilization" or "regional society." See also DeWitt [1989] who is more direct in his references to a "California civilization" (vii).

ica; and, second, the contours of a history and character that students of twenty-first-century economics, politics and culture need increasingly to take into account if their reflections and predictions are to match national and international reality. Those contours, far from being summed up solely by synonyms of material wealth which seem to be one conventional stance towards Californian uniqueness, require far more comprehensive terms of art. This chapter argues that, properly applied, such terms of art may help reveal that California is possibly the only major characteristically twenty-first century civilization worth recording today.[3]

What single set of signifiers helps mark off the unique characteristics of California? Once California had settled into American rule around the late nineteenth century, the first serious efforts to capture those characteristics by a host of Californian writers, thinkers, explorers and academics settled on the majesty and towering presence of California Nature – along with concern that human and social life would always sense its own inadequacy before such natural greatness.[4] Perhaps the most imposing such statement, certainly the most prestigious at the time, is the lecture given by Harvard philosopher George Santayana to the Berkeley Philosophical Union in 1911 in which Santayana asked his California audience to pay more attention to the mountains and redwoods of their environment as stimuli to break what he called "the genteel tradition" in American philosophy and inaugurate a California philosophy reflective of its natural grandeur. In the presence of such "a virgin and prodigious world," Californians must sense "a non-human beauty and peace" which should "stir the sub-human depths and the superhuman possibilities of your own spirit," since "everywhere is beauty and nowhere permanence, everywhere an incipient harmony, nowhere an intention, nor a responsibility, nor a plan." In short, Californians must learn "to salute the wild, indifferent, non-censorious infinity of nature," as a consequence of which they would be simultaneously inspired to "speculation."[5]

---

3   A sensitive statistic to follow in the future relations between California and the United States may well be the balance of payments between California and the U.S. federal treasury in terms of fiscal outflow to the federal government. Whereas until 1987 there was a net fiscal inflow from Washington, D.C., since that period there has been a net outflow. In 2002 the imbalance set a record for any U.S. state in its relation to the federal government (succeeding the 2001 record imbalance, also involving California). In short: "As has been the case for more than a decade, California subsidizes the rest of the nation at unrivaled levels." California Institute for Federal Policy Research [2003], 8. For figures to 2005 see Table 2.
4   See the account in Starr [1973], 417–33, specifically drawing on George Santayana, Joseph Le Conte, and Luther Burbank. Also the study of Californian landscape and imagination by Wyatt [1986].
5   "The Genteel Tradition in American Philosophy (1911)," in Santayana [1967], 62, 63, 64.

Table 2
California's Balance of Payments with
The Federal Treasury, 1990 – 2005

Year	Federal Taxes Paid*	Federal Spending Received**	Taxes per capita+	Spending per capita++	Spending/Tax #
1990	135,497*	117,636**	4,551+	3,951++	0.89#
1991	137,071	128,639	4,517	4,240	0.89
1992	137,581	141,913	4,460	4,600	0.93
1993	143,298	149,383	4,593	4,788	0.95
1994	152,768	153,952	4,860	4,898	0.98
1995	163,140	153,831	5,156	4,861	0.94
1996	177,479	156,075	5,557	4,887	0.93
1997	195,099	160,884	6,027	4,970	0.92
1998	213,694	161,909	6,503	4,927	0.90
1999	235,772	168,676	7,065	5,055	0.87
2000	276,393	175,967	8,158	5,194	0.81
2001	265,608	188,758	7,718	5,485	0.82
2002	241,625	206,417	6,922	5,914	0.82
2003	233,626	219,706	6,608	6,214	0.79
2004	250,373	232,387	7,004	6,501	0.78
2005	289,627	242,023	8,028	6,709	0.78

* = Federal Taxes Paid to Federal Government
** = Federal Spending Received
\+ = Federal Taxes Paid to Federal Government per capita
++ = Federal Spending Received per capita
\# = Federal Spending Received Per Dollar of Tax Paid

Source: Tax Foundation Special Report No. 158, "Federal Tax Burdens and Spending by State";
U.S. Census Bureau
Consolidated Federal Funds Report 2005

According to California's historian Kevin Starr, Santayana's suggestion may be read to claim that "the true key to the success of California as a civilization" would be "its interior life in relationship to its environment."[6] Taking Santayana's cue as our starting-point, let us flesh out the breadth of this reference. Certainly, if California is something other than an economic statistic, it must reside in features discernible in its flora and fauna, its environment and ecosystem.

First, that ecosystem is unique. Even its geological basis stands out for originating tectonically from the subduction of the Pacific tectonic plate under the North American plate, thus producing what would eventually become an "island" of biodiversity.[7] As a result, "California has environmental diversity and richness

---

6 Starr [1973], 423.
7 "No other concept in geology is as important to understanding how California came to be so diverse than that of plate tectonics, plates sliding about on the surface of the earth." Schoen-

unparalleled anywhere in the world." Moreover, "this astounding array of Californian vegetation exists in close juxtaposition."[8] Indeed, "there is more climatic and topographic variation in California than in any region of comparable size in the United States."[9] Belonging mainly to the Mediterranean climate group, California displays far greater variety in species and landscape than other similarly classified regions of the world. It has eleven of the world's major soil groups and ten percent of all soil types in the United States, some of which are astonishingly old. Each vegetation group has its own habitat, soil and local climate, resulting in fifty types of vegetation, in a landscape that encompasses the highest as well as lowest points in the contiguous United States.[10]

Second, with regard to the human component to this ecosystem, California has been occupied for probably fifteen thousand years by native Californians who cared for it in a manner that shaped its appearance for the Spanish conquistadores who began its conquest from outside after 1535. This native Californian population formed the most populous native American region north of Mexico – possibly 310,000 at the time of European intrusion – and lived in small groupings of two to five hundred individuals "in small well-defined territories under the tradition and authority of a leader who almost always was a male." What is of even greater significance is that, as a result, native California was "one of the most linguistically diverse areas in the world", with "perhaps as many as one hundred mutually unintelligible languages."[11]

The argument of this chapter regarding Californian uniqueness thus begins with the juxtaposition of these natural and human indices. What gives "California" its unity and constancy is the fact that historically its environmental diversity was matched by its human diversity down to the presence of a uniquely rich variety of languages. That native Californians related to their natural environment in small groupings and developed languages that replicated the diversity they experienced over vast periods of time is an important key to understanding Californian history and destiny. Once the longevity of this uniqueness is granted, it becomes no accident that contemporary California is presently interpreted as posing the challenge to world history of a "new society of the new millennium"

---

    herr [1992], 58, 58–62; also Francis & Reiman [1999], 5–9, and McPhee [1993]. My thanks to Colin Day for these references.
8   M. Kat Anderson, Michael G. Barbour, and Valerie Whitworth, "A World of Balance and Plenty: Land, Plants, Animals, and Humans in a Pre-European California," in Gutiérrez & Orsi [1998], 12.
9   Schoenherr [1992], ix.
10 Anderson, Barbour & Whitworth, "A World of Balance and Plenty: Land, Plants, Animals, and Humans in a Pre-European California," in Gutiérrez & Orsi [1998], 12–47; Bakker [1971]; Schonherr [1992].
11 William S. Simmons, "Indian Peoples of California," in Gutiérrez & Orsi [1998], 56, 48.

reflecting "the state's growing diversity," in short, it carries the overall "viability of a multicultural society."[12]

If then there is an inner historical "essence" to "California," it might be worded as nothing less than, in the full natural and human sense of the word: *Biodiversity*.[13]

1.

To grasp the continuity of this thread from its beginnings, it is vital not to begin a history of California with its somewhat problematic absorption into the United States of America between 1848 and 1850, nor even to start with the arrival of the archetypal conquistador Hernán Cortés at La Paz, Baja California, on the third of May 1535, but with the fifteen thousand years of native Californian stewardship that established the matrices for humankind's affair with California. This wider context means, of course, that "California" as a reality and event precedes the United States of America, as well as even New Spain and the United Mexican States (the political entities that first baptized the ecosystem as "California"), and that therefore there is no intrinsic logic why California might not supersede such cultural and political limitations in the future.

Taking this "native" California as our necessary point of departure, one central fact stands out. The California ecosystem with which we are familiar was dramatically transformed after 1850 by European and American incursions. In contrast, the California that the conquistadores first encountered in 1535 and 1542, and then more permanently during the 1769–1823 period of Alta California missions, already reflected millennia of productive interchange between humans and wilderness:

---

12 Rawls & Bean (2003), 552; Gutiérrez & Orsi (1998), ix.
13 Notwithstanding their deep suspicion of the "myth of Paradise" against which Raab and Jones direct their collection of recent essays on California archaeology, the authors nonetheless conclude: "The state's coastal, desert, mountain, valley, and other environments provide perhaps *the most diverse range of settings for prehistorical cultural development of any region in North America*. The huge cultural-environment variability that existed in these settings during the 12,000 or more years of California prehistory offers the promise of a vast natural laboratory for comparative research" (emphasis added). Raab & Jones [2004], 211. Perhaps one reason for the authors' inconsistency in this regard is that they remain victims of a commonplace Platonist reading of the word and concept "paradise."

"What is labeled as 'wilderness' in today's popular imagination and on current topographic maps actually harbored human gathering and hunting sites, burial grounds, work sites, sacred areas, trails, and village sites. Today's wilderness was then human homeland."[14]

By their constant allusions to natural spaces as gardens, parks or orchards, the earliest non-native Californian descriptions of this landscape confirm awareness that the environments had been already modified by humans. Judiciously tended by native Californians, the forests had been more like tended gardens – cultivated woodland – with clear open spaces allowing for remarkable vegetative, fruit and floral growth while at the same time facilitating a human way of life that was neither "agriculturist" nor "hunter-gathering" – to employ the conventional vocabulary of anthropology – but true "wildland management," transforming the ecosystem into a category "between true wilderness and the domesticated garden" – a condition attested to by the earliest explorers' descriptions of California "as unsurpassed in beauty and biological wealth." In short, what native Californians confirmed for the fate of California civilization was the innate possibility "for humans to tend and use wildland resources *and* coexist as part of sustainable and diverse ecosystems."[15]

Hence, when Hernán Cortés, the recent conqueror and destroyer of Mesoamerica's mightiest power, Tenochtitlán, baptized as "California" the land that his exploring fleets first discovered on that third day of May, 1535, in Baja California, the identification was propitious. Cortés was drawing very probably on the "pulp fiction" of his day, the interminably long best-seller romance begun as *Amadís de Gaula* in the late fifteenth century and continued in 1510 by Garci Rodríguez de Montalvo as *Sergas de Esplandián*, which included a chapter on the miraculous, if "infidel," island of California: "Know ye that on the right hand of the Indies there is an island called California, very near the Terrestrial Paradise," ruled by the black "infidel" Amazon queen Calafía and her female Amazon warriors and marked by plentiful gold and griffons. Since Bernal Díaz del Castillo, the intrepid recorder of Cortés' triumphs over the Mexica, had already compared the grand vision of the Aztecs' capital city, along with its countless towers, pyramids and civic spaces, to the images in *Amadís de Gaula*,[16] it is understandable

---

14 The following summary is based on M. Kat Anderson, Michael G. Barbour, and Valerie Whitworth, 'A World of Balance and Plenty', in Gutiérrez & Orsi [1998], 14. See also Fagan [2003].

15 Gutiérrez & Orsi (1998), 38 (emphasis in original). In this volume see William S. Simmons, "Indian Peoples of California," who points out "how closely and responsibly California hunter-gatherers identified with the animals, plants, and physical terrains of their tribelet worlds" (72).

16 "These great towers and cues and buildings rising from the water, all made of stone, seemed like an enchanted vision from the tale of Amadis." Díaz del Castillo [1963], 214 (citing *Historia veradera de la conquista de Nueva España,* 1904, II, 418).

that Cortés should apply the name of a mythical island recorded in Montalvo's sequel to what appeared to be in reality an extensive island. This misinterpretation of the Baja California peninsula was faithfully recorded in canonical maps of the subsequent two centuries characteristically displaying an "Isle of California" west of the North American continent, notwithstanding practical confirmation of Baja's peninsular status as early as 1539, and required the official statement of the Spanish government as late as 1747 that "California is not an island."[17]

Yet the insular allusion would appear quite appropriate, whether or not the application, as differing interpretations contend, reflected admiration or irony over the land that had been discovered by Cortés' original squadrons. Montalvo located Queen Calafía and her Amazons on the infidel side of the Christian-Moorish spectrum where she was defeated by Prince Esplandián and converted to Christianity, but her realm, at least for the conquistadores, bears the patina of the Islamic world which had just been roundly defeated by the conquest of Islamic Granada in 1492 as partial counter to the Ottoman conquest of Christian Constantinople in 1453 (the scene of the great struggles in the *Amadís de Gaula* pageantry). The very term "conquistador" refers originally to the Spanish destroyers of the Islamic domain of al-Andalus (Andalusia), and its final conquest in 1492 released new energies, but also similar attitudes to Islamic grandeur, that the primarily Andalusian crews carried with them to the New World.[18] In later reflective works these conquistadores recalled how deeply their quests and adventures had been inspired from youth on by literature drawing on Greek romance and Persian chivalry.[19]

The bare word ("California", "Kār-ī-farn") itself therefore goes far towards suggesting "island" and "paradise." Coincidentally the ecosystem of native California had already revealed itself as a "paradise," if by paradise is understood the original Persian meaning of the word as a "walled garden."[20] Moreover, the fact that this "enclosure" itself – very close to the meaning of "mountain" in Old Persian in terms of a sacred celestial space – is concretely an "island" is confirmed by specific ecological facts. Studies of California, whether concerned with its human history or its ecology, willingly play with this notion of "island,"[21] and all

---

17   Ferdinand VII issued a royal decree in 1747 that stated: "California is not an island." Cited in Iris H. W. Engstrand, "Seekers of the 'Northern Mystery': European Exploration of California and the Pacific," in Gutiérrez & Orsi [1998], 105 (note 7).
18   See Thomas [1993], 293, 359; statistics on the predominantly Andalusian contingent of New World explorers (58, 652 (note 17)).
19   Thomas refers to Francisco Aguilar's reminiscences of the 1560s. Thomas [1993], 61.
20   For the Persian etymology of "pairidaeza," the basis for the Greek "paradeisos," see Moynihan [1979], 1–2.
21   E. g. Bakker [1971], McWilliams [1973], Polk [1991].

things considered, the word captures something essential about the Californian ecosystem: "there is ecological validity in thinking of California in insular terms." Relatively "isolated by sea, mountain range, and desert, this area has developed in its own way and at its own pace; evolutionary history here has woven numerous distinctive patterns of interaction between life form and the land." In this sense, it "is truly an 'island called California,' a singular piece of country with extremes unknown in more temperate or less diverse regions."[22] Even though the colonial processes initiated by Columbus which eventually disrupted all habitats in the New World also reached California from the earliest conquistadorean presence, California's remoteness and "its unique physical and cultural geography" delayed the process to well after its effects on the rest of the New World: "California – because of its distance from the initial European colonial emphasis in the Caribbean and Mesoamerica – was spared for 277 years the ravages of change that accompanied the founding of missions, presidios, and pueblos."[23] Eventually, it is true, invasive peoples, cultures, germs, plants and animals did succeed in forever changing the California ecosystem that had prospered at the hands of native Californians, but the delay itself is part of the story of Californian uniqueness. Even in the late nineteenth century travellers encountering California for the first time saw fit to extol its relative climatic and topographic remoteness: "The United States has here, then, a unique corner of the earth, without its like in its own vast territory, and unparalleled, so far as I know, in the world.... Except a tidal wave from Japan, nothing would seem to be able to affect or disturb it."[24]

2.

As with the rest of European colonization of the New World, the coming of Hispanic imperial priorities to California proved disastrous for the native population as well as habitat. The effect of this European presence prior to American annexation in 1848 may be summed up in three stages: (1) the period of Spanish "benign neglect" from 1535 to 1769, (2) the activist period of Spanish colonization from 1769 to 1823, and (3) the establishment of the United Mexican States after 1821.

Between 1535 (more specifically 1542 when the Spanish explorer Juan Rodríguez Cabrillo landed in what became San Diego harbor or "Alta California") and 1769 the Spanish government took minimal interest in its westernmost

---

22 Bakker [1971], xi, 309. See also Gordon [2012].
23 William Preston, "Serpent in the Garden: Environmental Change in Colonial California," in Gutiérrez & Orsi [1998], 260.
24 Warner [1891], 5.

American province. Then, after 1769, following the building of missions in Baja California starting in 1697, the Bourbon regime, replicating patterns of increasing imperial efficiency by the European powers in the eighteenth century, constructed twenty-one missions to establish a concrete presence on Californian soil. While the primary aim was to forestall the potential incursion of French and Russian forces into this region, it also began the gradual process of assimilating the native Californians, bringing in the first fruits of an Hispanic Mediterranean economy, and producing in time a modest yet distinctive population that would eventually be known as *californios*.[25]

In 1804 the Spanish government established separate administrations for Alta (Upper) and Baja (Lower) California, as a result of which the term *Las Californias* was often employed for the entire region. However, by 1821 the breakup of New Spain led to the creation of an independent Mexico, and in 1822 both Alta and Baja California were made part of a single California within the Mexican republic. Both Spain, and subsequently Mexico, negotiated with the United States on border treaties, the American acquisition of the Louisiana Purchase from Napoleonic France in 1803 having established the U.S. as the predominant outside power bordering on Alta California. The 1819 U.S.-Spanish Treaty – which included the sale of Florida to the U.S. – confirmed the line of the 42nd degree latitude, and these negotiations also served in the 1828 U.S.-Mexican Treaty for the international boundary to run from the Rocky Mountains along the Sabine River north to the 42nd degree all the way to the Pacific Ocean.

Both Spanish and Mexican rules accelerated the process of displacement and diminution of native Californian culture. Mexican secularization of the missions, which paradoxically abandoned native Californians formerly working on the missions to *californio* exploitation, and the granting of huge tracts of land to what became a ranchero economy based on cattle caused serious depletion of the native population from around 300,000 to less than half that figure immediately prior to the American intrusion. *Californios*, a sparsely populated yet emphatically hierarchical society reflecting Hispanic class patterns, were quick to distinguish themselves as "men of reason" (*gente de razón*) from native Californian "savages" (*gente sin razón*), and did not hold back from sending out hunting parties to scatter and dissolve the native Californians. On the favorable side, these same *californios* acquired an apparently deserved reputation among outsiders for the largesse of their hospitality and an elaborate code of ritual and festivity.[26]

---

25 See Osio [1996] and Beebe & Senkewicz [2001] for translations of primary Hispanic and *californio* texts.
26 Douglas Monroy, "The Creation and Re-creation of Californio Society," in Gutiérrez & Orsi [1998], 178, 173–195; and more generally Pitt [1966].

Mexican rule over California remained highly volatile, however. Not only did the *californios* stay close to the coast in relatively small kin, social and communal groupings, thereby abandoning the hinterland of mountains and the Great California Valley to the growing invasion of American settlers crossing the American continent in search of the Pacific coast, but also gubernatorial rivalries among Alta California clans stimulated autonomist tendencies among *californio* patriarchs that further unraveled Mexican control over its most outlying province. Around 1845 these variegated tendencies meshed on the eve of the Mexican-American War of 1846–8 to create a flurry of factional politics within Alta California that might well have led to a breakaway Californio Republic. At the same time *agents provocateurs* sent in by the U.S. government found allies among American settlers in the hinterland ready to dismantle Mexican rule by first declaring a "Bear Flag Republic" and helping to bring in direct U.S. control through a series of political and military moves that culminated in the solid defeat and treaty surrender of Mexican forces by early 1847. A year later the Treaty of Guadalupe Hidalgo transferred almost all of "Greater California" to direct U.S. rule.

3.

In 1848 Alta California became part of the United States and in 1850 Congress accepted California as a U.S. state. In between, American Californians gathered in 1849 to frame a constitution among themselves in order to select what became the present boundaries of American California, and – in terms of the blazing dispute at that time between "free" and "slave" states in the American Union and the overall issue of secession – to resolve firmly to constitute a free state, with no barriers toward immigration by "free negroes" and aiming at becoming "a model instrument of liberal and enlightened principles."[27] Although some members of Congress were indignant over the Californians' presumption in constituting themselves as a political organization without prior federal involvement (let alone guidance and control), important pressures that arose exactly at the same time led to the unprecedented acceptance of California – without any intervening period as a federal territory – as the thirty-first U.S. state, thus breaking the exact tie between the 15 "free" and 15 "slave" states.

---

27 On this Monterey constitutional assembly, see the excellent study by Johnson [1992], 101–138; also Brands [2002], 281, 269–304. As Brands notes, it was these Californians who decided to restrict California to its present boundaries, partly because of discomfort of association with the Mormon presence in Utah and partly because of their desire to avoid involvement in slave-state issues associated with what became the territory of New Mexico. California, it was early determined, would be resolutely a "free" state.

Those pressures stemmed from a unique event that occurred at exactly the same two-year period of transition from occupation to statehood: the discovery in January 1848 of gold in California. By the time the constitutional representatives had arrived in Washington, D.C., California's population well exceeded the required number for statehood, and a massive economic transformation had been initiated through the flood of "argonauts" in search of gold that transformed California overnight into a functional advanced economy – at least in comparison with any territory west of the Mississippi River. In the singular words of Californian historian Carey McWilliams: "In California the lights went on all at once, in a blaze, and they have never dimmed."[28] As thousands of "Argonauts", utilizing any available means of transport from overland caravans to sea passages around the tip of South America or through the Panama isthmus, poured into California, an infrastructure sprang up to support their countless needs and to serve the mining operations that overnight became necessary. These immigrants came from all parts of the world, including refugees from the recent European revolutions of 1848 as well as from the Chinese Taiping rebellion of the same period. Suddenly a new kind of multiethnic "diversity" became part and parcel of Californian history.

It came, however, at the fatal cost of another kind of diversity. The prior inhabitants – primarily the native Californians, who after a discrete period of attempting to benefit from the gold profits were forcefully driven out of their lands and increasingly fell victim to new strains of disease, and the Hispanic *californios*, who notwithstanding international treaty assurances were soon deprived of their property by cunning Yankee appropriation of land claims through court proceedings – both found themselves relegated to subordinate minority status. Thus the transition to a new political order, which might have meant a less violent absorption of newcomer Americans into the more steady patterns of *californio* rule and a native Californian handling of much of the ecosystem, became a signal for the entirely new mode of social, economic and political life that not only shocked California into the dramatic fast pace of development that has since marked it, but also jolted American society and, in turn, world history proper over the next half-century.

On the pragmatic level, a vast range of entrepreneurial activities were almost immediately launched in both manufacturing and service industries. Housing and mining industries took off as the rapidly growing population created a huge demand for food, clothing, and shelter. California agriculture and farming expanded both in staple products and in efforts to develop consumer interest in an increasing variety of crops, vegetables and fruits. In turn, mining, business

---

28 McWilliams [1949], 25.

and agriculture stimulated the development of banks and financial institutions not only for California but also for adjoining territories. Eventually pressure grew from the alliance of government and railroads to connect California with the rest of the nation by 1869, thus propelling a further leap in the Californian economy as breadbasket for the U.S. and also enabling the U.S. itself to embark on a period of unprecedented industrial growth that by the end of the nineteenth century had raised the latter to its present status as a world economic superpower. These multiplier effects no less affected economies in Latin America, Asia and Europe. Finally, the injection of California gold into circulation provided a worldwide boost to the liquidities of industrial capitalism. Small wonder then that an intrepid columnist for the New York Herald Tribune in the 1850s, one Karl Marx, attributed his most recent empirical reflections on capitalism to the stimulus of the Gold Rush beginning in California; by 1880 Marx was even pinpointing California as the "shameless" edge to the American capitalist experience.[29]

But the impact of the Gold Rush on both California and America also provokes broader speculation. If the United States had flirted with becoming a fully entrepreneurial society well before this historical stage, it is really only after the Gold Rush and its multiplier effects that, as one commentator has pointed out, the Puritan ideal of the "City on a Hill" was permanently replaced by the entrepreneurial standard of "El Dorado," an unabashed militancy on behalf of the "pursuit of happiness" by a consumer society less concerned with merit and sin than riches acquired at (almost) any cost. This "new dream" of "instant wealth, won in a twinkling by audacity and good luck" as represented by the agonies of the argonauts, became the "American Dream," of which the "California Dream" would constitute its most radical expression. To be sure, the "no-fault ethos" of this "new era of the entrepreneurial spirit" brought unprecedented wealth and comfort for many, indeed for much of the rest of the world in the next century and later; but it also meant wholly new forms of "speculation, corruption, and consolidation on a scale unimaginable before" discovery of that first fatal gleaming nugget.[30]

---

29 Gerald D. Nash, "The Global Economic Significance of the California Gold Rush," in Rawls & Orsi [1999], 276–292; on Marx: 288–9. Marx-Engels [1927–32], 34 (5 xi 1880): 478.

30 Following Brands' reading in his last part, "The New El Dorado (America in the Age of Gold)," in Brands [2002], esp. 441–444. See also McWilliams' important statement on the "restless energy" of America: "But it is only in California that *this energy is coeval with statehood.*" McWilliams [1949], 25 (emphasis added).

4.

In California itself over the next half-century (1850–1900) such consolidation brought together railroad ownership, real estate monopoly, and exclusive water rights. Whether in the original urban areas of San Francisco developing and benefitting from the Gold Rush and the silver lode in Nevada or, somewhat delayed by the gradual rate of transportation links with San Francisco and the rest of the continent, in the Southern Californian desert range that came up with that unique urban/conurban plant of "Los Angeles" or "Southern Cal," the great Californian captains of industry worked relentlessly toward maintaining a seamless system of control uniting business and government.

Particularly the South Pacific Railroad (SP) has been aptly described as a "Gilded Age plutocracy, California style," composed of the Big Four alliance of Leland Stanford (California governor and future founder of Stanford University), Mark Hopkins, Charles Crocker and Collis P. Huntington, all Gold Rush immigrants who then went into business, railroads, steamship enterprises, land holdings abetted by friendly federal government grants, irrigation projects, hotels and urban real estate.[31] Such massive concentration ensured that the more enlightened dreams for a California composed of middle-class farmers and citizens along Jeffersonian lines would be undermined at the outset of American rule.

Perhaps the most imposing achievement of such collusion was the successful completion of the Owens Valley project in 1913 appropriately creating an Imperial Valley economy and bringing water to the desert expanses of Southern California on a scale that would serve the greater area of a rapidly burgeoning Los Angeles. Against all pre-industrial probabilities the fantastic conurbation called Los Angeles had by 1930 exploded to become the largest American city west of Chicago: the ultimate "matrix city for the United States in the twenty-first Asian Pacific century," cunningly constructed by cooperation among city fathers and an apparently bottomless American appetite to seek out homes and bliss within this "Southern California Raj."[32] What has been called an "epic of real-estate development" from the 1880s on, pumped up and funneled by massive advertising campaigns to the rest of America, became a permanent feature of the Californian economy to the present day. By 1930 one could legitimately refer to "a golden age of California as a regional American civilization."[33]

At the other extreme, a very different dream for California had also become a permanent fixture of Californian civilization. The "utopian" instinct to create

---

31 Following Starr [1985], 200ff.
32 Starr [1990], 392.
33 Starr [1990], 393.

new forms of individual and social life through experimentation, communes, cooperatives, general culture, and eventually the reformism of Progressivist politics originally reflected respect for the unmatched diversity of the Californian ecosystem. While the Californian agricultural economy was dangerously narrowed at first to the production of wheat for a bursting population, this same diversity of Californian soils and climate was already being noted and exploited by a growing number of viticulturists and fruit growers. With five major regions for planting and its basically stable Mediterranean climate, rich and variegated soil, it is not surprising that the agribusiness represented by a "handful of wheat barons" would be rejected as a monopolizing undertow of the mining industry well before the latter had begun its permanent decline by 1880. Moreover, the new availability of the American national market for foodstuffs after 1979 through transportation and refrigeration technology enabled Californian growers to transform American diet and drink between 1880 and 1920 in the direction of fresh fruits, vegetables and native wines.

The earlier exponents of such innovations fed a spate of utopian ventures in California,[34] although increasingly this new economy went hand-in-hand with more pressing capitalist priorities. Nonetheless, it also helped produce among its practitioners a mode of life that, reflecting the exigencies of such agriculture, emphasized, according to its more eloquent boosters, the priority of "aesthetics" in the dramatically beautiful human and natural landscapes that emerged as the privileged focus of "orange culture," a culture that was emblazoned elsewhere through orange crate illustrations of the image of fin de siècle California as "the point most desirable to attain for the fullest joys of living."[35] Particularly in conjunction with the simultaneous praise of the Californian climate as the most salubrious for health, longevity, and the cultivation of ultimate human bodily beauty, this image seemed a final confirmation of the "mountain of paradise" (*Kār-ī-farn*) metaphor of California as the land of the Hesperides itself with its fabled Golden Age "apples," the very concretion of a "Mediterranean" civilization that not only drew together the more rhapsodic comparisons by "Euro-Californians" of California with France, Italy, Greece and Spain, but also the Mediterranean of the Holy Lands and of Islamic al-Andalus and North Africa.[36]

Of course, this idyllic image hid facts of land monopoly and corporate control that no less ensured that Californian civilization would remain dependent on further developments in industrial and capitalist cycles. The varied ethnic elements making up farm labor supply – from Chinese, Japanese, Indian and

---

34 See the account in Hine [1966].
35 Edward James Wickson, cited in Starr [1985], 139; also Sackman [2007].
36 See "An American Mediterranean," in Starr [1973], 365–414.

Filipino to Latino workers – suffered modes of deprivation that only became Californian political issues during the Depression period of the 1930s before receiving national exposure in such literary classics as John Steinbeck's *The Grapes of Wrath* (1939). On the more urban level, however, monopolization had already awakened reformist concerns before 1900, and between 1910 and 1915 Progressivist legislation and in some cases direct Progressivist rule at the local and state levels fuelled important adjustments in the disparity of benefits from Californian natural wealth. Progressivism then received a far more important boost during the Depression period of the 1930s along with the tremendous stimulus to the Californian economy brought about by the outbreak of war in 1941 as California became the center for industrial and military activities in the Pacific theatre. By 1945–1955 Californians could claim some of the most advanced legislation and benefits arising from the governmental sector at both state and federal levels.[37]

5.

In terms of its direct entry into world history as a power in its own right, the story of contemporary California takes up two stages. In the first stage (1920–1945), California rose to the status of a regional civilization. In the second stage, mainly as a result of the second world war, California would begin its entry into the ranks of the world's major civilizations.

Between 1920 and 1945 Californians developed a new more casual style of life, from home design, clothing, diet, sports and "outdoorsness" to a generalized commitment to the "pursuit of pleasure" that placed them apart from the rest of the United States. These tendencies not only promoted fantasy, esotericism and utopianism that made California the most receptive culture for heterodox religiosities and communities. Such tendencies also came together in the pragmatic domains of art and technology to create one of the more enduring cultural industries of the twentieth century: "Hollywood." Generating wealth and subcultures connected with film, literature, and overall media production, Hollywood turned into one of the greatest bonanzas for the California economy, diversifying itself over the rest of the century to link up with theme parks like Disneyland on the one hand and the computer economy of multimedia on the other.

More than any other industry, Hollywood also benefitted from the unprecedented diaspora of Central European refugees in the arts, philosophy and literature who fled European fascism and anti-Semitism in the 1930s to find homes and

---

37 McWilliams [1949] is especially interesting for his futuristic expectations of California as of 1949.

professional opportunities in the Southland. Even where they were not engaged in screenplays for the film industry, many such refugees produced some of their most vital and personal works in California.[38] While a substantial number would eventually return to Germany and Central Europe after the war, in such cases as that of screenwriter Prague-born Frederick Kohner California proved sufficiently congenial for him to stay and compose the classic surf novel *Gidget* (1957) which inspired a bevy of surf films and turned surfing into yet another exemplar of the Californian life of pleasure. Based on the beach life of Kohner's teenage daughter, *Gidget* eventually helped provide a new icon for the 1960s: the "California Girl."[39]

At the same time it is a revealing coincidence that the real estate originally called "Hollywood" was owned by the Theosophical Society and served as locus for a Pythagorean institute "Krotona" committed to the spiritual transformation of western civilization. Eventually, the Society moved to the Valley of Ojai near Santa Barbara which served to inspire the Indian meditative master J. Krishnamurti to a series of enlightenment experiences in the late 1920s.[40] Another branch of theosophy, led by Katherine Tingley, managed to create an entire community, replete with temples and Greek open-air theatres, at Point Loma near San Diego.[41] On a less esoteric yet still influential level, the founder of the "Wizard of Oz" stories, Frank Baum, moved to Southern California where he completed the body of writings of Oz, probably confident that he now dwelt concretely in Oz proper. This "Oz" strain in Californian civilization may also be the traced to the later efflorescence in the 1940s of a "Berkeley-Big Sur bohemia"[42] associated with the name and presence of Henry Miller after the New York native moved from Europe to Big Sur, the "Tibet" of California, and encouraged an ebullient mix of politics, sex and esotericism – supported by the theories of Wilhelm Reich and other transplanters of Freudian radicalism to California that would form the Human Potential movement – that helped give birth to the later Beat and hippie movements of the 1950s and 1960s.[43]

---

38 See Chapter 3 below.
39 Kohner [2001]. A particularly rhapsodic version of the "California girl" for popular consumption is provided in the *Time* magazine issue on California in 1969 ("California: A State of Excitement"). Time [1969]. By contrast, the 1991 *Time* issue on California is more reflective of the flattened economy of the early 1990s ("California: The Endangered Dream"), leaving out the "California girl" theme. Time [1991].
40 See Ross [1989] and Ross [2004]; also Blau [1995], Lutyens [1975], Lutyens [1983].
41 See Greenwalt [1955].
42 Following Starr [2002], 212, but see also Herney, Rideout & Wadell [2008] on a prior "Berkeley Bohemia" in the early twentieth century.
43 See Leonard [1988] and Kripal [2007].

Somewhere between Hollywood and this Berkeley-Big Sur bohemianism, California also succeeded in producing exemplary academic standards of intellect at its great institutions.[44] Such excellence was responsible not only for epochal discoveries in the pure sciences of astronomy and related astrophysical fields, but also for the more pragmatic sciences of jet propulsion, atomic fission and the construction of both atomic and hydrogen bombs. It was in the Southern California of George Ellery Hale's and Edwin Hubble's observations at Mount Wilson and Mount Palomar that the theory of a universe of galaxies and nebulae and of an endlessly expanding cosmos was first articulated and confirmed, while it was in the Northern California of Robert Oppenheimer's Berkeley circle that atomic theory led to the Manhattan Project that was eventually realized on sacred native land in Los Alamos, New Mexico, that had been personally recommended by Oppenheimer himself.[45] What is perhaps less well known, and reflective of that esoteric dimension in the California imagination even in its most stringently cerebral moments, is that Hale and his followers took themselves equally seriously as members of a scientific brotherhood committed to meditation and ritual redolent of ancient Egyptaic and Zoroastrian circles.[46]

6.

The second stage begins when such elements – the "California" style of life, the willingness to risk new modes of living and esoteric communitarianism, fantasy, scientific cosmic speculation, and the pragmatics of that designer of dreams, Hollywood – became *American* standards mainly through the effects of the second world war and its immediate aftermath (1945–55).

After 1945 American society was largely shaped by the pragmatic transference to daily American life of the California style founded in the California 1920s and 1930s. By the same token, California had become all the more essential to Cold War considerations that dominated much of the American political scene between 1948 and 1989. A major recipient of defense expenditures from 1941 to 1950 and after, California spawned an imposing body of aviation industries that continued to be central to its own and the U.S. economy throughout the cold war. More

---

44 E. g. the University of California (at Berkeley and then later also at Los Angeles), Stanford University, the California Institute of Technology, and the University of Southern California.
45 See Jungk [1958] and Cassidy [2005].
46 Following the account in Starr [1997], 61–89. In his attempt to create "a scientific Athens amidst the orange groves" in the Pasadena of the California Institute of Technology, Hale drew on Egyptaic as well as Florentine Renaissance Neoplatonic motifs. Hale was called "Priest of the Sun, Zoroaster of our time" by newsmagazines (77). See also Hale [1924] and Hale [1926].

viscerally, California produced two of the most visible expressions of political alternatives for the next twenty years: on the one hand, its governor Earl Warren who as Chief Justice of the U.S. Supreme Court from 1953 continued the liberal progressivist message of California into U.S. law and practice to the extent that the "Warren Court" became the favorite whipping boy for American conservatives and reactionaries; and, on the other hand, Congressman Richard Nixon whose cold war politics, originally nurtured in Californian battles, brought the full brunt of what has been termed Southern Californian "plutocratic conservatism" to the American political landscape and facilitated the later conservative turn in American politics associated with former Californian Governor Ronald Reagan during the 1980s.

As of 1962, the year in which California permanently surpassed New York as the most populous U.S. state, the transference of Californian civilization to American daily life had been largely completed. From this stage on, California was more explicitly accepted as the vanguard of the American project, and over the next forty-odd years California has largely fulfilled such expectations. Californians launched the protest movements of the Sixties, the ecology and environmental concerns of the Seventies, the spread of a computer society starting in Silicon Valley in the Seventies before becoming the PC force of the Eighties and the worldwide web and dotcom phenomena of the Nineties.[47] California also came to stand for the forces of political upheaval on the American scene, from the minority outbreaks of the Sixties led by such groups as the Black Panthers and the random violence of urban life in the Eighties and Nineties to citizen selfishness starting with Proposition 13 in 1978 severely limiting civic responsibilities toward the imposing social and material programs that had been achieved in the earlier part of the century.

Relentlessly growing in population, power, and influence as the center of America's Pacific concerns, California has therefore made its way to the world's major economic ranks while giving off an endless set of worries intermixed with film noir fixations over the meaninglessness of "L.A.", the groundlessness of culture under the sun, and science-fiction fantasies of Armageddon.[48] National newsmagazines continue to rush to publicize the apparently inevitable collapse of Californian civil society in the more recent crises of state budget and political recall movements.[49] Still, at the very least, these same apocalyptic accounts

---

47 See the special issue on "California" in Look [1966] and George Leonard's account of the New York "establishment's" strong reaction to the issue's claim of California's new preeminence. Leonard [1988], 240–248.
48 See, e. g., Davis [1990] and [1998].
49 See, e. g., Newsweek [2003], Steinhauer [2009].

recognize that if California "goes," so may everything and everyone else in the American, and eventually world, economy.

7.

Are there underlying patterns to this complex mosaic of events and intentions making up Californian civilization? And, apart from concern with the heavy weight that the Californian economy brings to all aspects of global culture and globalization tendencies, are there strong reasons for non-Californians, including the rest of the United States, to care?

This section attempts one strong reading of such patterns by claiming that California represents "paradise" in world history, understood in the relatively testable sense that it has been built on millennia of biodiversity permeating ecosystem and human habitation and articulation.[50] Modern Californian history is therefore the story of a dialectic between such biodiversity and attempts both to preserve and to undermine it. To argue exclusively that such biodiversity has been irretrievably lost since the coming of the Europeans is to overlook the degree to which such challenges remain an extremely recent facet of Californian reality and, in any case, are being countered by contemporary efforts to regain and protect such biodiversity. Such continuity may be noted by looking at five literary examples from the recent past: John Muir, Robinson Jeffers, Henry Miller, Jack Kerouac, and Michael McClure.

Of these five, the most effective has been the body of works and both social and naturalist achievements attached to the name of John Muir. Muir is known as the remarkable naturalist and explorer who was fundamental to the creation of the first national parks, environmental groups like the Sierra Club, and the evolution of an environmentalist consciousness and movement in the United States. While all this is true, it is his body of writings that may well prove his greatest legacy. In a style halfway between romantic elegy and naturalist precision, Muir, perhaps even more than Henry David Thoreau, succeeded in capturing and preserving the miracle of contemplating the Californian "wilderness" before the great central valley of California was turned into the world's most successful agribusiness and the Yosemite Valley overturned by visitors. Above all, Muir pinpointed the sacred center of California as the towering Sierra Nevada mountain range guarding and nurturing the Californian landscape, and, within it, the Yosemite Valley proper. Coming upon the mountains through a Central Valley landscape "glow-

---

50 For an effectively illustrative presentation of California as a "visionary state," see Davis [2006].

ing golden in the sunshine" with its multitudinous flowers and the sweet honey, Muir was transfixed by their huge presence "reposing like a smooth, cumulous cloud in the sunny sky, and so gloriously colored, and so luminous, it seems to be not clothed with light, but wholly composed of it, like the wall of some celestial city." This brilliant vision Muir henceforth baptized the "Range of Light;" and once he had penetrated the heart of this "celestial city," he then went on to describe the entire Yosemite Valley (his home during 1868–73) as "an immense hall or temple lighted from above." Indeed, "no temple made with hands can compare with Yosemite," every rock of which "seems to glow with life."[51]

A quarter-century later a similarly dazzled explorer and author, the poet Robinson Jeffers, found the words to extol the Big Sur landscape connecting North and South California. In Jeffers' case, the landscape evoked an Hellenic quality that differed radically from the familiar orderliness of "genteel" classical readings. Jeffers' philosophy of "inhumanism" attempts to articulate its elemental strengths:

> Erase the lines: I pray you not to love classifications:
> The thing is like a river, from source to sea-mouth
> One flowing life. We that have the honor and hardship of being human
> Are one flesh with the beasts, and the beasts with the plants
> One streaming sap, and certainly the plants and algae and the earth they spring from
> Are one flesh with the stars.[52]

In a 1941 lecture at the U.S. Library of Congress Jeffers explained that his position might be likened to "pantheism," but it was more of a "feeling" or "certitude" that "the world, the universe, is one being, a single organism, one great life that includes all life and all things; and is so beautiful that it must be loved and reverenced; and in moments of mystical vision we identify ourselves with it."[53] In a further letter to a correspondent, Jeffers amplified his thoughts: "This whole is in all its parts so beautiful, and is felt by me to be so intensely in earnest, that I am compelled to love it, and to think of it as divine." Humans could contribute "ever so slightly" to this overriding "beauty of things" by making their own lives and environment beautiful, but such contributions were not overly important or necessary to the whole. Yet this beauty went hand-in-hand with the unquestioned cruelty and torture and suffering in things. The living wildness of Big Sur – its eagles, falcons, condors and cougars – penetrated the core of Jeffers himself; as one visitor described Jeffers at the time, "something utterly wild …. crept into his mind and marked his features." This wildness enabled the poet to articulate the underlying female energy of the

---

51   Muir [1961], 2; Muir [1962], 4.
52   "The Double Axe," cited in Karman [1987], 51–2.
53   Jeffers [1956], 23–4.

cosmos proper as *shakti* – possibly reflecting the more compassionate cult of the Madonna, "la Conquistadora," in his home town of Carmel where he built his own tower to gaze like a hawk upon the thunderous seascape.[54]

The case of Henry Miller and his particular infatuation with the Californian ecosystem carries a further elaboration of this vision. After years of expatriate existence in Paris and a galvanizing experience of Greece, Miller was forced to return to the United States during the second world war. He set out to cross the United States by car, and in his ill-tempered account of that odyssey, *The Air-Conditioned Nightmare* (1945), recorded what he considered to be the most frightful aspect of American society, namely its total disengagement from nature.[55] Eventually, however, Miller ended up in Big Sur, and his paeans to the landscape and the life of its inhabitants took on a typically Millersque tone of mixed humor and awe: "It was here at Big Sur that I first learned to say *Amen*!" Here, that is, Miller continued to live as the conflicted and farcical person his writings invariably reveal, without however the hard edge of the bad humor of underachievement of his earlier self. Like the hero of his title, Hieronymous Bosch and the latter's associations with the Brothers and Sisters of the Free Spirit in which the millennium of paradise had been presumably attained, Miller confessed that thanks to California, he now truly dwelt in "paradise" – albeit one which "contains flaws (Paradisiacal flaws, if you like)."[56]

Against these reconciliations may be contrasted the more tortured case of Jack Kerouac as the ultimate Beat literary antihero. Kerouac's *On the Road* (1957) had already provided the classic Beat equivalent to Muir's walk across the continent to Yosemite Valley and Miller's wild drive from New York through the Old South to Los Angeles. However, in *Big Sur* (1962) which recounts his stay there in 1960, Kerouac revealed how far he had come to the end of his particular road of alcoholism and paranoia. Big Sur rewarded him at first with what he called "marvelous insights": "Don't call me eternity," its blue sky told him, "call me God if you like, all of you talkers are in paradise: the leaf is paradise, the tree stump is paradise, the paper bag is paradise, the man is paradise, the sand is paradise, the sea is paradise, the man is paradise, the fog is paradise." Yet, though Kerouac "spoke the language," he turned away from it even if his self-deceptions could

---

54 Cited in Karman [1987], 70,40, 92, 136. Ultimately Jeffers' "Aphrodite," the final manifestation of the wild goddess in his poetry, utters the warning: "Something is lurking hidden/ There is always a knife in the flowers. There is always a lion just beyond the firelight." Jeffers had received an extensive classical education since the age of five, had studied in Europe, and studied both medicine and forestry at American universities. At the same time, like Muir, he was known for his physical energy in mountaineering and mountain-climbing.
55 Miller [1965], 16.
56 Miller [1957], 32, 25.

not be hidden in this light and space: "All my tricks laid bare, even the realization that they're laid bare itself laid bare as a lotta bunk." Eventually Kerouac seems to have undergone a complete breakdown, and the only fitting survivor of his ordeal is the closing onomatopoetic poem "Sea: Sounds of the Pacific Ocean at Big Sur:"

> Sho, Shoosh, flut,
> ravad, tapavada pow,
> coof, loof, root, –
> No, no, no, no, no, no –
> Oh ya, ya, ya, ya, yo, yair –
> Shhh—[57]

Finally, the body of writings and text gesticulations of Kerouac's colleague Michael McClure shows how far such gestures could be carried in a more positive manner and developed into a proper philosophy. While McClure's own environmentalist explanation of the origins of Beat thought seems, at least historically, problematic, it is certainly applicable to his own considerable production (as well as to that of another environmentalist Beat poet and thinker Gary Snyder).[58] McClure's "meat"[59] approach toward the symbiosis of humans, animals and nature works partly because McClure's own poetic persona straddles the boundaries between cub lion, outlaw and dissident:

> THIS LIFE IS STAR LIFE:
>   SISTER DEER AND I
>   SEE STARS WITH STARS.
>   Brother puma
> bites his lover's neck and she sees
> multidimensioned
>   shapes of light.
> What is in space for roses and for berries
>   is the life
> that's whirling there
>   WITHIN
> – within the organelles of cells
> and the imagined time they took to crumple selves
> Into a racing thing that's standing in the rains
>   and still beyond the reach of brains.[60]

---

57   Kerouac [1962], 29, 33, 178–200, 186.
58   See the discussion in McClure [1993], 4–5. McClure notes that it was when he met Sterling Bunnell after his arrival in San Francisco in 1954 that he was introduced to Californian nature: "With him I was able to watch coyotes and foxes and weasels and deer, and walk through savannah country, hike through the foothills, go over the mountains, and to the seashore and look into tide pools" (3).
59   See, e. g., McClure [1963].
60   "To Glean the Livingness of Worlds: Replying to Rilke's Eighth Elegy," in McClure [1991], 92. For a more recent example of the Buddhist turn in McClure's poetry, see McClure [1999].

8.

These five examples may be taken as sound testimonials to the persistently transformative impact of California Nature. Even so, how does this exalted account of "California" through its "Range of Light" and "celestial temple" relate to the "lowlands" of the rest of California's material civilization? Henry Miller already teases a suggestion with his emphasis on joy and release, and even Jack Kerouac agrees, however much Kerouac himself failed to incorporate the laughter and exhilaration that stems from the encounter with Californian natural reality. True, these "ecstatic" aspects to the California ambiance often enough lead down into a "Hollywood Babylon"[61] as well as into the recorded excesses of the Human Potential (Beat and hippie) and New Age movements that have proved popular among a substantial minority of natives and outsiders.[62] Yet, at the very least, it is such indefatigable "pursuit of pleasure," whether physical or spiritual, that can be related not only to the particularly manic manner in which California entered an incipient American capitalist and industrial society, but also to more sophisticated responses to the California landscape.

As seen in art history where something like a higher plastic reality is often the object of Californian artists, architects and designers, such factors have enabled a remarkable set of aesthetic achievements that temptingly suggest possibilities, if not attainments, of a larger synthesis. From the earliest American period, Californian art linked up with European and American standards, and in such cases as the Art and Crafts movement it has been argued that California might have served as the most imposing case of arts and crafts influence throughout a wide variety of social sectors.[63] Modernism and surrealism also had some of their finest articulations on the West Coast, and abstract expressionism may well have originated not so much in New York as in important features of certain Californian painters.[64]

One indication of such Californian efflorescence is the arts movement of Dynaton, a temporary coalescence of three artists, Wolfgang Paalen, Gordon Onslow-Ford and Lee Mullican, during the late 1940s and early 1950s in the San Francisco Bay area. A continuation of the art magazine *Dyn* begun by Paalen in Mexico during the early 1940s, Dynaton (from the Greek for "possible") achieved

---

61 E. g. Anger [1965] and Anger [1984]. However, for the "utopian" dimension of Hollywood cf. Brown [2002].
62 See, e. g., Kripal [2007] and Schou [2010].
63 Between 1900 and 1915 California was "the culmination of the Arts and Crafts movement in America." Wilson [1993], 33.
64 See Susan M. Anderson, "Journey into the Sun: California Artists and Surrealism," in Karlstrom [1996], 198, and Landauer [1996]; also Barron, Bernstein & Fort [2000].

a rare fusion of the painters' simultaneous concern with Amerindian cultures, Zen Buddhism and spiritualism, the new physics, extraterrestrial life, psychology meditation, and, finally, "the vital quiet in California nature."[65] In the words of Paalen, Dynaton meant "limitless continuum in which all forms of reality are potentially implicit. Possibilities are a part of nature. Nature is what we can know of realized possibilities."[66] If Dynaton had no clear successors, it nonetheless provides a suggestive parameter of the level and quality of synthesis with which the California temper continues to engage.

Still, short of pursuing such lofty standards, Californian civilization does often enough express itself in darker tones of *noir* and even despair. Whether in the caustic novels of Nathaniel West[67] or in the Hollywood film noir tradition, such as *Double Indemnity* and *The Blue Dahlia* (1946) screenwritten by Californian thriller author Raymond Chandler (the former script based on a book by Californian novelist James M. Cain), the individual invariably comes up hard against a frenzied and unstable background of atomistic forces in chaotic play.[68] Sometimes a narrow suggestion of redemption is found precisely in the struttings of a lost idealism that does "the right thing" while still "playing all the angles," such as the hero Rick in the classic Hollywood film, *Casablanca* (1943),[69] or even in the alienated postures of the cinematic "rebel without a cause" or motorcyclist "wild one."[70] It is difficult to separate these gestures as responses either to the continued acceleration of an entrepreneurial society gone (almost) mad or to what California's more acute writers and poets have pointed to as the uncompromising truthfulness of its Nature. Yet this very question underscores the claim that no answer can ignore the need not only to incorporate cynical readings but also one that touches on the "utopian other" in the California experience.

---

65 See Dyn [1943] for an example of Paalen's commitment to Amerindian art.
66 Dynaton Reviewed [1977], 6.
67 *Miss Lonelyhearts* (1933), *Day of the Locust* (1939), in West [1962]. West died of an automobile accident in 1940.
68 A good introduction to the film noir is Hirsch [1981]. Although Hirsch does not emphasize the role of California, his extensive account of the literary tradition helping to give rise to film noir clearly privileges the Californian contributions. Also Starr, "The Boys and Girls in the Back Room: Minimalism and the California Novel," in Starr [1997], 286–319.
69 Following Starr [2002], 165.
70 The events of the film *The Wild One* (1953) starring Marlon Brando were vaguely related to a motorcyclist Fourth of July weekend takeover of the Californian town of Hollister in 1947.

9.

In the final analysis "California" belongs to world history as a major civilization – distinctive from the "United States of America" – because it is the most packed symbol of elements otherwise difficult to decipher in the unprecedented voyages of discovery and exploitation first launched by Europeans in the fifteenth century and forming the very beginnings of the globalization process. If California has been rightly labeled "a questing sort of state,"[71] it may well be because California symbolizes the ultimate object of that endless quest to the West, toward the "Hesperia" sought by mythical Aeneas as Virgilian founder of ancient Rome that in the fifteenth century came to be associated with island-hopping from the coast of west Africa across the Atlantic Ocean in hopes of reaching the fabled "Indies," themselves forming yet another body of islands from Zipangu (Japan) to Ceylon.[72] Even after discovery of the huge size of the future South America as a continent around 1500, it was still felt that Columbus' landfall among the Caribbean islands augured a further set of isles – rather than a North American "continent" – eventually working its way to the Indies and "Cathay" proper. Along that extensive thalassic highway, the "Isle of California" became a fixture of imagination, and eventually of unrepentant ambition.

As one commentator has noted, "it is well known that islands excite the imagination of the maturing individual… the island image emerges as a significant symbol in evolving consciousness. The island is a controllable, perfectible world in miniature."[73] In such terms, the Island of California, this veritable "Mountain of Paradise," carries a standing challenge not only to Californians proper, but also to the rest of the contemporary world caught up in a globalization process that first took off in the fifteenth and sixteenth centuries when it was first literally discovered that "the salt seas of the world are connected; that all countries possessing sea coasts are mutually accessible by sea;" and that "eventually the existing networks" are "embraced in a super-network, so to speak, of ocean routes encircling the world."[74]

Naturally such a challenge is intended for both Californians and non-Californians. Yet unlike non-Californians, Californians proper remain imbedded in the land, its ecosystem and its history that we have briefly traced, and these factors should invariably transcend the priority of any limited historical reading. For Californians proper, this deeper commitment means that the purely academic

---

71 McWilliams [1973], 374.
72 Polk [1991], 24–5. See also the interesting psychological reading of California as the ultimate Egyptaic descent into the underworld, afterlife, or "voyage to the West" in Rickels [1991].
73 Polk [1991], 27.
74 Parry [1981], ix, xv.

topic of "California civilization" is really the nature of their identification with the ramifications of that final deathbed message from the last native Californian, "Ishi," to his latest "fellow" Californians: "You stay, I go."[75]

---

75 Kroeber [1961], 238. I put "Ishi" in quotation-marks since it was not his personal name, which remained a private possession, but a native Yana word meaning "man" that Californian anthropologist Alfred Kroeber gave him for practical reasons of identification. Ishi was considered a member of the Yahi, a subgroup of the Yana; more recent research suggests that he was of mixed native Californian origins. See Starn [2004].

Chapter 2
Bordering the Civilization of Greater California: An Inquiry into Genealogy, Treaty-Making and Influence[1]

"When they first saw him, a goal they had all harbored would suddenly germinate."
Garci Rodríquez de Montalvo, *Sergas de Esplandián*[2]

At the beginning of all great civilizations there is Naming: baptism. With naming comes genealogy. Then follow the sighting – and the siting – of that which was named. All this collectively sculpts the history of borderings, which must be necessarily both literarily articulative and pragmatically grounded. Because these two aspects to the act of bordering are perduring, there is never a final moment of settled borders. Which is not to claim that there are no borders. Only that they are malleable – and potentially revolutionary.

The "creation" of "California" is of this order of invention. Not invention out of nowhere, but invention out of the richest stratum of Western classical thought and genealogizing, one that traces back to the epic-tragic fall of ancient Troy and the ensuing ventures by its noble citizenry to ground new Troys throughout the world. One such achievement was the ancient Veneto; another, and far more prodigious, was the foundation of ancient Rome – along with all subsequent Latin (and "Latino") civilizations. From this Roman fount followed a host of lesser Troys in western Europe, all more or less wedded to the primacy of the Trojan pedigree of Aeneas, son of the goddess Aphrodite and the Trojan prince Anchises. Around the eighth-ninth centuries C. E. there is plain evidence that the surviving clerical spokesmen for the classical tradition (however much christianized) had extended the Virgilian gesture on behalf of Rome to the domains of the Franks in Celtic Gaul (Fredegar) and of the British in the British isles (Nennius).[3] These ideological identifications proved important to the eleventh-century Norman conquerors of Anglo-Saxon Britain who remained equally concerned with the pedigree of their French-Norman base ("Normandie"). Thus it is not surprising that the same medieval ideologists for the Trojan genealogy of "Britain" – Geoffrey of Monmouth, Wace, Benoît de Sainte-Maure – were often equally committed to tracing the lines of their patrons, the Norman kings. This meant that, as is invariably the

---

1 An earlier version of this chapter was published as "Bordering the Civilization of Greater California: An Inquiry into Genealogy, Treaty-Making, and Influence," *Western Humanities Review*, 60:2 (Fall 2006), 27–50.
2 Montalvo [1992], 518 (Little translation); Montalvo [2003], 825.
3 E. g. *Chronicle* (650); *Gesta regum Francorum* (720).

case, epic matter – the "Matter of Troy", the "Matter of Britain" – ended up indissolubly mixed up with political matter. Even as such works headed in the medieval direction of espousing chivalry and amor in the forthcoming flood of *romans de geste*, British novelas, and *romans antiques*, they became no less exemplars of the burgeoning literature on statecraft in a steady succession of *libros des caballerías y los de principes* spreading throughout western Europe and down into the Iberian peninsula.

For all the variety of works between Geoffrey of Monmouth's standard *Historia Regum Britanniae* (c. 1138–9) and Garci Rodríquez de Montalvo's *Sergas de Esplandián* (1510), a reasonably clear line of texts is documentable from the Trojan foundation of Britain, the Arthur of the knighthood of the Round Table and the caballeros of the Reconquista, to the emergence of the "California" theme. Geoffrey's classic first laid out the Trojan foundations of Britain in a manner recapitulated by all succeeding chroniclers of the Arthurian cycle, while Montalvo first put the "Island of California" on the mythico-genealogical map by refashioning the four books of the medieval *Amadís de Gaula* (1508) along with the fifth volume to the Amadis cycle that he himself composed called *Sergas de Esplandián*.

Moreover, the consistency of this line carried with it a generally pro-Trojan reading in terms of the sources that were primarily used for the epic treatment of the "Matter of Troy." Instead of Homer – who was mostly unavailable during the European middle ages – or Virgil – who had been used by the Carolingians – medieval chroniclers from Oxford to Toledo largely depended on two works of the Roman period, one by a certain Dictys the Cretan *(Ephemiredos Belli Troiani Libri)* and the other by a Dares the Phrygian *(De Excidio Troiae Historia)*, on the ostensible claim that both authors had been actual eyewitnesses at the Trojan conflict, whereas in fact the texts attributed to them probably date through Latin translations to original Greek works of the first and second centuries CE.[4]

Particularly Dares' pro-Trojan account was followed by Benoît de Sainte-Maure's highly influential *Le Roman de Troie* (c. 1160).[5] The latter became the basis for a variety of Iberian works more or less entitled *Crónica Troyana* (composed

---

4   A Greek fragment of Dictys (its fictional original was supposedly composed in ancient Phoenician) connected with the Latin translation was discovered in 1899–1900, proving such an origin; speculation also suggests a Greek origin to the Latin Dares. If so, the Greek original of Dictys can be dated to 66–250CE and the Latin to the fourth century CE; the (possible) Greek origin of Dares to the first century CE and the Latin to the early sixth century CE. Following Frazer [1966], 3–15. Frazer calls these two works part of "the anti-Homeric tradition" for contradicting Homer at several points. Cf. also the Latin of Dares in Dares the Phrygian [1873].
5   Benoît explicitly thanks Dares and Dictys as his sources at the start and end of his narrative. Benoît de Saint-Maure [1998], 44–47, 632–633.

in, alternatively, Galician, Portuguese and Castilian).[6] Following his master, Benoît de Sainte-Maure made sure to reassert the absolute primacy of Troy as the paradigmatic polis for European culture.[7] Moreover, for a variety of reasons these works were happy to exploit Dares' starting-point of the expedition of Jason and the Argonauts as the origin of the disputes leading to the Trojan war.[8] For one thing, the Argonaut expedition brought in Heracles whose reaction to a snub by Laomedon, the Trojan king at the time who refused temporary hospitality to the traveling Argonauts, led to a first destruction of Troy by Heracles himself, the killing of Laomedon, and abduction of his daughter – and the future Trojan king Priam's sister – Hesione whom Heracles handed over to his erstwhile ally Talomon, king of Salamis and father of the warrior Ajax.[9] Heracles of course plays an essential role as mythical founder of a variety of Hispanic locations, all more or less focused on the "Pillars of Heracles" leading out from the Mediterranean Sea into the Atlantic Ocean. The outgoing route eventually extended on to Galicia (the northwest region of Iberia), a prominent stopover for journeys to little Britain ("Brittany") and great Britain ("Britain"), as well as to the larger world of "Gaul" (whether Belgium, France, or even Wales). Meanwhile, Geoffrey's account of Aeneas' kin Brutus setting off from a Latin-Roman base to seek out his own fortune and kingdom in the "west" through the Pillars of Heracles and Galician Coruña in order to reach the Loire valley of Gaul in alliance with a king "Corineus" (*Corineus, Cornubia, Corualles, Cornwall*) supported a multiplicity of accounts of "Brutuses" – some identified with a Roman consul of 146 BCE

---

6   E. g. Parker [1975] for the *Historia Troyana* and Lorenzo [1985] for the *Crónica Troiana*. See also Montero Garrido [1994] for his reflections on *El Victorial*.
7   See the introductory comments to Benoît de Sainte-Maure [1998], 12, and the author's extensive description of the unrivalled beauties of Troy and Ilion, concluding: "Onc ne fu rich maïstrie/N'a faitement ne curteisie/Don't l'on eüst delit ne joie,/Que ne trovassent cil de Troie" (lines 3169–3189), 124; also lines 2995–2998 (114).
8   In contrast, the original Homeric material begins in the *Kupria* (authored ostensibly by Arctinus of Miletus) with Zeus' desire to bring down population growth by inciting a struggle through the dissensions to be caused by the Judgment of Paris; in addition, Dictys' account also does not begin with Jason and the Argonauts. Both Dares and Benoît de Sainte-Maure give great emphasis to a meeting of Paris and Helen on the isle of Cythera at a temple consecrated to "Vénus" prior to the famed abduction. Dares the Phrygian, in Fraser [1966], 141; Benoît de Sainte-Maure [1998], 152–153.
9   There are original Greek sources for these themes. Thus Apollodorus (of Athens) recounts in his *Library and Epitome* the chaining of naked Hesione (cum jewelry) to a rock before a sea monster (no doubt on the analogy of Andromeda) who was saved by Heracles, who himself then failed to get his just reward from Laomedon. Apollodorus ii.5–9. Significantly Montalvo includes a closing vision of a naked woman at the top of a moving cliff approaching his heroes on the sea, grabbing Esplandián's magic sword – an obvious parallel to the Arthurian legend – that Esplandián had drawn at the start of the *Sergas de Esplandián* as the start of his exploits, and taking it back down into the sea. Montalvo [2003] [180], 809.

associated with the mythical foundation of Hispanic Toledo – that sufficiently matched the mythical wanderings of Heracles to appeal to Iberian demands for inclusion in the conventional Trojan genealogy. The result was a substantial body of written material from the period that confusedly mixed "Heracles" (*Hércules*) themes with those ascribed to "Brutus" (*Bruto*).[10]

On the other hand, none of these chronicling gestures firmly established a separate Trojan foundation for any given Iberian or Spanish sovereignty. Rather, they strongly encouraged inclusion *within* the still exemplary model of Gallic and Arthurian supremacy upheld by the foremost Norman and Breton writers of the middle ages. Accordingly, by 1200–1400 when such narrative influences gave rise to the evolution of the *Amadís de Gaula* theme through a body of *Ur-Amadís* texts (in Portuguese, Castilian, even French), the primacy of "Great Britain" (*Gran Bretaña*) and of "Arthur" (*Arturo*) had become unchallenged in asserting a Trojan pedigree for heroes fictionalized and celebrated by Iberian writers such as Montalvo. Far from questioning this British supremacy – and therefore the eponymous centrality of "Brutus" or "Brute" of Troy – Montalvo either accepted the conventional account or himself located his hero Amadís and the latter's son Esplandián in a mythical line of kings of Great Britain that included the brothers Falangris/Falangriz and Lisuarte – Amadís' grandparents –and that more than once underscored the redemptive arrival and return of Geoffrey's and Wace's King Arthur for Montalvo's vision of a future aion.

1.

Indisputably the founding text for the very concept of California is Chapter 157 of Montalvo's *Sergas de Esplandián* published in Sevilla in 1510. There in the midst of the gathering clouds of war between Esplandián's European-"Greek" Christian alliance and an infidel enemy led by Armato, King of Persia, over Constantinople as the exemplary polis of Christendom, Montalvo introduces the Island of California (*isla California*) ruled by the redoubtable and beautiful black Amazon queen Calafía (*una reina muy grande de cuerpo, muy hermosa*) whose domain Montalvo magically locates to the "right side" of the "Terrestrial Paradise."[11]

This much is a commonplace of California research. What is less often observed is that far from being a momentarily picaresque gesture by the author in

---

10   Geoffrey of Monmouth [1958] I [12], 19. See references to "Hércules/Bruto" in Montero Garrido [1994–1995], 208, 214, 226–227, 239 (note 227).
11   Also: "una isla llamada California," "la gran isla Californ[i]a," and "la Ínsola California." Montalvo [1991], [157, 182], 752.

the course of his more central narrative concerning a culminating confrontation between true believers and infidels over Constantinople, the introduction of this Island of California plays a critical role in Montalvo's overall narrative stratagem not only with regard to the *Sergas de Esplandián* itself but also to his entire restructuring of the preceding four-part Amadís cycle. By his own account, Montalvo claimed to have basically edited the first three parts of that cycle, reconfigured the fourth part to his new priorities, and entirely composed a new fifth part in which California and its Calafía figure.[12] His purpose was not only to inject into the traditional Amadís cycle a degree of coherence and meaning not available in the earlier Ur-Amadís material – characteristically concerned with the chivalric wanderings of knight errantry and amor, the stuff of medieval *chansons de geste* – but also to introduce a new gravity to the destinies of the hero Amadís and his crusader-conquistador son Esplandián.[13] Himself a city father (*regidor*) in the proudly castilian city of Medina del Campo, Montalvo participated actively in the final ten years (1482–1492) of military campaigns to retake the last Islamic city-state in western Europe, Granada, and in his own work reminded his reader (as well as the newly-instituted Spanish crown of Ferdinand and Isabella) of the duty to continue an international struggle against the infidel, particularly now that the historical center of Christendom, Constantinople, had itself fallen in 1453 to the Turk.

There is therefore a strongly compensatory element in Montalvo's refashioning of the Amadís cycle by shifting its fulcrum to the birth and subsequent deeds (*Sergas*) of Esplandián. Montalvo's Esplandián is the son of his hero Amadís, who has already ascended to the throne of Great Britain on approval of King Lisuarte, father of Amadís' beloved, Oriana, and whose act is sanctioned by the British lords through a formal investiture in the "New Troy" of London.[14] In contrast however to the knight errant Amadís, Esplandián represents the serious line of *conquistadores* who were completing the conquest and expulsion of the "infidels" in Spain itself during the author's lifetime.

---

12   This interpretation of Montalvo's larger aims follows the important readings of William T. Little. See Little in Montalvo [1992], 13.
13   Esplandián opposes "las aventureas de la Gran Bretaña, que más por vanagloria y fantasía que por otra justa cause las más dellas se tomavan." Montalvo [2003] [55], 363. Still, he describes his own destiny as: "a mí me conviene seguir aquello para que nascido en este mondo fue, buscando y provando las cosas furra de toda la orden de natura." [5], 142.
14   Hence Montalvo makes sure that the chapter on the birth of Esplandián forms the middle of the cycle (Book III, Chapter 66). "New Troy" is the term Geoffrey of Monmouth applied to London. Geoffrey of Monmouth [1958], I [17], 27. The investiture of Amadís is recounted in Chapters 63–64 of the *Sergas*. The word "sergas" itself is quite unique in Spanish and may be directly linked to the word "deeds" (ἔργα) with which ancient Greek myths clarified the character and essence of their deities. See Little in Montalvo [1992], 67 (note 1).

Not surprisingly then, the most compelling theories for the origins of Montalvo's "California" are "pagan" or "infidel," undoubtedly reflecting influences from Islamic themes on Hispanic mythmaking ever since the Islamic founding of the Iberian emirate (later caliphate) of al-Andalus (Andalusia) in the eighth century. Already the eleventh-century text of the Christian *Song of Roland* lists "Califerne" among the oriental people arrayed against Charlemagne.[15] Accordingly, as we earlier noted, contemporary commentators have come up with a host of competing theories regarding the possible origins of the word itself. Thus "California" could have stemmed from an Old Persian word "Kār-ī-farn," meaning "Mountain of Paradise" and linked in Persian mythology to the magical mountain of Qaf that is associated with Persian chivalric and indeed mystical Sufi themes.[16] Or it might have referred to the Arab-Berber combination of *Kalaa* (strong fortress) and *Ifrène* (a Maghreb or North African people) and be related to Beni Hammad, an actual centre of civilization around the ninth-eleventh centuries in North Africa which was known by "les Occidents" as "la Kalaa par excellence des Berbères," with the Ifrenes as their principal representatives.[17] Or, finally, a long list of words similar to "California" in Montalvo's work suggests associations with the Arab word referring to the ultimate Islamic leader and "follower" of Muhammad the Messenger: *Caliph* or *Calif.*[18] In fact these alternative explanations may well be compatible inasmuch as, given the high prestige of Persian culture in West Mediterranean Islamic societies at that time, al-Andalus and north Africa were major transmitters of Persian themes and myths.[19] In his conscious attempt at fictionally reversing through his own work the 1453 defeat of Chris-

---

15 The listing states: " cil d'Affrike e cil de Califerne" (line 2924).
16 Carnoy [1922], 227; Polk [1991], 131; McWilliams [1949], 3.
17 Hunt and Sánchez [1929], 36–7, which is based on Boissonnade [1923], 159–162. This is the "official" account given by the State of California in Appendix J of California's Legislature. Wilson & Ebbert [2000], 271–2.
18 See the argument by Little in Montalvo [1992], 456 (note 1). Some similar names listed by Sales Dasí [1998]: *Calafes, Calaferes, Calaferis, Calafre, Calaphere, Calaferis* (156). Also califas in Montalvo [2003] [123], 643. There is also the lingering argument over the resemblance of "khalif" or "caliph" to the Greek word for beauty καλά as in the account of Sebastián de Covarrubias in 1611 who stated regarding *calipha*: "The word, if it is Greek, seems to mean the beautiful, or resplendent one." Cited by Little in Montalvo [1992], 407 (note 2).
19 There are alternative accounts as well, such as links with an ancient city in Armenia "Caliphia" and with an Armenian queen "Dorotea." Such accounts may well be connected with ancient pre-Islamic Armenian-Persian associations. Nonetheless, the Perso-Andalusi-Maghrebi link would appear to be the canonical one for Montalvo's particular imaginal. Sales Dasí [1998], 155 and 155 (note 23); Montero Carrido [1994–1995], 207 (note 111). Cf. also Sokol [1949], who associates "California" with medieval legal references to a Roman noblewoman "Calefurnia" which may go back to "Calpurnia," a woman of a noble Roman family in the time of Caesar (23–26).

tendom by the Ottoman Turks, Montalvo's had his fictional pagans and infidels led not by the historical Turks but by quasi-mythical Persian rulers, emphasized that a key to the latters' hopes was the participation of the infidel Calafía and her Californian forces in the assault on Constantinople, and finally made sure that the conflict itself in Montalvo's own version was fanned by a prior struggle over a "forbidden mountain" (*la Montaña Defendida*) presumably marking the physical border between the Persian and Greek worlds.[20]

Thus Calafía and California's intervention are no mere colorful interlude for its creator Montalvo but absolutely central to the forthcoming world-historical conflict between his conquistadores and pagans. When Armato, King of Persia, succeeds in abducting the key Christian magician Urganda, he embarks on a grand plan to expand his empire and become the greatest ever Persian sovereign by taking Constantinople and the "Greek" realms. His message to potential allies that they "again" (*agora nuevamente*) face a challenge from a "knight [Esplandián] descended from the Trojan Brute" (*un cavallero descendiente del troyano Bruto*) who has given his name to the isle of Great Britain (*por causa del su nombre Bretaña la Grande la intituló*) establishes the larger epic nature of this forthcoming struggle.[21] As the pagan forces gather by land and sea, thunder toward Con-

---

20 If the Amadís cycle begins in the period of the "passion" of Christ, or 30–33CE (Montalvo [1991], 227), the best dating for the events of the *Sergas* is 313–400CE, or the early period of a Christianized Roman Empire. See Little in Montalvo [1992], 75 (note 16). This vaguely corresponds to Geoffrey of Monmouth's genealogy of Christian Roman figures immediately preceding the period of Uther Pendragon and his son Arthur for the fifth century; Arthur would defend "Britain" against the forthcoming Saxon raids somewhere between 450 and 538CE according to historical attempts to chronologize his deeds. Indeed, Geoffrey's Britons remind the first Roman invader Julius Caesar of the common ancestry of Britons and Romans back to "Priam, father of us all." Geoffrey of Monmouth [1958] IV [1], 66. For the most part, however, Montalvo's account of the battle for Constantinople historically most resembles the titanic war between Chosroes II of Sassanid Persia and the Byzantine emperor Heraclius in the early seventh century, when Persian forces actually laid seige to Constantinople and which ended in a resounding defeat for the Persians and the Roman capture of their capital Ctesiphon ("Ctesifante" in Montalvo). This war so depleted both empires that Islamic armies in the first decade of peace (630s) succeeded in destroying the Persian Empire and depriving the Byzantines of most of their Asian and African holdings.

21 Montalvo [2003] [123] 643. Curiously enough Little does not think that this very clear statement of Trojan ancestry is believable to Montalvo's readers because they would have taken anything a pagan would say as a lie. Little incorrectly adds that there is no other evidence in Montalvo's work to justify this Trojan genealogy, but already in the *Prólogo* Montalvo invokes the great heroes of Troy. Montalvo [1991], 222–223. Still, Little does concede that Montalvo would expect his readers to note the parallels between the Christian defense of Constantinople and the heroism of the original Trojan defenders of Troy. Montalvo [1992] 407 (note 4). Carlos Sainz de la Maza states that this link marks "con alguna inexactitud la tradición, defundida en castellano a partir de Alfonso X – que bebe en Geoffrey de Monmouth" of the Trojan origin

stantinople, and drive back the crusaders in a bloody and potentially fatal battle, Montalvo exploits the ensuing pause and recovery of the dead and wounded to inject California into the fortunes of his war. Admitting that this sudden shift is with regard to "the strangest thing ever found anywhere in written texts or in human memory," Montalvo introduces California as the element that paradoxically will provide the city which is on "the verge of being lost" with its "salvation" precisely from its "new danger."[22] Formally the danger is that Queen Calafía, her formidable Amazon warriors, and her griffons, will now lead the pagan forces and ensure Armato's victory with their superior warrior qualities (as well as the aeronautic technology of their griffons); indeed Calafía's initially fierce attack on the Christians wreaks such havoc that it brings Esplandián himself rushing from the forbidden mountain to the battle site. Yet Calafía remains in spirit a knight errant seeking the traditional goals of fame and glory.[23] Accordingly she submits a challenge of individual combat to the Christian side, a challenge accepted by Amadís and Esplandián. As a woman however, she is laid low by the matchless beauty of Esplandián himself and subsequently loses the arranged personal combat with his father Amadís. Her burgeoning love for Esplandián ensures that at the crucial moment of the subsequent key battle over Constantinople she will keep her forces from helping Armato and thus guarantee Esplandián's ensuing total victory on sea and land.[24]

Unfortunately for Calafía's love, notwithstanding her conversion to the "true" religion of Christianity, she cannot hope to marry Esplandián, since Montalvo's priorities require that his hero ascend to the imperial throne of Constantinople and Greece proper by marrying his true love (and Emperor's daughter) Leonorina. Still, Calafía does receive the important compensation of marriage to Esplandián's cousin Talanque. It is this final genealogical move by Montalvo that completes his absorption of his invented California into the genealogical line from storied Troy and also provides a surprisingly open future for his future Californians stemming from the reign of Calafía and Talanque in sharp contrast to the inaction that he designs for his European heroes, Amadís in Great Britain and Esplandián in Greece.

---

of British Brute. Montalvo [2003], 643 (note 572). Also Montero Garrido [1994], 210–223 and Sales Dasí [1998], 157 (note 32).

22   Montalvo [2003] [157], 727.
23   Calafía is also extremely proud of the richness of her (non-European, non-Christian) lineage: "Mi linage es muy alto, que, sin aver memoria del comienço, vengo de sangre real." Montalvo [2003] [178], 799.
24   By the end of the work Esplandián, now Emperor of Greece and Constantinople, will go on to conquer Persia and Armato as well. Montalvo [2003] [182], 813.

Whereas Esplandián is the son of Amadís, whose direct parentage is from "Gaul" (possibly "Wales"), Scotland ("Ecossia") and "Little Britain" (Brittany) and whose links with the kings of Great Britain he owes to his marriage to Oriana, daughter of King Lisuarte, Talanque is the son not only of Amadís' "Don Juan" brother Galaor (thus carrying at least the same parental connections as Esplandián) but also of Julianda, niece of the benign sorceress Urganda and, most importantly, daughter of Falangris/Falangriz (and of Urganda's sister Grimota). Falangris is in fact Lisuarte's brother and his predecessor to the throne of Great Britain.[25] In short, unlike Esplandián, Talanque's blood connections to the line of British kings – and hence, through Brute, to Troy proper, the original polis model for Montalvo's Constantinople – are impeccable. Besides, his mother Julianda is the Greek scholar who translates the whole work of the *Sergas* itself from its presumed "true" author Helisabad (who "wrote" it in Greek) to our "Author" Montalvo (for a genealogical chart of the Isle of California, see Figure 1).[26]

This newly reformed Californian kingdom of Calafía and Talanque is just getting its start at the end of Montalvo's vision. In fact it is endowed with a far more open-ended future than his avowed heroes who remain the specified rulers of Great Britain and of Greece. In the very middle of his work Montalvo as "Author" admits to an internal hesitation about concluding the project – biographers associate this doubt with possible personal difficulties of the 1491–2 period marking the imminent fall of Granada in which Montalvo was involved – and he is only reinvigorated to his task by Urganda's urgings and explanation that all his heroes will be frozen like sculptures in an abyss so that they can be brought back to life after Arthur himself is reawakened by Morgan le Fay to reign again over Great Britain with Montalvo's knights joining him in the real and final reconquest of Constantinople from the Turks.[27]

Unfortunately this arrangement leaves very little opportunity for deeds and fame for the immediate children of Montalvo's original heroes and ladies. Accordingly, these *infantes* head out to join Calafía and Talanque in California

---

25 This is very clearly stated in Montalvo [1991] [I, 3], 267: Falangriz "reinava en la Gran Bretaña," but, dying "sin heredero," passed on his rule to his brother Lisuarte. Also 268 and Montalvo [2003] [63], 398.

26 It is worth noting the supremacy of the Greek language in Montalvo's account. His heroes are quick to learn foreign languages. Amadís knows his Greek, German and Persian; Esplandián certainly knows his Greek. The "true" author of the *Sergas*, Helisabad, writes in Greek and Julianda translates it to the "Author's" language, presumably castilian Spanish. All this reflects the larger tradition that Greek was the language in which the *libros de caballerías* were supposedly written. See Daniel Eisenberg, *A Study of Don Quixote*, 71, cited by Little in Montalvo [1992], 67 (note 1). "Esplandián" itself is presumably a Trojan name. See Pierce [1976], 47.

27 Montalvo [2003] [98–99], 524–550; [183], 818–821.

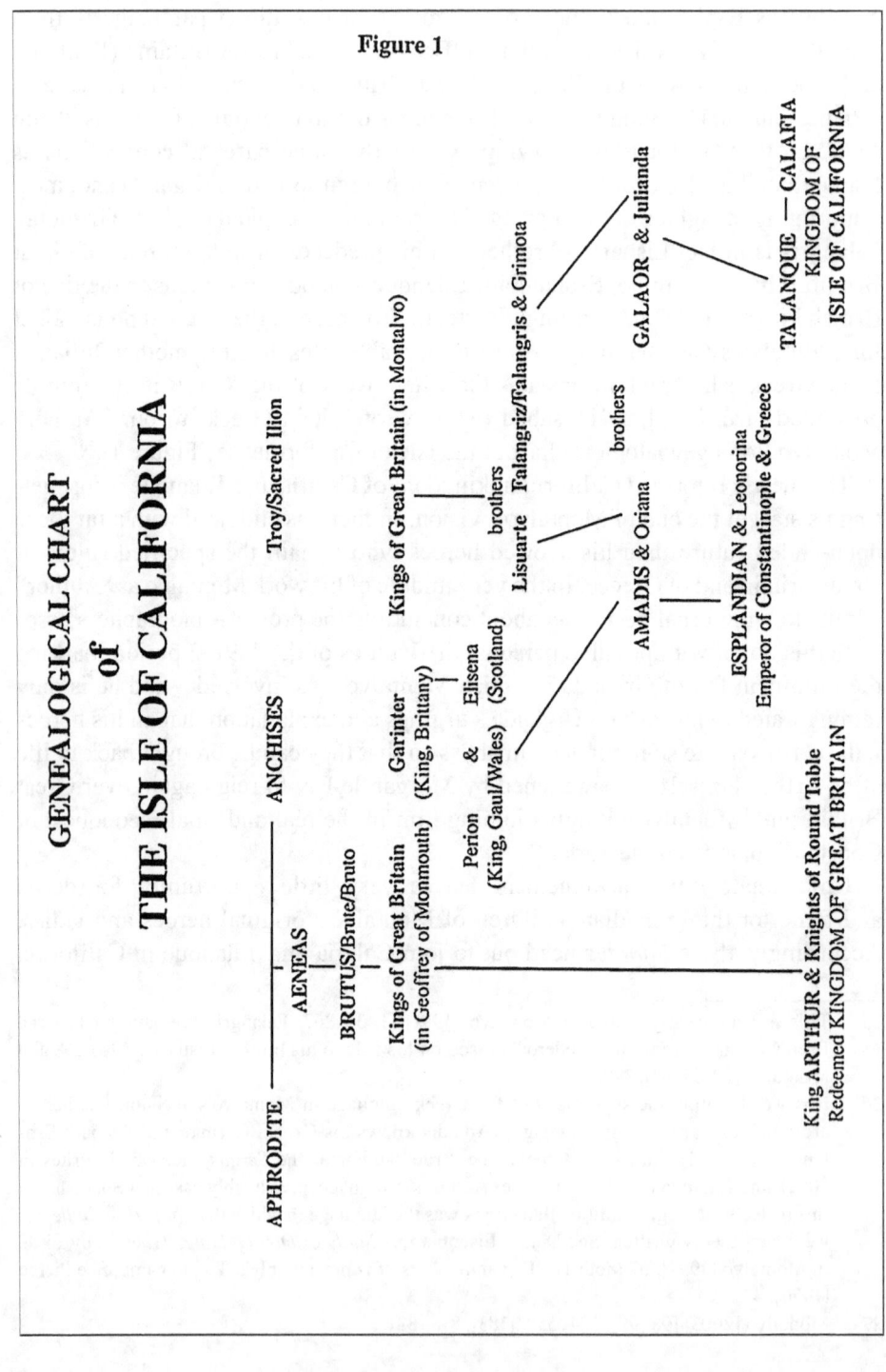

Figure 1

itself, renewing older patterns of knight errantry (*como cavelleros andantes*). Significantly enough therefore, Montalvo ends his entire narrative by focusing on Talanque and Calafía joining with their friends to conquer other islands. Given their encompassing love, Talanque accedes to Calafía's request to put aside the maidenly ways she has adopted since their marriage and, along with her female warriors, to join him and his men in martial deeds. Indeed, as queen and women prove their battlefield metal anew, the new California conquers the neighboring Island of Argalia where Calafía and Talanque meet a remarkable sage whose destiny it will be to write a book of great wisdom which will recount all the great deeds awaiting both the future Californians and the denizens of Contantinople.[28]

2.

If it is Garci Rodríquez de Montalvo who largely invents California in this manner, it turns out to be Hernán Cortés – the greatest of all conquistadores – who sites and names it. After the inventive *genealogical* bordering of California, there thus follows the first *geographical* bordering of it.

Hernán Cortés is justly celebrated (and, alternatively, pilloried) as the great conqueror of the Aztec Empire. Yet that achievement was completed by 1521; for the rest of his life Cortés was obsessed with finding the proper route to the South Seas, as a result of which efforts he should also be celebrated as the discoverer of "California." After sponsoring explorations by subordinates in 1533, it was Cortés who on May 3, 1535[29] landed on and named as "California" a body of land around what is now La Paz in Baja California.[30] Whatever his larger intentions, the name was applied more widely as Spaniards continued their sea explorations

---

28 Montalvo [2003] [178], 802; [182], 814; [184], 822–826. Montalvo's work in fact also spawned a host of imitative works chronicling the deeds of Esplandián's children, such as "Lisuarte of Greece."
29 See the evidence in the reference to "Mapa de la *Nueva tierra de Santa Cruz* [the area of La Paz, Baja California], extreme meridional de la *California* descubierta por Hernan Cortes el 3 de Mayo de 1535" [emphases in original], along with references to his act of possession, in Torres Lanzas [2000], 19–20. Also the documentary citation in León-Portilla [1985], 105–106.
30 The most plausible version of the claim that Cortés "named" California is by Little. Noting the number of writers between 1550 and 1654 who "refer to the place Cortés landed as *California*," Little goes on to consider "the unproved assumption that Cortés is responsible for the definitive naming": In "the absence of documentary evidence of the real event (for example 'I, Hernán Corté, do hereby declare the name of this bay and this island or peninsula to be *California*.'), it is sufficient to note that Cortés demonstrated such depth of education and a propensity for mythicizing actions in the conquest of México that it is reasonable to postulate a link between Cortés and Rodríquez de Montalvo in the naming of California." Little [1987], 34 (note 2).

of the baja (or "lower") California coast and by 1539 had more or less discovered that this body of land was not an island but a peninsula; accordingly, shortly thereafter in 1542 the first Spanish landing in what is now San Diego harbor by Juan Rodríguez Cabrillo initiated the Spanish affair with the "alta" or upper California coast.[31]

That Cortés' "California" very probably stems from Montalvo's thematics is confirmed from several directions. In the first place, evidence that the Amadís body of works was among the literature carried and imbibed by the conquistadores seems incontrovertible: Bernal Díaz del Castillo, the intrepid recorder of Cortés' triumphs over the Mexica in 1519–1521, compared the grand vision of the Aztecs' capital city Tenochitlán or Mexica, with its countless towers, pyramids and civic spaces, to the images in *Amadís de Gaula*.[32] In the second place, Cortés himself, in his fourth letter to Emperor Charles from Mexico, expressly referred to the existence of Amazons in the province of Ciguatán, a claim that purportedly confirms his familiarity with "the *californianas* in *Esplandián*."[33] In both cases, it should be noted, faced with such an unprecedented (and probably unrepeatable) contact with an alien civilization, the only concrete parallels the conquistadores could draw upon from personal experience and European reports were the great Islamic cities of Al-Andalus and Renaissance Venice.[34]

On a broader scale it seems clear that Montalvo's own fixation with islands reflects the fascinating reports coming into Spain after 1492 from the Columbian discoveries in the Caribbean archipelago; indeed it has been suggested that Montalvo's own invention of the two key islands in his narrative – *Isla Firma*, the Montalvo equivalent of Camelot or the ideal domain of chivalry, and the *Isla*

---

31 Details are provided with excellent maps in León-Portilla [1985]. The first map containing the word "California" is by Domingo del Castillo in 1541 (facing 136).
32 "These great towers and cues and buildings rising from the water, all made of stone, seemed like an enchanted vision from the tale of Amadís." Díaz del Castillo [1963], 214; see *Historia veradera de al conquista de Nueva España* (1904), II, 418. The author himself came from Montalvo's home town of Medina del Campo and his father was, like Montalvo, a *regidor*. Thomas [1993], 702 (note 54).
33 Little [1987], 14; Cortés [1986], 298–300, and Anthony Pagden, 502 (note 21) referring to Leonard [1944] on Velázquez's instructions to Cortés to search for the "nearby" Amazons. Little also notes that Nuño de Guzmán claimed in 1530 that the mythical Aztlán was only ten days away from Amazons by the Sea; presumably they were rich, possibly goddesses, and quite white (14). Finally, it has been suggested that Cortés' familiarity with the tall women of Tehuantepec, from which several of his California voyages of discovery set out, may have been the models for Amazons. Marks [1993], 280 (León-Portilla [1985] cites a 1532 document on "el puerto de Tehuantepeque" (86)). For an eloquent twentieth-century description of these *tehuanas*, see Covarrubias [1946], 243–296.
34 Thomas [1993], 292–293.

California itself – resulted from the effects of these reports on his imagination.[35] Such effects would have been compatible with the overall reading of the globe after a century of Portuguese and Spanish explorations into the blue waters of the "Ocean Sea" of the Atlantic. In imaginal affinity with Aeneas' Trojan quest for a new home to the west called "Hesperia," fifteenth-century island-hopping starting with the Canary, Madeira and Azores Islands suggested the possibility of a continuous line of such islands all the way to the fabled "Indies" themselves, which also formed a rich body of archipelagoes extending from Zipangu (Japan) to Taprobana (Sri Lanka or Ceylon). Even after the discovery of South America around 1500 more or less quickly led to its recognition as a "continent," it was still felt that Columbus' Caribbean landfall augured a further set of islands to the north – rather than a North American "continent" – that eventually worked its way to the Indies and to "Cathay" proper. Along this extensive thalassic highway, the "Island of California" – partially confirmed and mythologized through the discovery of the peninsula of Baja California – provided a convenient and alluring fit.[36] Indeed, as we earlier noted, notwithstanding practical confirmation of Baja's peninsular status as early as 1539, canonical European maps of the subsequent two centuries continued to display an "Isle of California" west of the North American continent as late as 1747.[37]

This naming of "California" was then gradually extended to what became known as Spain's Far West frontier and borderlands. Generally speaking, these lands became identified as: (1) *California* proper – either administered as the two units of Alta and Baja California – *Las Californias*[38] – or as one unit; (2) New Mexico or *Nuevo México,* concentrated around the already highly functional civic units of the Pueblos and Zuñis located along the upper Rio Grande valley; (3) and Texas. In other words, "California" or "the Californias" was applied to a far larger body of territory than the present U.S. state of California and to the present Mexican states of Baja California.

In terms of actual explorations during the initial century of colonial assertion, Spain was mainly concerned with New Mexico (see Map 2).[39] From the wander-

---

35 Avalle-Arce [1990], cited by Little in Montalvo [1992], 340 (note 1).
36 Parry [1981]. The connections between Sir Lanka as a possible "terrestrial paradise" in accordance with Biblical injunctions and the location of Montalvo's "California" on the "right" side of the Terrestrial Paradise is explored in Little [1987] and Sales Dasí [1998].
37 See Chapter 1 above.
38 Originally *Las Californias* could mean a presumed cluster of islands (one conjecture imagined them in a circle) to be called California, before it referred generally to Upper and Lower California. See Polk [1991], 117 and Plate 17b.
39 Regarding the territories within the present U.S. state of Arizona, the key figure for its gradual colonization was Father Eusebio Francisco Kino who came up from the province of Sonora to establish his missionary work in the late 1690s along the Gila River and Santa Cruz River. In

ings of Alvar Núñez Cabeza de Vaca in 1536 to the better-known expedition of Francisco Vásquez de Coronado in 1540, these earliest ventures settled on those communities which inspired tales of the existence of the seven cities of Cíbola (the smallest of which presumably exceeded Mexico City) and their reported mounds of gold.[40] More practically, it was after 1598 that Spaniards resolved to formally colonize this New Mexico, the crown declaring in 1609 a royal colony to be maintained at government expense. Nonetheless, subsequent onerous Spanish rule over the native population unleashed the Pueblo revolts of 1680, and notwithstanding stern Spanish reaction, these wars actually worked to the benefit of the neighboring peoples, the Navajos and Apaches, who were growing increasingly bellicose thanks to the spread of horse and rifle technology. As a result, during the eighteenth century the Spanish were in effect forced to agree to "a Spanish-Pueblo" alliance in New Mexico which turned it into a mere "fragment of empire."[41]

In California itself, outside of sea explorations to seek out fishing and pearling possibilities along the long Pacific coast, Spain constructed no permanent presence for its first two centuries of claims over the territories. Only as late as 1697 did the government begin a mission network, starting in Loreto, for controlling the land and native peoples in Baja California, followed in 1769 by a more ambitious formation of missions that by 1824 would reach San Francisco and Sonoma in alta California, just below the first – and brief – Russian colonies in northern California. These steps, of major importance for Bourbon Spanish policy of forming a more efficient empire comparable to similar reorganizations by other such colonial powers as Britain, France and the Netherlands, clearly show Spanish fears of being outflanked in these western frontiers by similarly acquisitive European powers. Unlike rule over the New Mexican Pueblo who already had their own longstanding civic settlements, the California missions forcibly moved

---

this region Father Kino created the first mission at San Xavier del Bac in the Santa Cruz Valley and continually pressed for further creation of a Spanish *villa* or city-colony on the Colorado River which could serve as a base for direct overland links with alta and baja California. Unfortunately the Spanish government was otherwise occupied with European wars during 1697–1713 ("The War of the Spanish Succession"), and the direct land route from Sonora across Arizona into California was only established some fifty years later. Wagoner [1975], 77–93. Of great value are Father Kino's 1701 and 1702 maps of the region, the former headed "Passage Par Terre a la Californie" and the latter labeled "Tabula Californiae." See Burrus [1965]. According to Polk [1991], 295–302, Kino is credited with scientifically confirming the continuity of California with the North American land mass.

40   White [1991, 6. As White notes, the Spaniards were faced with 130 effectively independent Zuñi villages, each one populated with 400 to 2,000 people.

41   White [1991], 13; also Spicer [1962] for a more detailed account of native American groupings and Spanish policy during this period.

Map 2

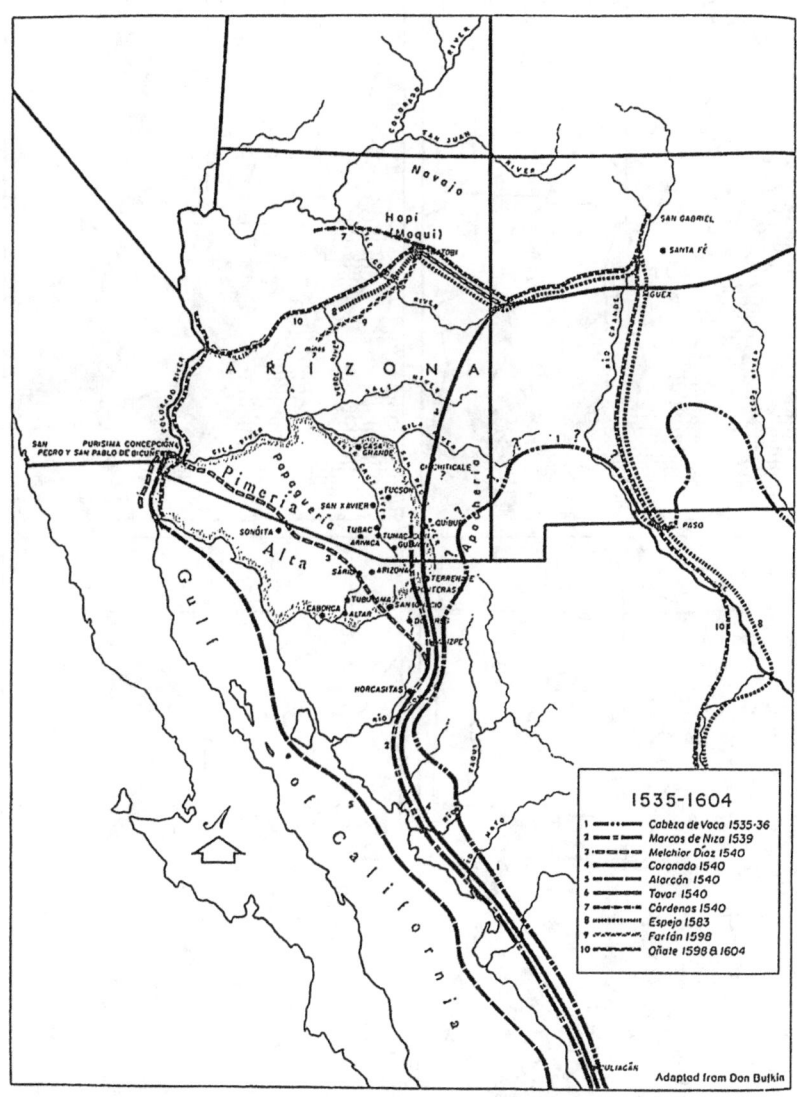

Routes of the early Spanish explorers
By kind permission of Jay J. Wagoner

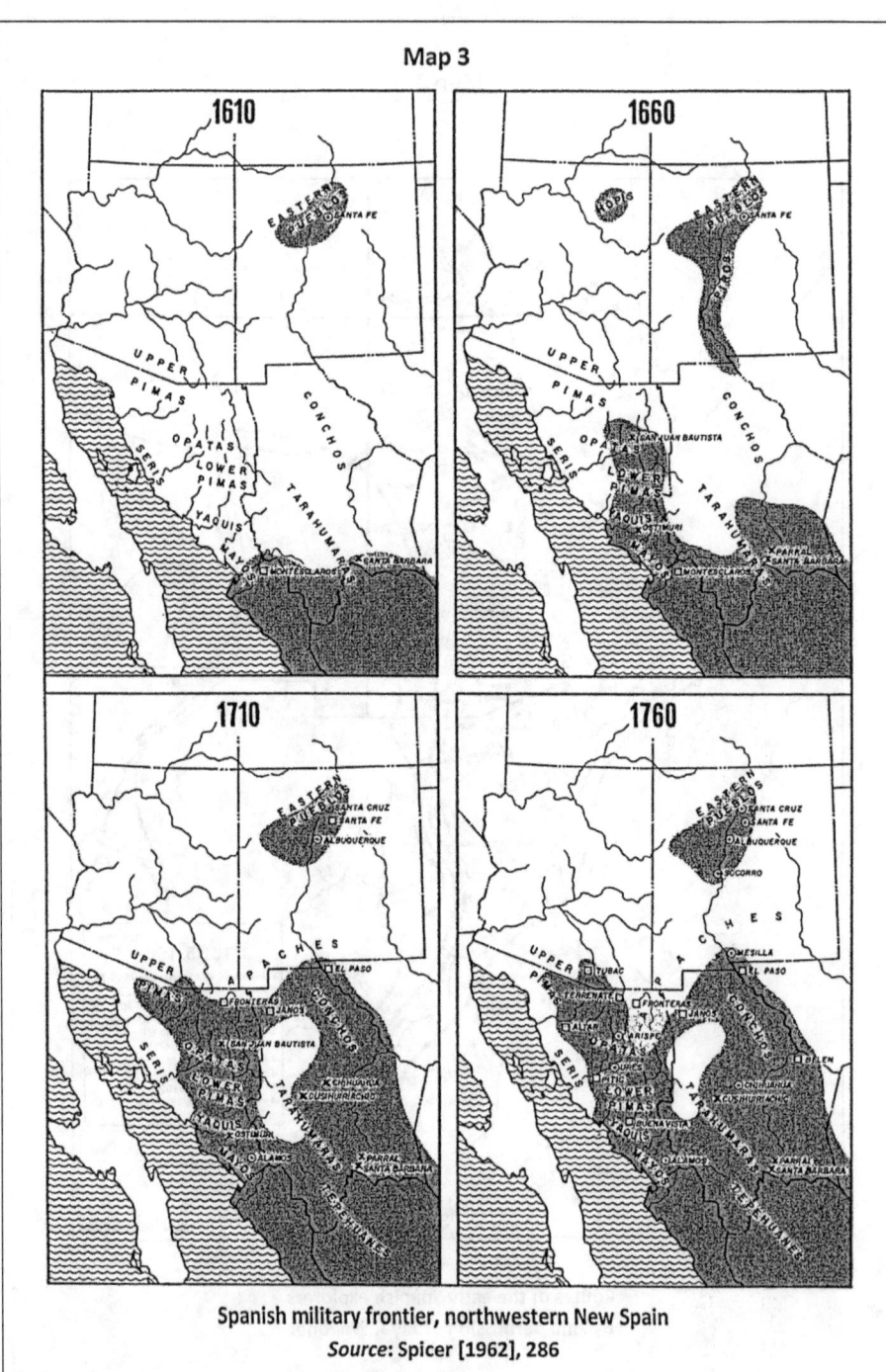

Map 3

Spanish military frontier, northwestern New Spain
Source: Spicer [1962], 286

native populations from their smaller localities to residency and labor in the missions themselves (see Map 3).

Aside from these coastal connections along the baja and alta coasts, Spain did not seriously fuse its Californian and overland territories directly until 1774 when Juan Bautista de Anza connected California to Sonora, and land links were consolidated around the Gila-Colorado route between Sonora and California (see Map 4). At this stage the Spanish more or less held a loose alliance with the Pueblos in "small, isolated villages along the Rio Grande" that were continually threatened by increasingly powerful nomadic enemies and a "string of equally beleaguered missions and presidios" in Texas pressed by such varied groupings as the Comanches, Utes and Apaches.[42] In short, whatever the impressive cartographic pretensions of New Spain's Far West borderlands, the reality was significantly more modest, at a time when the "last of the conquistadores," Father Junípero Serra, embarked on his mission system along coastal alta California.[43] He was backed by a Spain understandably concerned that notwithstanding its formal claims over California, Spain's colonial rivals France, Russia or Britain could well decide to move in if the land remained generally unoccupied.

Late eighteenth-century Spanish policy was therefore one of "defensive expansion" and it proved largely successful by 1800. For one thing, Spain benefitted from the defeat of France in the Seven Years War and the Peace of Paris of 1763 in which France passed on its Louisiana territories to ally Spain rather than relinquish them to the victor Britain. For another, during this period Spain was generally successful in coming to terms with the Comanches and, to a lesser extent, the Apaches. Finally, Spain worked hard to integrate its Far West provinces into Mexico proper with particular concern for the vulnerability of California. As part of its overall reorganization of these lands, it established separate administrations for Alta and Baja California in 1804.

Unfortunately for these measures, it turned out that the real danger to New Spain came more from within. An explosive set of revolts first set up by the Napoleonic takeover of the Iberian homeland in 1808 led, after over a decade of violent civil war in New Spain itself, to the establishment of an independent Mexico in 1821. Thus the fate of *Las Californias* passed on to the fate of the new state of Mexico itself. This would pertain to a series of interrelated issues: *within* Mexico, first, to the struggle between "liberal" secularization forces and elements of the pro-Spanish guard which had been defeated but remained unbowed, and, second, to the future legal and political relation between the home provinces of Mexico around the capital city – where the real power and status of the new

---

42   White [1991], 30.
43   See Engelbert [1956].

Map 4

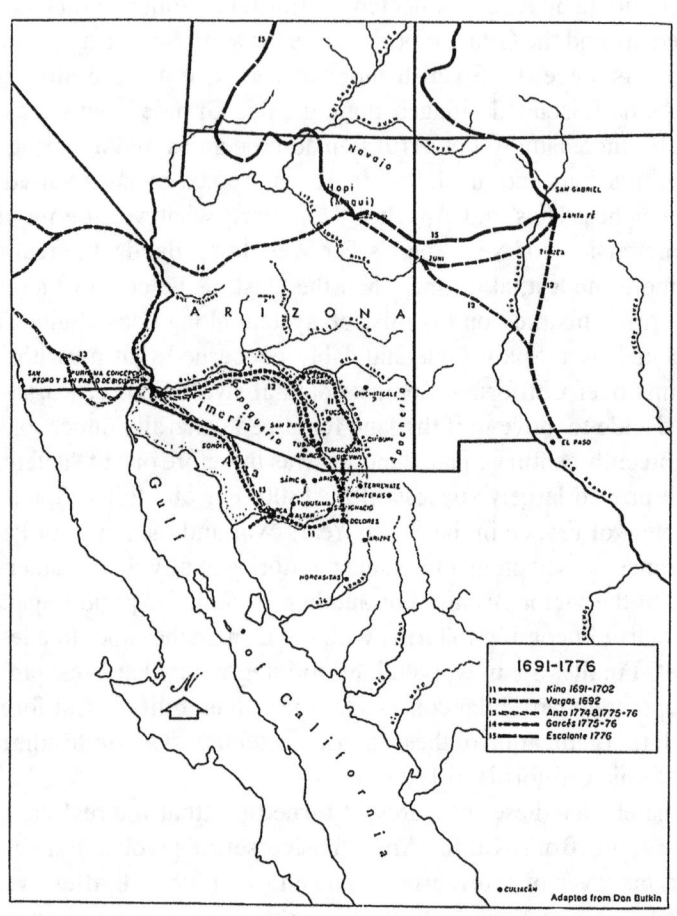

Spanish exploration routes in Arizona 1691-1776
By kind permission of Jay J. Wagoner

state lay – and the outer provinces including California; *beyond* Mexico, to the new regime's relations with the usual set of acquisitive colonial rivals Britain, Russia, and France, as well as an entirely new political power, the United States of America, which had supplanted the French (and the Spanish) in the Louisiana territories since 1803.

In 1800 Napoleon reacquired the Louisiana territories; in 1803, rather unexpectedly he sold them to Jefferson's America.[44] Suddenly, New Spain veered from reconsidering briefly its border concerns about France to worries about an apparently expansive and neighboring continental power. In the short run, Spain and the U.S. came to an agreement in 1819 with regard to common borders. Besides the sale of Florida to the U.S., Spain agreed to a common border starting with the Sabine River in the Gulf of Mexico, continuing along the Red River and the south bank of the Arkansas River "to its source" until it reached the 42nd North parallel, thence along the 42nd parallel all the way to "the South Sea," or Pacific Ocean, as the northern border for New Spain's Far West territories.[45] This border agreement then became the basis for the boundary negotiated by the United States and the new Mexican government in their subsequent treaties of 1828 and 1831.[46]

As provinces within these dispensations, *Las Californias* could be formally regarded as extending eastward well into territories located west of the continental divide, i. e. the line between watersheds heading west (e. g. the Colorado River) and those heading east (e. g. the Rio Grande River). In fact, outside a few minor efforts to colonize what is now called Arizona,[47] effective control by Mexico only included Californian settlements hugging the Pacific coast until the next substantial body of settlements concentrated along the upper Rio Grande river at Santa Fe and Taos (see Map 5).[48] Santa Fe itself functioned as the crossroads for the

---

44   For an account of François Barbé-Marbois, the French negotiator who sold Louisiana on behalf of Napoleon, see Potton [2007]. My thanks to François Logerot for this reference.

45   See Article 3 in Document 41, treaty with Spain of 22 February 1819, in Miller [1933], Vol. 3, 5–7.

46   Article 2 in Document 60, treaty with Mexico of 12 January 1828 and 5 April 1831, in Miller [1933], Vol. 3, 407–408. Article 3 calls for a commissioner and surveyor to fix the line "with more precision" (408–9).

47   In 1824 the Mexican government combined the provinces of Sonora and Sinaloa under the name Estado Interno de Occidente, with Arizona south of the Gila River becoming part of this new state; in 1830 this Estado Interno de Occidente was divided, with Sonora, along with southern Arizona, becoming separate. North of the Gila River, the land was described on maps simply as "Los Yndios Gentiles" ("the gentile, or heathen, Indians"). It was "vaguely claimed" by both the Mexican territories of New Mexico and California, but "it was colonized by neither." In effect, "it is little wonder that nobody in Arizona really knew who governed." Wagoner [1975], 162.

48   The New Mexico settlements were in fact substantially more populous than the Californian. Weber [1988], 92.

Map 5

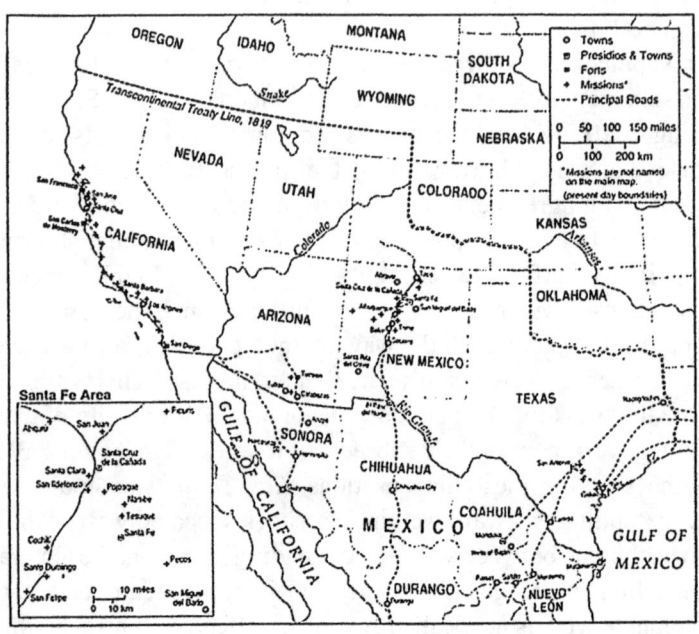

The Spanish-Mexican rim, 1821
By permission of Oxford University Press

main set of trails linking together the Mexican Southwest: the east-west trail (the "Santa Fe Trail") went from the U.S. at Independence, Missouri, through Santa Fe to the California coast at Los Angeles pueblo (the "Old Spanish Trail"), and the more important north-south trail (the "El Camino Real") directly linked Santa Fe and New Mexico to Mexico proper at Chihuahua.

In 1839 the Mexican government reorganized its "Californias" into the single department of California (one of 24 comprising the republic), with district capitals at San Juan Bautista, Los Angeles, and La Paz.[49] Formally then, at the very moment when Mexico succumbed to U.S. arms in the war of 1846–8 by its acqui-

---

[49] Miller [1998], 61, 64, on the decrees arriving in Santa Barbara from Mexico on 15 November, 1838 and the decree by Juan Bautista Alvarado of 25 February 1839 reflecting new regulations.

52

escence to the terms of the Treaty of Guadalupe Hidalgo of 1848 transferring "California" to the United States, California formed a single administrative unit (with three district capitals) within the Mexican state, and this department covered more or less the present U.S. states of California, Nevada, Utah, slivers of Wyoming and Colorado, much of Arizona – and Baja California. Of these territories only Baja would remain with Mexico; the others would be legally and politically separated from the present U.S. state of California by fundamental territorial adjustments during 1848–1850 within the newly expanded U.S. union. Paradoxically, then, the breakup of this "Greater California" directed attention to its nature and destiny just when it had ceased to exist as a single unit.

3.

If California begins with a Trojan-classical genealogical conceit going back to Aphrodite and Anchises, and is then sited by the concrete determinations of conquistadores and ensuing imperial efforts to hold on to this massive territory, this Greater California marks in turn the first clarification of a new ethos, that of the *californios*, emerging from the relatively recent settlement of missions, presidios and pueblos that was established by Spanish imperial policy.

The *californio* ethos, it needs to be underscored, proved dramatically different from – and ultimately opposed to – the priorities of the new Mexican state that was simultaneously struggling to establish its sovereignty over a widely extended and loosely held body of territories. Not until the Constitution of 1857 and the era of Benito Juárez (1857–1871) did Mexico's liberals succeed in establishing a modicum of stability for Mexico, but that came well after the severe amputation of Mexican sovereignty between 1836 and 1853 with the respective losses of Texas, California, New Mexico, and southern Arizona to the United States. During the heyday of *californio* society, 1833–1855, the presidency went through no less than 35 changes.[50] These changes reflected swings from what the liberals espoused in the Constitution of 1824 as a federal and decentralized solution regarding republican governance to conservative efforts after 1829 to reorient power back to Mexico City and the central provinces at the expense of the borderlands.

However, even with the best will in the world among its political rivals, the young state would have faced considerable obstacles.[51] The temporary allevi-

---

50 Weber [1988], 109.
51 As Weber argues, a clear account of this period is unfortunately hard to come by in the face of the eventual American takeover of Mexico's far western lands. While American accounts, even granted more recent politically correct sensitivity, still follow the story of an inevitable American expansionism into the West ("manifest destiny"), the Hispanic-Mexican versions,

ation of external pressures around 1800 had given way in the early nineteenth century to renewed conflict with the nomadic Apaches as well as to a new force entering the equation. While Indian tribes struck with such vigor on the borderland Mexican settlements that the new government lost sustained access to its border population and military compounds, American settlers and wanderers increasingly made their way into these relatively ungoverned areas and often bargained with Indians to the detriment of Mexican border stability. In particular, "mountain men" – a general sociological term to cover wanderers, traders, fur trappers and general undesirables – used the nomads to weaken Mexican authority for their own personal gain and trafficking.[52]

The obvious response would have been to increase military protection of these borders. But not only was it an intrinsically more difficult task now that the Spanish treaties with the Indians had subsided and the means available to Indian raiders skyrocketed through deals with Americans. Given the continued civic strife and instability between Mexican liberals and conservatives, it was also the case that qualified officers were hardly attracted to the troubled borders. For them it made much more political sense to secure posts close to or in the capital in case of sudden shifts in political fortunes.[53] As for the solution of bringing in American settlers into these relatively unpopulated border provinces, Mexico did temporarily change the Spanish policy of exclusion of foreigners, only to find that Americans pouring into areas contiguous to the U.S., such as the state of "Coahuila y Texas," far from assimilating into a Mexican self-identity, retained their yankee allegiances and thus served as a potential fifth column for breakaway tendencies.[54] Finally, even where liberals thought they were laying the foundations of an improved civic order, their measures proved ambiguous and often self-destructive. Liberals fought to secularize the missions, presumably in order to free the native population from church oppression, and they established the legal equality of Indians. Unfortunately such emancipation increased the capacity of the native population to fight Mexico; meanwhile, in California the closing of the missions generally turned the native population into landless and oppressed workers while

---

equally spellbound by the *Norteamericano* juggernaut, seem loathe to face this rather disconsolate period in their history. As a result, the kind of archival investigation of Spanish and Mexican sources that might break down present mythologizing is as yet lacking. Weber [1988], 89–104.

52 Weber [1988], 117–132; also Wagoner [1975], 242–258 for Arizona.
53 Weber [1988], 111.
54 The Mexican government did attempt to bring colonizing expeditions to California at a time when, according to one participant, "in Mexico to speak of California was like mentioning the end of the world." Nonetheless, eye-witness reports glorified California as "a land which in time would be one of the richest." Janssens [1953], 11.

californios exploited the opportunity to seize church lands and carve up the territory into massive rancherías displacing the natives.[55]

Following such events from the far north, *californios* became steadily more frustrated with Mexican policy and action during the two decades of Mexican rule. Indeed, immediately after independence in 1821, the hispanic-speaking residents of California already began referring to themselves as *Californios* rather than *Mexicanos* and developed strong hostility to Mexicans as *la otra banda* ("the other side").[56] On top of the constant shifts of governance from the capital, *californios* complained constantly of the central government's shortcomings in providing the necessary financial resources or even protecting them from raids by foreigners. Even when troops and settlers were sent, *californios* were furious that they tended to be convicts and *cholos* ("scoundrels"). Moreover, rather than showing sensitivity to *californio* regionalism, Mexico City tended to appoint Mexican rather than *californio* governors to rule the region. Finally – a grievance shared with other parts of the borderland provinces – *californios* were angered that the capital never fulfilled its promises to turn the borderland territories into states within the United Mexican States.[57]

The two decades of Mexican rule were therefore rent by at least two major efforts at *californio* autonomy. The first in 1836–8, shared with other borderland provinces, followed the abolition of the federal Constitution of 1824 and its replacement by the draconic Constitution of 1836 under President Antonio López de Santa Anna.[58] This new constitution ended the system of states and territories and turned New Mexico, California and Texas into departments governed from the center in a manner resembling the previous Spanish bureaucracy. The borderland revolts eventually led to an independent Lone Star State for Texas – the first serious amputation of Mexican lands – while both New Mexico and California temporarily returned to the fold.[59] Nonetheless, at its peak in 1836, the *californio* revolt under native governor Juan Bautista Alvarado produced a Californian "Declaration of Independence" stating that "California is erected into a free and sovereign state, establishing a congress that shall pass all the particular laws of the country," albeit within the compass of the (then suspended) 1824 fed-

---

55 Weber [1988], 101.
56 The Mexican-born Governor José Figueroa in 1833 "noted that the *californios* looked upon Mexicans with the same animosity that Mexicans viewed Spaniards." Weber [1988], 115.
57 Miller [1998], 26–7. Thus, Miller writes, by "1836 the Californios had developed a strong prejudice against Mexico and Mexicans who arrived from *la otra banda*" (45). Also Pitt [1966], 7.
58 Miller [1998], 41–46; White [1991], 39.
59 Weber [1988], 109.

eral constitution.⁶⁰ Eventually California did come to an agreement with the new government along with the latter's 1839 restructuring of California into a single department, but Alvarado for one remained concerned about California's exposed position: in the words of a French visitor, "too weak by itself to be independent and too backward in civilization to administer itself."⁶¹

Thus it needed only a further accumulation of grievances toward the central government, after its selection of General Manuel Micheltorena to govern California in 1842, to set off the second major and final *californio* revolt. An ally of Santa Anna, Micheltorena brought with him an army of *cholos* he was unable to control.⁶² Erupting in 1844, the *californio* revolt succeeded in driving out the governor and his men by 1845.⁶³ His "departure marked the end of Mexico's direct rule of California – that is, he was the last governor sent from central Mexico." At the same time civil strife had broken out in Mexico City itself during the same period 1844–1845.⁶⁴

Such were the specific political conditions under which California would be dragged into the American-Mexican War of 1846–8. Already during the 1840s *californios* had become exceedingly worried about the continued intrusion of American settlers across the mountains into Californian lands unoccupied by the *californios* themselves who remained segregated along the coast. Quite apart

---

60 Miller [1998], 50. Don Agustín Janssens, who was an eye witness to these events, insists that the revolutonaries' original aim was "the proclaiming of independence from Mexico" since "the plan of independence for California" had been "conceived for a long time." Nonetheless the original insistence on expelling Mexicans was soon modified in deference to the Mexicans among the participants. Janssens' account also reveals the degree to which Mexicans were generally hated by the *californios*. Janssens [1953], 50, 51, 53. Along with his boyhood friends Vallejo and Castro, Alvarado seems to have been a reader of Cervantes, Rousseau, Voltaire, and a history of Jacobinism, while Vallejo apparently had a copy of Fenelon's classic *Les aventures de Telemaque*. Miller [1998], 16, 31.
61 Captain Abel Dupetit-Thouars of the French vessel *Venus*, cited in Miller [1998], 56. More generally, cf. the valuable reminiscences of Alvarado, who was governor of California 1836–1842, in Alvarado [1876].
62 Janssens notes that "Californians applied to these troops, the epithet of *Cholos*." Janssens [1953], 117.
63 In a bold letter to Micheltorena, Alvarado as co-leader of the rebels proudly proclaimed: "The *sons of California* will do us justice, and we will shed our blood rather than *permit our country* to endure this infamous oppression." Cited in Miller [1998], 106 (emphasis added).
64 Miller [1998], 110, 102–110. After the departure of Micheltorrena, political and miliary government in California came under the temporary control of the *californios* Pío Pico and José Castro. As Pitt [1966], 22, states, already California was seen as occupying at this stage "the status of an international outlander." Later, according to Pitt, *californios* would partly blame their eventual downfall by the 1880s to "a failure to break completely with Mexico when it lay within their grasp to do so in the 1840s, which would have enabled them to appear before their Yankee conquerors as their own masters" (278).

from the potential for strife between *californio* and yankee settlers, it was becoming increasingly apparent that the newcomers would in time swamp the Spanish-speaking population in numbers.⁶⁵ Far from merging with *californio* society, yankee settlers largely created their own American settlements and retained close connections with the home American Republic. Unfortunately, rather than maintain a united front, *californios* remained caught up in their own kinship conflicts as well as a continuing hostility between the north (Monterey and San Francisco) and south (Los Angeles). Meanwhile outside powers such as France, Britain, Russia, and the United States made veiled suggestions of placing California under their protection, or even annexing it outright.⁶⁶

A gathering of *californio* leaders in April 1846 reveals the difficulties of the situation as seen by the elite. Some argued that California should put itself under a French protectorate, granted that France was also Catholic; others suggested joining a contiguous republic like the United States.⁶⁷ One retired captain Don Rafael Gonzalez declared: "*Viva* California, free, sovereign, and independent." What was not apparently seriously contemplated was further association with an unreliable Mexico.⁶⁸

As it turned out, initiative was stolen from the *californios* by the unexpected putsch later in 1846 by an American newcomer John C. Frémont who instigated a local yankee revolt in Sonoma which turned into the so-called "Bear Flag Republic" – an apparently California Republic – to be passed on to the United States. As *californios* massed to repel this threat, they found out almost simultaneously

---

65 See Chapter 1 above.
66 The controversial question of U.S. designs on California in 1845–1846 was nicely settled by the persistent research and inquiries of California philosopher Josiah Royce. Notwithstanding later claims by John C. Frémont, U.S. President James Buchanan's instructions to U.S. consul Thomas Larkin prior to the outbreak of war between Mexico and the U.S. were simply to assure Californian authorities – already recognized as only under "nominal" relation to Mexico – of U.S. goodwill and sympathy, to "induce them, if possible, to separate voluntarily from that country [Mexico]; to promise them, if they did separate, our kind offices as a *sister republic*." Royce [1970], 107 (emphasis added). Larkin's ultimate aim was "first, an independent republic managed by Californians, Yankees, and Europeans", and second, "an American military protectorate in an arrangement just shy of annexation." Pitt [1966], 21, following Hawgood [1958].
67 Pio Pico later states that as governor he sent the emissary José Maria Covarrubias to negotiate with a British admiral that if Mexico was disinterested in protecting California, "obliging us to rebel against it, California would place itself under the protection of His Britannic Majesty." Pico notes that "the prominent people" in Los Angeles were disposed to proclaim independence and "they pressed me to declare it," but he felt it was too "dangerous" if it was not done with the approval of José Castro controlling the northern towns and he was unable to contact Castro. Pico [1973], 123
68 "viva Califorinà libre, soberana è independiente." Alvarado [1876], V, 138; Miller [1998], 115–7.

that a more general war had broken out meanwhile between the United States and Mexico. Remarkably enough, among the borderlands only the *californios* offered any effective resistance to the American invasions, even winning a battle in November 1846 before surrendering in January 1847.[69] The terms of surrender, which turned out to be more or less those of the final agreement of Guadalupe Hidalgo in 1848 for all participants, guaranteed parity for the *californios* in the new American order in terms of citizenship and property claims (see Map 6).[70]

Greater California – the lands, minus Baja California, that were transferred to the U.S. – did not itself survive political-legal truncation,[71] but this in fact reflected voluntary actions taken by the new Californians. The U.S. had suddenly swallowed an immense amount of territory without really being prepared for knowing how to deal with it. Creation of something like an activist expansionist federal apparatus developed in the course of facing the problems attached to annexation over the next half-century.[72] Between 1846 and 1850 the federal government was entirely unclear about its strategy. However, within California itself annexation took place simultaneously with the single most important economic event to hit the territory in its history. As we earlier noted, the 1848–9 Gold Rush transformed California overnight into a functional advanced economy, and it was the Californians themselves – primarily the yankee settlers who had helped bring about the U.S. annexation – who, meeting in 1849 to frame a constitution for California, resolved to constitute a "free" state and in effect draw the present boundaries of the U.S. state of California. These borders reflected the Californians' discomfort with Mormon presence in Utah as well as their unwillingness to associate with the possibility of "slave" tendencies in the "New Mexico territories."

---

69 White [1991], 79–80.
70 These promises were generally betrayed over the next thirty-odd years of property litigation. Similarly the use of bilingual markers only lasted the first thirty-odd years. See in particular Pitt [1966].
71 When the present lands of Arizona north of the Gila River became officially part of the U.S. in 1848, "there were no Anglo-American settlements there." Wagoner [1975], 277. The Gadsden Purchase of 1853 eventually settled the international border in such a way that the U.S. acquired additional territory which the Mexican President Santa Anna found worthless. The agreement at least allowed Mexico to retain a land passage to Baja California. In negotiating for additional land, U.S. diplomats had at their disposal several proposals, many of which included offers for Baja California. See the account in Wagoner [1975], 288–297. There is also the quixotic failed effort by the American Southerner-adventurer William Walker to create a Republic of Lower California in 1853 with its capital at La Paz. See May [1973] and Harrison [2004]. See Chapter 6 below.
72 See the thoughtful analysis in White [1991], "The Federal Government and the Nineteenth-Century West," 55–178.

Map 6

Map used for negotiations for the
Treaty of Guadalupe Hidalgo 1848
Source: U.S. Library of Congress

Californians therefore set up the manner of their entry into the Union in 1850 as a state without any intervening period spent as a federal territory.[73] Whereas the other territories between California and the Mississippi were characteristically forced to spent long periods as territories under direct control of federal agencies, the U.S. state of California from the outset was an active participant in U.S. politics thanks to its suddenly burgeoning population and economic muscle. Eventually the "Utah" territory set up in 1850 became the states of Nevada (1864) and Utah (1896), with pieces going to Wyoming and Colorado, while the "New Mexico" territory, also set up in 1850, became the states of Arizona (1912) and New Mexico (1912), with a southern sliver going to Nevada (see Map 7).[74] Of these integral parts of the original Greater California to be incorporated into the U.S., the U.S. state of California alone was able to lessen federal intervention in its affairs and over the next half-century build up an economic base containing the only two substantial urban and metropolitan concentrations (San Francisco and Los Angeles) in the American West.

By the 1890s, thanks to growing profits for American farmers in the new global economy as well as to the beginnings of Southern Californian boosterism (cultivated by the railroads, city fathers and real estate speculators), settlers from the American midwest began the long sustained immigration into California proper – rather than stopping in between – thanks to the health and climate attractions of the state.[75] From this significant influx of people and their savings, California took off in the early twentieth century as by far the most dynamic economy in the American West. While the rest of Greater California remained subordinate either directly or indirectly to federal policy and control, the California of the 1920s succeeded in creating an independent engine for growth concentrated on an increasingly diversified set of industries from oil and agriculture to Hollywood. Even the 1930s depression hit California less hard than the other Western states; in fact California became the choice of asylum for dispossessed Western farmers ("Oakies") of the decade, while significant elements of California culture were shaping the affluent ethos that would then become the American standard of the 1950s. When around 1940 the U.S. turned to a war economy, California was

---

[73] Judson A. Grenier, "'Officialdom': California State Government, 1849–1979," in Burns & Orsi [2003], 137–168.

[74] Even though Nevada's entry in 1864 – due to voting patterns related to President Lincoln's election strategy (in fact against the Californian John C. Frémont) during wartime – was not long after that of California's in 1850, Nevada's senators in the 1870s and 1880s characteristically preferred to live in San Francisco in acknowledgment of the latter's "financial and cultural influence on Nevada." White [1991], 392. As recently as 1949 McWilliams could unapologetically describe Nevada as "simply a satellite of California." McWilliams [1949], 351. See Chapter 6 below.

[75] White [1991], 190–191; Starr [1973] and [1985].

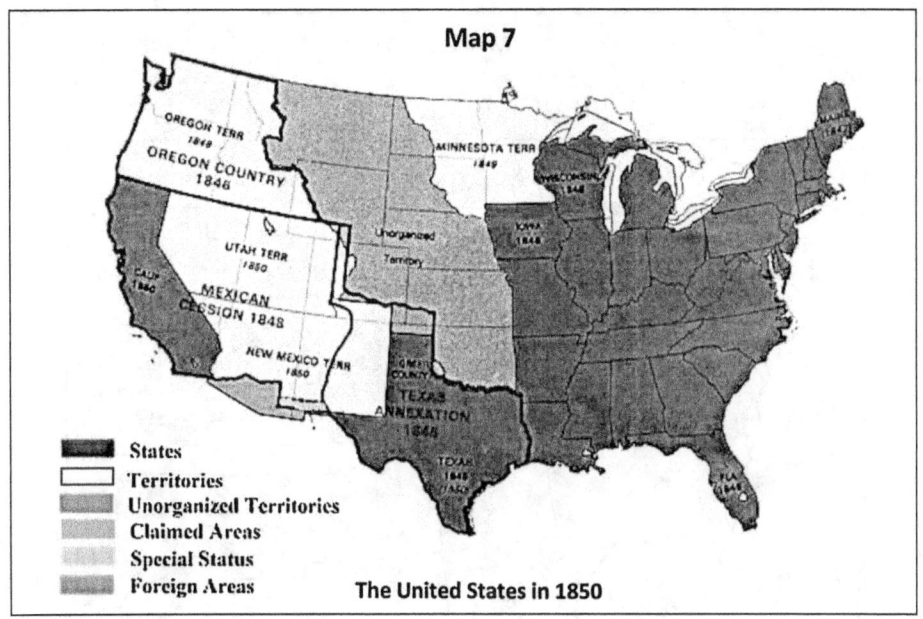

Map 7

The United States in 1850

Legend:
- States
- Territories
- Unorganized Territories
- Claimed Areas
- Special Status
- Foreign Areas

the favored site for federal largesse in the creation of a full employment economy: by 1945 even East Coast analysts were granting California's emergence as a powerful manufacturing presence in the world economy. These gains continued to accumulate during the 1950s and 1960s as California became the most populous state in the American Union and began its first forays into the top list of world economies (see Map 8).[76]

4.

It is arguable that this story of Californian preeminence in the American West could be recounted by using simply the starting point of the Gold Rush. According to this perspective the California that is generally recognized was "born" suddenly and dramatically at that time and grew in bursts and starts to its present status thanks to its function largely within the expanding American union and economy of the late nineteenth and early twentieth centuries. As part of this story it could be added that the Californian economy easily dwarfed its Western neighbors and turned them largely into its "colony" for such primary needs as water and raw materials. To this extent, there might be something like a general

---

76 The best introductions to these periods of Californian history and economy are Starr [1996], [1997], [2002]; cf. also White [1991].

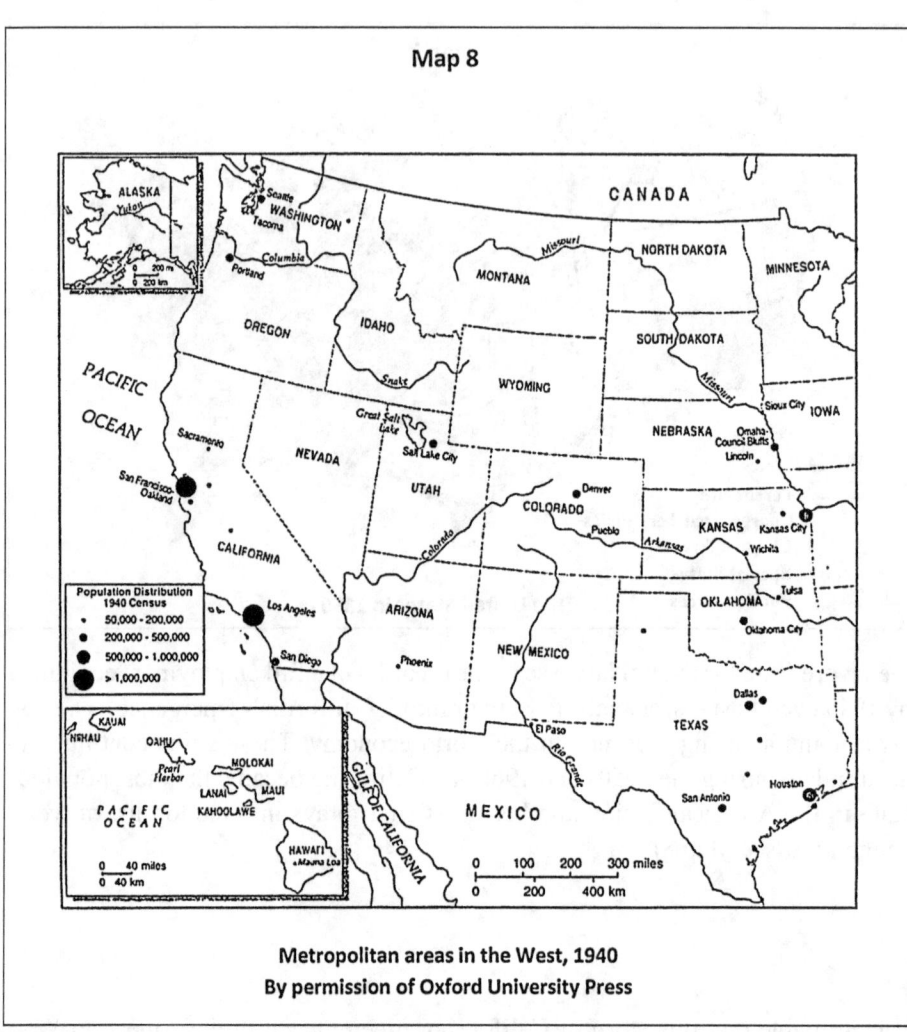

Map 8

Metropolitan areas in the West, 1940
By permission of Oxford University Press

"Greater California" – but only in the sense that California has relentlessly moved "to dominate its own resource-rich western hinterland."[77]

From a different perspective, there is also the increasingly popular slant that brings in some of the wider cultural features of Western history, namely the manner in which the American West originated from the American victory over a

---

77 See, for example, Kotkin & Grabowicz [1982], 246–254, on "California's Colonial Policy" for the late 1970s, a period of growing self-identity by the West as well as temporary hubris related to its favored status in relation to the oil crisis of that decade. Also the 1949 perspective of McWilliams on California's leadership role in the West. McWilliams [1949], 362–367. For more detail, see also Chapter 6 below.

Mexico whose continued shadow over these lands augurs the longterm reality of an "Aztlan" or "MexAmerica" for the entire Southwest.[78] Such rereadings occasionally lead to the proposal that thanks to large and steady immigration of Mexicans into these borderland areas, the Anglo-Protestant cast of the region is being permanently changed, Guadalupe Hidalgo reversed, and perhaps something like a future hispanic "Republica del Norte" uniting the borderlands around 2080 is on its way.[79] Such hopes are presumably backed by empirical studies of the fluid nature of the borders between the U.S. Southwest and northern Mexico in terms of population movements and economic developments in newer urban centers.[80]

Conveniently enough for this chapter, Samuel Huntington, the same theorist who has introduced the theme of a "clash of civilizations" into contemporary discussion, has targeted these same patterns in his worries over the very viability of the American Union as based on its original Anglo-Protestant ethos.[81] In other words, present-day controversies over the overall relevance of the category of civilizations (and their "clash") for post-Cold War global realities and the theme of a permanent hispanic transformation of Greater California and the American Southwest belong to a single conceptual package. Our theme of the "bordering" of the "civilization" of a "Greater California" joins this debate from the perspective of its own priorities.

It is important first to be clear beforehand about the parameters of the debate. One needs to acknowledge the political nature of the very articulation of theories and speculations on the history of civilizations and their finitudes, since such speculation invariably touches on ideological sensitivities in the interrelated areas of political power, international politics ('the states system," the "global system," the "balance of power"), and "culture" ("high" as well as "low"). Since international systems supposedly perform some sort of normative role for cultural flowering or contraction, attempts to adjudicate between finite moves within politics, both domestic and external, and the normative dimension of such entities invariably invoke the vaguer, if more seductive, presence of temporally longer and spatially more comprehensive entities called "civilizations." Concerned about the "late-civilizational" corruptions and decadences of the West in the early twentieth century, the German writer Oswald Spengler came up both

---

78 Or for that matter a "Mexifornia" according to Hanson [2003].
79 Huntington [2004], 246, citing a professor at the University of New Mexico.
80 See, e. g., Langley [1988]; Herzog [1990]; Lowenthal & Burgess [1993]. For the U.S. state of California, recent projections envisage the "Latino" share of the 2020 population at 43.0% compared to 33.7% for "Whites," 12.7% for "Asians," and 6.7% for "Blacks." Actual 2000 figures were: Latino 32.6%, White 47.1%, Asian 11.0%, and Black 6.5%. California Budget Project [2005], 3 (Figures 2 and 3).
81 Huntington [1996] and Huntington [2004].

with his metapolitical messages regarding a "decline of the West" (*der Untergang des Abendlandes*) and a cyclical account of the life-stages of a given list of historical civilizations as relevant primarily for fellow Germans. Subsequent histories of philosophies concerned with the rise and fall of "civilizations" have often shown comparable tendencies, even if they have been expressed in language less charged than Spengler's.[82]

An acknowledged academic expert in international politics, Huntington shows solid credentials in his readings into more sophisticated versions of the taxonomy of civilizations since Spengler. Still, his work is driven by his distinctly American concern over the post-Cold War global world of the 1990s.[83] The list of major civilizations he provides – which he reasonably claims is generally compatible with comparable lists – comes to, more or less, eight (Western, Islamic, Sinic, Japanese, Hindu, and possibly Orthodox, Latin American, and African), and the nub of Huntington's concern is that a future world politics is being determined by the potential for conflict between these civilizational clusters, their "fault lines" forming the scenes for most contemporary hostilities and reflecting the present tendencies by humans to identify ultimately with the "civilizations" – the largest complex for identification in historical time and space – to which they sense that they belong.[84]

Hence, it is as both "a patriot and a scholar" that Huntington has reappeared in more recent reflections on the American component of one of those major civilizations called the Western (covering Europe, the United States and other such settler states as Australia, New Zealand, and Canada).[85] That component seems increasingly driven by a self-identity reduced to the basic American "Creed" of the original documents creating the United States such as the Declaration of Independence and U.S. Constitution. For the rest, not only have race and ethnicity been dropped – a step which, incidentally, receives Huntington's approval – but also contemporary multiculturalism has undermined the very Anglo-Protestant base of the union, which included such features as the one language of English, Protestant Christianity, and English notions of the rule of law.[86] In practi-

---

82   For an easy introduction to Spengler and cyclical historians from Nikolai Danilevsky to Arnold Toynbee and Pitirim Sorokin, see Hughes [1952].
83   As Huntington frankly puts it, his work is "meant to be an interpretation of the evolution of global politics after the Cold War." Huntington [1996], 13. For a helpful list of the texts on civilization that Huntington himself has employed, see 324–325 (note 1).
84   Huntington is very clear that he is not claiming that such identifications are somehow final: in other periods such identification has gone toward the nation, and no doubt there will be changes in the future. Huntington's claim is therefore simply concerned with the historical present.
85   Huntington [2004], xvi.
86   Huntington [2004], xvi.

cal terms, the single source of danger for this undermining of Anglo-Protestant America is the hispanic "invasion" along the southern border of the United States, which unlike all previous flows of immigration, is massive, continual, at least semi-permanent, contiguous (as well as unique for coming from a Third World economy directly into a First World economy) and embodied in individuals who, far from attempting assimilation into the American union, more often than not retain non-American loyalties and cultural-linguistic practices, such as the Mexican. As pragmatically confirmed in the changing profiles of such American cities as Miami and Los Angeles, Huntington argues, the recent ideologies of bilingualism and multiculturalism that provide one influential articulation of this type of population transformation seem more directed to the breakup of the American Union than its further flourishing.

Of course, as Huntington himself grants, all civilizations unfold under the ultimate certainty that they too will come to some future end. Moreover, the kind of American Union that he is describing only succeeded in claiming loyalties as late as around the 1850s and especially after the American civil war – a rather short time period within the temporal parameters of civilizations. These generalities need not however dim efforts to prolong the vitality of a very unusual and in important respects imposing civilizational construct from which hundreds of millions have benefitted. In effect, the Hispanic-American borderlands betray a typical case of the kind of civilizational fault-line and potential conflict about which the author of our epoch of civilizational clashes has already warned and against which the self-professed patriot of the Anglo-Protestant American Union inveighs. At the very least, the case of Huntington shows how difficult it is, if not impossible, to engage dispassionately in the study of the history and fate of historical civilizations without introducing ideological priorities that might seriously slant that engagement.

Granted this much, let us pursue our own slant – rather than deny one – and see what happens to the Huntington problematic. This chapter has narrated the bordering of a civilization we call Greater California to remind readers that the original cartographic and political entity called *California* – or, at some stages, *Las Californias* – was considerably larger than the present U.S. state called California. As it turns out, this larger region comprising "Greater California" itself belongs to the theme of the relations – economic, political, and demographic – between the U.S. state of California and its Southwest-state neighbors, relations that for the most part may be read as domination by a prodigious economy centered on the U.S. state of California over these same neighbors. Even today after some thirty years of Western self-identification and national adoption of many external traits of the Western stylistics of Reagan-era politicians, it is the metropolitan areas of this American West – centered in the conurbations of southern and northern California – that dictate terms to the increasingly challenged and shrinking role of the rural West and its ethos.

By positing a "civilization" of Greater California that is different from the American civilization of Huntington's account of Anglo-Protestant priorities, we provide an alternative terminology for grasping this phenomenon, backed by a narrative that shows a far longer – and therefore possibly more salient – set of historical factors at play in shaping this civilization than an account coming out of a purely American set of conditions. This difference can be elaborated even within the more discrete studies of "California" which have read it as a dynamic "regional civilization" emerging by the end of World War II. Supplanting such accounts, our own narrative regarding its "bordering" helps make more sense of the present status of this geographical region as well as the relevance of the hispanic "problematic" – at least as formulated by Huntington.

If it is true, as Huntington asserts, that no civilization will probably prosper if it is limited to a "creed," however impressive, but must also call upon far more organic and material realities such as ethnicity, religion, language and customs, our bordering of cultural phenomena labeled "California" is rich with its own mythological and imaginal propensities. Dating back to a genealogical conceit that establishes its legitimacy from the most important pedigree of the entire Western classical tradition of thought – namely, the Homeric polis of Troy – California was invented as a generative symbol of a chivalric, albeit "infidel," isle that inherited the culturally multivalent implications of that tradition along a thalassic highway used by hispanic explorers to find a route to the fabled Indies. What they in fact found and named as California was indeed in many ways, as we have earlier argued, an ecological "isle" and it did turn out to reward the conquistadorean imaginal in due course with the only kind of gold that seems to have counted for incipent capitalist societies, namely, the impact of a gold rush that eventually kicked into operation a competitive society capable of operating and succeeding within modern economic indices of growth. But well before that discovery, a society had been gradually emerging called the *californio*, one which identified itself as primarily *Californian* rather than *Mexican*, and which was making its first tentative moves toward something like an independent political reality when it was swamped by American "manifest destiny."[87] It would be a mistake to simply read the ongoing products of this California as solely hispanic, since much of what it has since become – particularly during 1900–1960 – is largely due to the Californian variant of the Anglo-Protestant ethos which Huntington rightly

---

87 As Pitt [1966], 7, notes, "the native-born ceased calling themselves *Españoles* or *Mexicanos* and began to insist on the name *Californios*" (emphasis in original).

praises for its accomplishments.[88] But if culture means anything, it surely entails the importance of acknowledging and internalizing histories even where the particular proponents were, for the moment, on the losing side. Similarly, from another perspective, any primarily hispanic reading of California which prefers to avoid the 15,000-odd years of native Californian cultivation of the "ecological" isle of California would be sadly inadequate – and in its own way unpardonably ideological.

If then the "bordering" of the civilization of Greater California changes the character and implications of the Huntington problematic to one of working through the concept of an already ongoing civilization that contains at its source a powerful Hispanic-American component (along with a prior vital native Californian contribution), that problematic becomes less a danger – since the issue is not one of primarily underscoring the standard of a threatened Anglo-Protestant ethos – than an opportunity to follow through on this same enterprise. In writing of civilizations, Huntington points out that his global theory is reserved for the "major" civilizations, but he often notes the equal presence of smaller entities that deserve the title of civilization, such as the rather diminutive "Anglophone Caribbean."[89] Obviously Huntington must grant the presence of civilizations that are less than "major" since the American civilization he espouses is a subset of the "major" civilization labeled the "West." The question that then follows regarding a civilization of Greater California is whether that civilization belongs to the same scale as the American, or whether it even qualifies – through both its continental and growing Pacific importance – as a "major" civilization at least at the level of what Huntington himself lists as the "major" civilization of Japan.

To answer this question is to admit how much present controversy over civilizations (major, middle and minor), carrying as it does larger political implications, could do with heightened sensitivity to the related themes of "California" borders and borderings that this chapter has raised. An imaginal that began with the love of the goddess Aphrodite for the Trojan prince Anchises, that baptized a great "isle" and continental land into cartographic being, and that in time sculpted the most distinctly twenty-first century civilization in the offing – the civilization of Greater California – deserves no less.

---

88 See in particular the accounts in Starr [1985] and [1990]; also McWilliams [1949].
89 Huntington [1996], 43.

Chapter 3
The coming of European speculative thought: Three Stages[1]

> If it is remarkable when a people has become indifferent to its constitutional theory, to its sentiments, its ethical customs and virtues, it is certainly no less remarkable when a people loses its metaphysics, when the spirit which contemplates its own pure essence is no longer a present reality in the life of the nation .... Systematic philosophy and ordinary common sense thus cooperating to bring about the downfall of metaphysics, there was seen the strange spectacle of a cultured people without metaphysics – like a temple richly ornamented in other respects but without a holy of holies."[2]

Granted that, as has been often trumpeted, the twentieth century was the American Century, all the more so has it been the California Century, as a formerly peripheral state on the west coast of the United States of America ascended to a ranking of anywhere between fifth and eighth economic power in the world. And granted that a civilization of this global ranking may need to display, following the citation from the philosopher Hegel above, something like its own "metaphysics," the theme of California and "speculation" deserves further reflection.

This chapter looks at California civilization and its relation to the European speculative tradition over three different historical stages. The *first* stage covers the emergence of Californian thinkers, primarily native son Josiah Royce and his fashioning of a philosophical idealism greatly indebted to classical German Idealism and its heirs; the *second* stage studies four major speculative works – Max Horkheimer and Theodor W. Adorno's *Dialectic of Enlightenment*, Bertolt Brecht's second version of his play *Galileo*, Thomas Mann's novel *Doktor Faustus*, and Franz Werfel's *Star of the Unborn* – composed by European émigrés as part of the massive Central European intellectual diaspora to California during the troubled 1930s and 1940s; the *third* stage then completes our survey with three contemporary European thinkers – Herbert Marcuse, Michel Foucault, and Jacques Derrida – who developed important aspects of their thought largely as a result of the California nexus.

---

1   An earlier version of this chapter was published as "California Civilization and European Speculative Thought: An Evolving Relationship," in *California History*, 85:4 (2008), 50–69, 73–75. My special thanks to Shelly Kale for her editing and selection of illustrations used in that version. The most important change in the present version is my inclusion of Franz Werfel after subsequent study of the Franz Werfel collections in the University of California, Los Angeles special papers collections. I am grateful to the Department of Special Collections for permission to access the papers.
2   Hegel [1969], 25.

1.

If *American* philosophy begins with a single work, it is very probably the Young Emerson's maiden essay *Nature* (1836), written not long after his 1832 pilgrimage to England and meetings with William Wordsworth, Samuel Taylor Coleridge and Thomas Carlyle, the British transmitters of European "transcendental" philosophy. Ralph Waldo Emerson's "transcendentalism," which he later clarified as philosophical Idealism *tout court*,[3] marks the first strong indigenous intellectual movement that claimed American priorities, and its primary concern was to free the religious mind from outdated sectarian standards narrowly associated with Puritanism and Presbyterianism in favor of the awe-inspiring spirituality of Nature as such.

Yet Emerson's glittering prose needed its embodiment, and it was only after meeting and befriending the younger Henry David Thoreau in 1837 that Emerson began to conceive a clearer standard of what his philosophical naturalism might portend.[4] In turn, however, Thoreau, himself the eventual founder of a distinctly naturalist genre of writing and speculation in America starting with *Walden* (1845–6), moved away from the more technically Idealist components of Emerson's Nature reflections to a far more precise and detailed understanding of the lived experience of environmentality and ecosystematicity. With Thoreau, Emerson's hopes for a new culture celebrating his advocacy of Nature were realized, but only to the degree that Emerson himself and his peculiar brand of Unitarian thinking became correspondingly outdated.

While *California* civilization is a phenomenon that easily predates the American conquest of the vast territories formerly ruled by Spain (and after 1821 by the newly independent United Mexican States), connections with formal speculative European thought really only begin after the American annexation of 1848, linking up, as might be expected, with such threads recently woven by Emerson, Thoreau, and (after 1855) Walt Whitman. These threads are nowhere more prominent than in the transmission of the theme of a spiritual Nature from the New England Transcendentalists to the first concrete experiences of California Nature that came to be specifically associated with the discovery and celebration of the magnificent Sierra Nevada mountain range and its centerpiece, the Yosemite Valley. By the time that Emerson himself made his first and only pilgrimage to Yosemite in 1870, it was in the company of the young naturalist explorer and writer John Muir.[5] Muir was destined to immortalize these ranges with his later

---

3   See "The Transcendentalist" (1843), in Emerson [1981], 92.
4   See Baker [1996], 106–107..
5   Baker [1996], 490–491; Beidleman [2006], 366, 367–368.

eulogies of them as the "Range of Light" and the Yosemite Valley as a veritable Temple of Nature. Moreover, in practical terms, it was Muir who helped establish the first true environmentalist organization, the Sierra Club, and was largely responsible for the establishment of the Yosemite region as the first U.S. National Park.[6] Muir's friendship with University of California professor and scientist Joseph LeConte, with whom he co-founded the Sierra Club, and whose own pilgrimage to Yosemite also took place in 1870, was itself followed by LeConte's career of practical, theoretical and spiritual geological celebration of Nature as California's unique gift to the American-European imagination. The LeConte connection meant that Muir's naturalist philosophy had its academic counterpart in LeConte's influence on a future generation of California students, academics and scientists along comparable lines.[7]

Among those students first graduating from the University of California at its campus in Berkeley and assiduously attending LeConte's lectures, Josiah Royce was a product of the Gold Rush immigration to California after 1848. Born in the mining town of Grass Valley, California, in 1855, Royce's professional career is the first clear case of academic or "technical" philosophy triumphant in the United States as Royce helped establish the preeminence of the faculty of philosophy at Harvard University between 1885 and his death in 1916.[8] The formal basis of Royce's reputation was his inauguration of an American brand of philosophical Idealism that owed a great deal to the stimulus of his year of study (1875–6) at the German universities of Heidelberg, Leipzig, and Göttingen, the latter location allowing him to follow in particular the lectures of Rudolf Hermann Lotze.[9] A convinced Germanophile (at least until what he regarded as the unpardonable German act of sinking the neutral ship *Lusitania* in 1915),[10] Royce was originally forced to pursue his career on the young campus at Berkeley as an English instructor before his new friend William James, the future founder of American philosophical pragmatism, helped him shift to Harvard after 1882. Hence the first genuine formal philosophical voice coming out of California is Royce's German Idealism, drawing above all on Kant ("the good father," in Royce's homage)[11] and later the Hegel of the *Phenomenology of Spirit*.[12]

---

6   See Starr [1973], 185–191.
7   Starr [1973], 425–428.
8   Kuklick [1977].
9   For Royce's German period, see Hine [1992]. Wilhelm Wundt and Wilhelm Windelband at Leipzig also proved important for Royce's later philosophical-historical writing. Royce [1893], 232; Clendenning [1985], 70.
10 See Royce's references to the *Lusitania* in his letters of 1915 and 1916. Royce [1970b], 628, 649.
11 Kuklick [1977], 144.
12 Cf. Royce's early notes for 1878–1882 in Royce [1920]. Also his continued admiration for this work which he taught regularly between 1889 and 1898. Cited in Clendenning [1985], 230.

Ultimately the German Idealist in Royce formulated what he himself came to dub a "constructive Idealism,"[13] closely affiliated with James' pragmatic bent while remaining committed to the primacy of a systemic totality that Royce learned from Hegel's historical dialectics.[14] This Idealism permitted Royce to retain the religious dimension of "God" or the "Absolute" in a philosophizing that – inspired both by Lotze and by LeConte – simultaneously accorded a speculative approbation to the Darwinian theory of Evolution as a more scientific articulation of the "romantic" philosophy of nature (*Naturphilosophie*) of the original Idealists Schelling and Hegel.[15]

Most relevant to our theme is what Royce drew from the Germany of his day for the cultural standard of his future California. Not only did Royce call upon the tradition of German philosophical Idealism for his speculative method, but he also drew on the Germany of the *Goethezeit* for his standard of what a truly civilized mode of being might be like in terms of converging thought and community.[16] This Germany – specifically the Weimar and Jena of Goethe and Schiller – showed both a commitment toward literature and the arts and toward protracted speculative thinking;[17] and this proved the standard that Royce's later advocacy both of "Provincialism" (the standard of regional enlivenment in cultural and creative practices) and of the "Absolute" (the goal and reality of speculative thought) meant to serve. Goethe *and* Kant – rather than Goethe *or* Kant – must be called upon to inspire Californians whose characteristic weakness of excessive individualism (the fault so glaringly exposed by the Gold Rush origins of American California) should be countered by more convivial and social tendencies toward "community." As Royce claimed shortly before his death, "I strongly feel that my deepest motives and problems have centered about the Idea of the Community."[18]

How specifically did this Roycean speculative thought impinge on his reading of Californian civilization? The author of two early books on California – one a novel *The Feud at Oakfield Creek* (1885) subtitled "A Novel of California Life" – and the other *California* (1886) – the first critical interpretation of California history – Royce remained obsessed with the unique traits of California Nature as the

---

Royce [1964] is a continuous celebration of this work.
13   Royce [1893], 235, 269.
14   Thus Royce claimed: "I may assert that personally I am both a pragmatist and an absolutist." Royce [1964], 258.
15   "The doctrine of evolution, I assert, is in heart and essence the child of the romantic movement itself." Royce [1893], 291; also xii.
16   For Royce gazing upon the *Goethezeit*: "Philosophy and life were then in far closer touch than, as I fear, they are today in the minds of many people." Royce [1964], 64.
17   For Royce's rhapsodic account of this period 1750–1805, and especially 1795–1805 (the peak of the Goethe-Schiller friendship), see Royce [1893], 170–171.
18   Royce [1969], i, 34.

key toward imagining a California civilization.¹⁹ In a later essay, "The Pacific Coast" (dated 1898, published 1908), which Royce explicitly marked as a continuation of his *California* history book, Royce returned to his younger euphoric reflections on the redemptive qualities of California Nature.²⁰

What made California Nature unique, according to the older Royce, was a "kindly nature" based on the predictable character of weather, including the long period of drought, mild climate and definite routine. It was a Nature that encouraged being grasped or visualized at a glance, with open clear views and outlines. Hence a peculiarly "intimate" relation between humans and Nature followed, augmented by a sense of geographical isolation from the rest of the North American continent: California was not merely an extension of the American West, it was unique.

Accordingly, California could be conducive to what Royce called a "harmonious individuality of the Hellenic type." Royce approvingly quoted an American east coast friend who experienced *fin de siècle* Californians as akin to the Homeric Greeks of the *Odyssey* for their independence of judgment, carelessness of what outsiders might think of them, freely choosing what they wanted to be, and cultivating a ready and confident speech.²¹ This distinctly Californian individuality did carry its dangers, Royce conceded, but at its best it meant people who were not easily caught up in enthusiasms and false prophets. Admittedly, California was no longer so isolated as a result of the new transcontinental railway connections and accompanying interweavings with the new U.S. industrial and world economies. Thus Royce concluded that the story of future Californian civilization would be the California bred by the Californian's intimacy with Nature and the economic-technological global forces bringing in values from the American eastern seaboard and the rest of the world. At its best, this relation to nature would continue to produce emotionally exciting and intimate relations to breed the "sensitive" Californian in what Royce baptized as "provincial California."²²

How does this reading of California civilization relate to Royce's commitment to the age of German Idealism and its future unfolding in America? Although Royce played with the idea of a book on Hegel at one time, his real hero was

---

19 Note that for Royce the Idealist, the "Californian's well-known and largely justified glorification of his climate" remained "the same expression of his tendency to *idealize* whatever tended to make his community, and all its affairs, seem unique, beloved, and deeply founded upon some significant natural basis." Royce [1908], 70 (emphasis added).
20 Royce [1908], vii.
21 Royce [1908], 205.
22 Royce took pride in the "rapid evolution of the genuine provincial spirit in my own state." Royce [1908], 70.

Goethe and he even entered into negotiations with a press to publish a book on Goethe.[23] The serious student of Goethe knows that the critical moment in Goethe's life came when the latter went down to Italy and Sicily in 1786 and experienced a metamorphosis in which he thought he directly intuited the Homeric Greeks of the *Odyssey*, particularly the hallowed isle of the Phaiakaians and the "magical garden" of their King Alkinous. Goethe then returned to his Weimer home and attempted to create a new Hellenic culture on German soil. This is all part of the complicated story of German culture-making in a Hellenizing direction which Goethe's Idealist admirers such as Schelling and Hegel supported, the creation of what Goethe's ally, the poet Schiller (on whom young Royce wrote extensively), called the ideal of the "aesthetic state of the beauteous shine."[24]

And this, for Royce, was the kind of ideal bringing together the formal philosophy of German Idealism and the cultural-social goals of German Romantics and Classicists. California had a unique role to play in bringing forth a Hellenic-Goethean civilization equally at home in "romantic" creativeness and Idealist speculation. Thanks to the intimate relation between the Californian individual and Californian Nature, a sensibility could arise reminiscent of the German Romantics that would nonetheless mature to a more serious scientific-evolutionary understanding of the meaning of Nature – for Royce the intention or realization of Spirit as such.[25]

As a young boy in Grass Valley, Royce had often gazed forth with his elder sister upon the distant blue mountains of the Coastal Range, dreaming of the oceanic realms beyond.[26] Growing up, he embarked on a lifetime articulation of what this intimacy with the real California – what we have called California Nature – entailed. Saturated in the model of the *Goethezeit* that presumably had united speculation and community, Royce later looked back and remembered this Grass Valley as his first taste of what he called "a new community."[27] At the end of his life Royce, who thought of himself as a "non-conformist disposed to a certain rebellion," hoped that he would be remembered as the metaphysical philosopher of the Idea of Community for this California civilization in the making.[28]

---

23   After his 1891 work *The Spirit of Modern Philosophy*, Royce planned a study of Goethe. He even signed a contract with the Century Company to write six articles as the basis for the biography. Clendenning [1985], 190.
24   See Chytry [1989], 56–58. For Royce on Schiller, see his early essay, "Schiller's Ethical Studies' [1878], in Royce [1920], 41–65.
25   "The world is the process of the spirit." Royce [2001], 381. Also 401 for Royce's reaffirmation of his commitment to philosophical idealism.
26   Royce [1969], i, 34; Royce [1908], 172–173.
27   Royce [1969], i, 31. Royce's final thoughts were concerned with his ideal of the "universal community" or "the beloved community." Royce [1958], 55; Royce [2001], 75–98, 376.
28   Royce [1969], i, 29.

2.

The second stage in the interrelationship of European speculative thought with the evolution of California civilization owes a great deal to the Californian creation of "Hollywood," that complex of cinematic and related literary and media industries constituting the "film business."[29] As home to the California film industry, the city of Hollywood had become (after incorporation in 1915 into Los Angeles proper) the site for its "movies" – originally referring to both the actors as well as the products of the newest of genres emerging out of modern technology. By the 1920s something like a studio system was fully in operation, but it was really only after 1929 with the technical achievement of the "talkies" that the big five of the studio system succeeded in driving out smaller rivals through their incestuous convergence of finance, industry, and the "creative" fields needed to fabricate "stardom."

The emergence of Hollywood as a distinctly twentieth-century sector of technological productivity belongs to the larger story of the astonishing growth of the California economy during that period. Besides film, this California proved at the cutting edge of a variety of industries, including oil, automobiles, agribusiness, real estate and water economics. By the 1920s the Greater Los Angeles area, already third in population behind New York and Chicago, was developing into the most distinctively twentieth-century metropolis in the world.

During these founding decades Greater Los Angeles had proved a magnet for European talent, but until Hitler's assumption of power in Germany in 1933 the Anglo component (the "British Raj") was the most marketable of that European presence.[30] After 1933, however, Central Europeans – both Jewish and non-Jewish – were driven for a variety of reasons – ethnic, political, and creative – to American shores.[31] Through the prospect often of Hollywood employment – or at least through friends and relatives benefitting from such employment – they ended up creating a "Weimar in Hollywood" or "Weimar on the Pacific," the cultural equivalent of Berlin and Vienna (as well as Prague and Budapest) in the interconnected communal spaces of Hollywood, Santa Monica, Pacific Palisades,

---

29 For early efforts at a serious appraisal of the Hollywood industry, cf. Rosten [1941] and Powdermaker [1950]; also Mordden [1988] for a history of the major Hollywood studios. The best recent study of Hollywood as "a central point of reference in the cultural economy of the modern world" in terms of being "one of the most highly developed agglomerations of productive activity anywhere, and a major urban phenomenon in its own right," is Scott [2005], 175, xi.
30 Taylor [1983], Morley [1983].
31 McWilliams [1973]; Starr [1997], 342–345; Palmier [2006], 490.

and Beverly Hills.[32] Thomas Mann, that eminently German representative of the Central European diaspora, only slightly exaggerated when he speculated that not even the Weimar of Goethe and Schiller could match such an assemblage of German-speaking intellectuals.[33]

The larger implications of this rush of Central European talent into the film industry and its environs have been treated in a variety of studies, some more scholarly than others. Fascinating as that subject is, the speculative contributions of the diaspora have received less attention. And yet the obvious fact remains that at least three major works in the history of twentieth-century European thought were conceived and completed in this region of greater Los Angeles dominated by Hollywood and its technological tributaries: Bertolt Brecht's *Galileo*; Thomas Mann's *Doktor Faustus*; and Max Horkheimer and Theodor Adorno's *Dialectic of Enlightenment*[34] – all more or less connected importantly with the *annus mirabilis* of 1947, a year which unfortunately also marked the onset of a new Californian and American anti-Communist fervor, as emblematized that fall by the House Committee on Un-American Activities (HUAC) hearings on the Hollywood Ten (to which Brecht was a European "eleventh"), that stamped an end to the creative interchange of progressive European speculation with its California receptacle.

Although students of Brecht, the Frankfurt School, and Mann have marked the fact of an American exile in their respective careers, there has been a perhaps less keen recognition of the exactness of the shared time that they experienced specifically in 1940s California. For example, Mann arrived in California in March 1941; Horkheimer in April; Herbert Marcuse (also a member of the Frankfurt School who will play a major role in our third stage) in May/June; Brecht in July; and Adorno by the end of November. Each followed very different itineraries to reach California – that of Brecht from Helsinki to San Pedro Harbor via the Trans-Siberian railway being undoubtedly the most spectacular – but all in effect chose the same Los Angeles reality – to be precise, Santa Monica and the Pacific Palisades – for the temporary home in which they would embark almost at the

---

32 "The notion of Los Angeles/Hollywood as Berlin or Vienna in exile is not far-fetched." Starr [1997], 342, also 347–348; Palmier [2006], 490. Bahr [2007] is now the classic study; see also Crawford [2009].

33 Cook [1983], 58. This connection is aptly captured by the photo of the Goethe-Schiller Monument in Weimar in Bahr [2007], 2 (Figure 1).

34 I have chosen to concentrate on these three major works, although it is also worth mentioning Horkheimer's *Eclipse of Reason*, Adorno's *Minima Moralia* and essays on modern music, and Mann's *Joseph and His Brothers*, as well as Brecht's reworking of the major body of his theatrical works.

same precise time on their respective contributions to Central European speculation concerning the crisis of the fascist period.

Thus, beginning in 1938 Adorno and Horkheimer foresaw a project vaguely directed toward a new work on speculative dialectics, or dialectical logic, in the tradition of Hegel and Marx;[35] but it was only once they were in mutual physical proximity in California that by late 1941 they were well on their way to the early key chapters of what became the Dialectic of Enlightenment project (originally called *Philosophical Fragments*, the present subtitle of the book).[36] Crucial financial help from a Jewish organization helped swing the project by 1943 to its bold speculations on the origins and character of anti-Semitism, and by May 1944 the work was available in a monographical version: the preface to that version is dated "Los Angeles, California." In fact, the final version published by Querido of Amsterdam in 1947 only includes one substantial addition in the chapter on anti-Semitism.[37]

For his part, Brecht, seeking to break into both films in Hollywood and plays on Broadway in New York, embarked on a major revision of his 1938 *Galileo* play. By December 1944 the new version was available in German, and through his friendship with Hollywood actor Charles Laughton (who would play Galileo in the first production of 1947) embarked on an English translation that was more or less completed by December 1945 (Brecht habitually added minor touches to his plays right up to production) and enjoyed its premiere at the Coronet Theatre in Hollywood in July 1947.[38]

Finally, Mann, who since 1904 had been vaguely playing out the idea of his own version of the Faust legend as part of his assumption of Goethe's mantle in German *Kultur*, took off on his most German novel *Doktor Faustus* in the spring of 1943, right after the completion of the last leg of his massive *Joseph and his Brothers* tetralogy. Between January and late February of 1945 Mann completed the all-important twenty-fifth chapter that "records" the dialogue between his protagonist and the Devil, and managed to finish the whole work by early 1947.[39]

All three works, notwithstanding their obvious membership in the German-language tradition, were almost from the start intricately connected with plans for English versions. Brecht's uncharacteristic eagerness to befriend and

---

35 Wiggershaus [1986], 202, 214.
36 The original title of the first chapter, "Dialectic of Enlightenment," became the overall book title while that chapter was then retitled "The Concept of Enlightenment."
37 The addition was mainly by Frankfurt School colleague Leo Löwenthal, later professor of sociology at the University of California, Berkeley. Löwenthal had helped write the prior sections of this part.
38 Following Cook [1983], 165–181. Also Brecht [1993], 358 (1 December 1945).
39 Mann [1992], 39.

exploit Charles Laughton for that purpose[40] actually led to the first production of the second version of *Galileo* in English rather than German, while Mann worked from the start with his English translator, Helen T. Lowe-Porter, even while he was composing the original German text, in order that her English version would come out simultaneously.[41] It is clear from comments in the text itself that Mann, then a U.S. citizen, was almost thinking more of an American English-speaking audience than a German.[42] Finally, Horkheimer made every effort – albeit unsuccessfully – to provide an early English translation of at least the key chapter, "The Culture Industry [*Kulturindustrie*]: Enlightenment as Mass Deception," even as he and Adorno spun out the body of heterogeneous topics that became the manuscript of *Dialectic of Enlightenment*.[43]

No doubt much of this concern for immediately available English versions reflected the exiles' temporary uncertainty over the future during these difficult years of German domination of Europe, the German invasion of the Soviet Union in 1941, the U.S. entry into the war against National Socialism in late 1941, and even the increasing assurance by 1944 of the favorable course of that campaign; indeed, some exiles, such as Mann himself, had become U.S. citizens during this period. But it also reflected the authors' positive valuations of the importance for an English-reading audience of the results of their respective labors at the very moment that the United States was emerging as the one undisputed superpower. The ominous political turn toward a virulent anti-Communism in America after 1947 proved a shock to the émigrés for whom America had largely implied the strongly welfare-state and European-internationalist policies of Franklin Roosevelt in which our authors originally undertook to complete their works. Not surprisingly, this dramatic turn in the political climate of the late 1940s helped hasten their permanent departure to new or reinstituted European homes.

How then do these works fit into our theme? As regards their target audience, all three probe the challenge of German fascism by attempting the most broad-ranging analyses and critiques of the overall problematic of what Adorno and Horkheimer call the "program of the Enlightenment." Certainly, all three works advocated the importance of intellectual speculation. Brecht's *Galileo* was

---

40 For Brecht's own account of working with Laughton on the translation, see Brecht [1993], 338–339 (December 1944). Brecht mentions that the biggest difficulty was translating Galileo's Scene 1 speech about the "new time" (339). Also 348 (14 May 1945).
41 Starr notes that "rarely has an important work of art been composed in such a condition of simultaneous translation." Starr [1997], 388.
42 Mann's narrator in fact confesses at the end of *Doktor Faustus* that the text is meant more for an American audience, a point noted by his translator in her introduction to the book. Mann [1948b], v; Mann [1948a], 764.
43 Rabinbach [1997], 167. Wiggershaus [1986], 764, points out that this shows how much the authors longed for a "US-American Publikum."

meant to be part of a "propaganda for thinking," and originally Galileo himself was positively presented as a "Schweikian" Galileo in tribute to the Czech fictional character who outsmarts his enemies through adaptability and cunning.[44] Mann's narrator Serenus Zeitblom is presented throughout as an eloquent defender of the classical humanist tradition of thought.[45] Adorno and Horkheimer assure their reader that their critique of the Enlightenment will be followed by a positive notion of enlightenment, the never achieved "Rescuing the Enlightenment *[Rettung der Aufklärung]*" project, although as Rolf Wiffershaus has argued, three later individual works succeed in part in realizing that project: Horkheimer's *Eclipse of Reason* (also conceived and executed in California), Marcuse's *Eros and Civilization*, and Adorno's *Negative Dialectics*.[46]

Still, these works draw much of their deserved reputation for the severity of their attacks on the conventional European Enlightenment tradition of Reason. Of these the one by Adorno and Horkheimer is the best known, not least for its memorable rhetoric: "The fully enlightened earth radiates disaster triumphant. The program of the Enlightenment was the disenchantment of the world *[Entzauberung der Welt]*", and this "disenchantment of the world" is nothing less than the "extirpation *[Ausrottung]* of animism."[47] Aiming at mastery "over a disenchanted nature," science and technology – "the essence of this knowledge" through computation (mathematics) and utility – seek knowledge only in order to exploit nature and thus dominate both nature at large and humanity: "Power and knowledge are synonymous."[48]

In Mann's case the charge against Enlightenment is subtly entwined with the career of his main character Adrian Leverkühn (from the Nietzschean motto "Leben kühn," or "Live boldly"), a musician whose father belongs to the tradition of Central European *Naturphilosophie*. That tradition was famous for penetrating the secrets of Nature by "tempting" her to reveal her secrets through the

---

44 In California Brecht continued work on his long-term project "Schweik in the Second World War." Cook [1983], 136.
45 This is clear from Zeibloom's introduction of himself in Mann [1948b], 7ff., and contrapuntally reiterated throughout the text.
46 Rabinbach [1997], 171, 197; Wiggershaus [1986], 6–7. The authors themselves stressed that their critique of enlightenment "is intended to prepare the way for a positive notion of enlightenment which will release it from entanglement in blind domination." Horkheimer & Adorno [2002], xvi.
47 Horkheimer & Adorno [2002], 3, 5; [1969], 7, 8. The same word "Ausrottung" is later used in the authors' excursion into the "Elements of Anti-semitism" in the claim that for fascists the Jews are not a minority but the "negative principle" on whose "extirpation" *[Ausrottung]* the happiness of the world presumably depends. Horkheimer & Adorno [1969], 151.
48 Horkheimer & Adorno [2002], 4.

alchemical and magical arts.[49] But what for the father had been a mystical quest moderated by reverence – and to that extent remained in the spirit of Comenius and Johann Valentin Andreae in the seventeenth century – is regarded by the son as a laughing matter, even though he himself is drawn to the archetype of the *Hetaera Esmeralda*, a transparent butterfly which loves shades, symbolic of an impure, albeit diabolically tempting Philosopher's Stone.[50] Leverkühn finds his alchemical equivalent in the world of tones: music, but a music that abandons the homophonic-melodic tradition of bourgeois humanism for the elementality of the equality of all tones – the triumph of dissonance – which will usher in a new age that no longer distinguishes between culture and barbarism but sees reason and magic as one.[51] In effect, Leverkühn is the quintessential German-Nietzschean seeker of the power of pure creation by his pact with the Satan within him. Lacking human warmth he embodies the psychological poles of pure intellectuality and pure instinct; hence, in exchange for the capacity to create works of startling genius, he is denied "love," that is, desire with human warmth.[52] As his devil easily perceives, Leverkühn's intellectual coldness drives him to his deepest yearning: "the aphrodisiacum of the brain [*das Aphrodisiacum des Hirns*]."[53] And he gets it, in the "little sea maid's knifelike pains," i. e. syphilis.[54] A complicated set of rhetorical moves, Mann's stance toward the Enlightenment might be summed up as a bourgeois humanist voice that is sensitive but impotent and a creative side that is powerful but blasphemous.

Then there is Brecht's Galileo, character and work. In the 1938 version of his play Galileo was the cunning Schweikian opponent of absolutism – whether in its seventeenth-century Church Inquisitorial garb or in 1930s Nazi fulminations – who outsmarted his opponents to eventually publish the truth of the new astronomy and physics.[55] The 1947 California version is instead the archetypal scientist who sells out the dignity of science to authority in order to be able to create atomic technology for a new barbarism. Brecht's new Galileo thus fits in

---

49 Cf. Mann [1948b], 13–20; also 132 on "the hermetic laboratory, the gold-kitchen: composition."
50 Mann [1948b], 14, 142, 232, 498.
51 Mann [1948b], 46–47, 193, 194. "Vernunft und Magie ... begegnen sich wohl und werden eins in dem, was man Weisheit, Einweihung nennt." Mann [1948a], 302. It is known that Mann wrote these difficult musicological passages by conferring with Adorno and later had to explain its dependence on neighbor Arnold Schönberg's twelve-tone system. Schönberg lived in financial modesty in Santa Monica. Mann [1948b], 511. See also Crawford [2009].
52 "...eine Liebe, der man die animalische Wärme entzogen hat." Mann [1948a], 113. Mann [1948b], 147, 69, 132.
53 Mann [1948b], 248, [1948a], 384.
54 Mann [1948b], 352, also 249, [1948a], 539.
55 Cook [1983], 13.

with Mann's as well as Adorno and Horkheimer's condemnation of the rationality of the Enlightenment to the extent it reduces knowledge to power and power to domination over a "disenchanted" nature.

How do these stances touch on the California environment in which they were conceived, developed and completed? The California of the 1920s and 1930s was already seen by its more indigenous writers, including John Fante, Dashiell Hammett, and Nathaniel West, as manifesting two outstanding traits. On the one hand, there was a continued fascination with its clear, keen nature and its unparalleled fertility, displayed in its innovative agriculture and more lately augmented by Southern Californian experimentations in flora and fruits made possible by the completion of the massive Owens Valley water project in 1913. On the other hand, writers were beginning to explore the spectacle of an entirely new style of life associated with the automobile, highways, supermalls, motels, and drive-in diners: in short, mass-culture paradise.[56] Both features betray the turn to what might now be called post-industrial technology: from leisure wear and stylistics, media, aviation, and services to the physics, astronomy and jet propulsion achievements that would eventually produce the computer economy of Silicon Valley. In short, serious issues of individualism, anomie, and simulacrum had already surfaced; and along with such concerns had come the exhilarating sense of being able to entirely recreate or refashion the self.[57]

These features clearly permeate our three texts. Whatever its fragmentary tendencies, *Dialectic of Enlightenment* owes its narrative cohesion to the relation between the opening chapter on the concept of the Enlightenment and the latter's contemporary manifestation in chapter two as the "culture industry" (*Kulturindustrie*) of "mass consumption."[58] Although Adorno and Horkheimer's analysis of this "culture industry" is meant universally, its entire tone depends on features of the California media industry, particularly films, but also radio, magazines, and even television. Any statistical listing of specific references in that chapter would give precedence to California phenomena: from Greer Garson, Betty Davis and Donald Duck to Orson Welles and that girl in the sweater ("den Busen im Sweater"), presumably Lana Turner.[59] Such specificity is hardly surprising, given that both Adorno and Horkheimer enjoyed a privileged view of a mass society in the making, along with personal daily contact with fellow Central Europeans who made their living in these industries.

---

56   See the excellent account in Starr [1990].
57   Starr [1997], 296ff.
58   In terms of the major divisions in the book, the intervening sections on the Odyssey and de Sade's Juliette are explicitly catalogued as "excursus" one and two, and the chapter on Anti-Semitism is a later edition. The final aphorisms are simply added on.
59   Horkheimer & Adorno [2002], 129, 138, 140; [1969], 125.

Brecht was, of course, one of these. He had hoped to break into the industry, although his only success was his script for Fritz Lange's *Hangmen Also Die* (1943) based on the Czech resistance movement that brought down the S. S. leader Reinhard Heydrich – until, that is, the *Galileo* premiere of 1947 that led to a Broadway production the same fall and winter.[60] As a Marxist, Brecht of course professed to be appalled by these fatuous stages of what Adorno and Horkheimer termed "late capitalism" (*Spätkapitalismus*).[61] Brecht's prior "America" had been the Chicago gangsterism he had exploited for his earlier play *The Rise and Fall of the City of Mahagonny*. Now he was living in the midst of L. A., this "Tahiti in the form of a big city" as he disdainfully called it,[62] preferring to hang out in familiar proletariat industrial districts of the San Pedro Harbor docks. L. A. after all was already seen by its own writers as the classic "laissez-faire dystopia."[63] Still Brecht needed L. A., *and* Hollywood ("Das Dorf Hollywood"), to confirm his convictions of imminent capitalist debacle, as suggested by his remorseless critique in the six-part "Hollywood Elegies" of 1942:

> The city is named after angels
> And one meets angels everywhere.
> They smell of oil and carry golden pessaries
> And with blue rings around their eyes
> They feed every morning the typewriters
> In their swimming pools.[64]

Still, for all his whining, Brecht did refashion his *Galileo* there as his greatest triumph;[65] its Hollywood premiere turned out to be the ultimate gathering of émigré

---

60 Unfortunately for Brecht's Dreams of Broadway, he had already fled America – and the tentacles of HUAC – beforehand. Brecht's journals record that the morning of 31 October 1947 he had an amiable meeting with Laughton who was donning "his galileo beard" and that in the afternoon he, Brecht, was "taking off for Paris." Brecht [1993], 372.

61 Horkheimer & Adorno [1969], 138. Brecht begins his stay by whining about "this mausoleum of *easy going*." Brecht [1993], 157 (1 August 1941, emphasis in original).

62 Brecht [1993], 199 (9 August 1941). Brecht goes on: "they have nature here, indeed, since everything is so artificial, they even have an exaggerated feeling for nature." Brecht's physical discomfort in a climate "with no seasons" is relayed on 21 January 1942 (193).

63 Starr [1997], 364.

64 "Hollywood-Elegien," in Brecht [1967], 849–850. As an interpreter of these poems notes, these "bitter and aggressive epigrams are only peripherally elegies." Whitaker [1985], 160. In his journals of the period Brecht notes that one critic looking at these elegies is struck by their detachment ("as if they had been written from Marx") but both conclude that this detachment is a general product of anyone living in L. A. Brecht [1993], 257 (20 September 1942). Kurt Eisler, for whom the elegies were composed, performed them for a small group including Herbert Marcuse (3 October 1942).

65 "Despite all the complaining and bitterness of Brecht's Los Angeles years, the *Galileo* he co-authored with Laughton may very well be his masterpiece." Starr [1997], 365.

Los Angeles and the Best of Hollywood, from Lionel Feuchtwanger and Igor Stravinsky to Charles Boyer, Ingrid Bergman, and Charlie Chaplin. And in terms of thematics, the great change in the California Galileo came to Brecht, as he himself stated, with the onset of the atomic age in 1945[66] and the dangers of a science gone wild, right in the midst of a civilization that was at the cutting edge of these very same innovations: for it was largely Californian technological thinking, from jet propulsion at Cal Tech and the new astronomy of Edwin Hubble at Mount Wilson and Mount Palomar observatories that proved the existence of multiple galaxies and an expanding universe, to Ernest Lawrence's cyclotron at Berkeley in tandem with Robert Oppenheimer's leadership of the Manhattan Project, that literally inaugurated that same atomic age. And these factors funneled into the most important change of the new *Galileo*, namely Galileo's self-denunciation in the penultimate act which ascribed to his own cowardice the prototype of a scientific subservience that broke up any progressive alliance between science and human emancipation.[67]

The case of Mann's relation to Southern California society is more diffuse. For him as a writer, California was Weimar in exile: a Central European could live out his entire day speaking and hearing only German.[68] Contact with the southern California flora and fauna proved an exhilarating experience for Mann akin to his former love for the similar Tuscan landscape. Already in 1939 he was remarking how the Beverly Hills area "thrilled" (*entzückt*) him – filled as it was with "a hundredfold charms of nature and life" – and he was speculating on whether to build his home there. By 1941, he was rejoicing in his own Pacific Palisades home with its countless "lemon trees."[69] There Mann, who of all our figures spent the longest period in California from 1941 to 1952, exploited his environment to experiment with the German language. As his daughter Monica later recounted, the "odd elegance of that distant shore, with its almost intangible beauty and worldly barrenness," deeply influenced his work and his beliefs: as Mann's own narrator concludes, the "democracy of the western lands [*die Demokratie der Westländer*]"

---

66 "The atomic age made its debut over Hiroshima in the middle of our work. Overnight the biography of the founder of the new system of physics read differently." Brecht, cited in Eric Bentley's "introduction" to Brecht [1966], 16.
67 Brecht [1966], 123–124, concluding:: "Any man who does what I have done must not be tolerated in the ranks of science." In a conversation on the work dated 30 July 1945 Brecht notes its emergent theme of the "decisive difference" between "'scientific progress pure and simple' and science's social and revolutionary progress." Brecht [1993], 350. On 20 September 1945 still working with Laughton on the play, Brecht states that "the atom bomb has, in fact, made the relationship between society and science into a life-and-death-problem" (355).
68 Cook [1983], 57ff.
69 Bürgin & Mayer [1965], 138 (March 29, 1939), 156 (July 1941). Mann (August 29, 1943), cited in Palmier [2006], 792 (note 125).

was to be "after all essentially in the line of human progress": it was "after all capable, by its own nature, of a transition into conditions more justified of life."[70]

If California provoked our authors to digest these latest stages of industrial society, the other aspect – California Nature – helped them sustain an intuition for a redeemed Nature. Even Brecht, notwithstanding his constant complaints about Southern Californian nature, could not resist the paradisiacal side of his friend Charles Laughton's sumptuous garden, as shown in Brecht's 1944 poem "Garden in Progress."[71] Mann for his part remained in love with his garden and home in the Pacific Palisades, an affection that not only permeates the last of his Joseph novels, *Joseph the Provider*, entirely composed in California, but also helped him articulate the "uncanny" Nature of Father and Son Leverkühn in *Doktor Faustus*: Mann was "enchanted by the light, by the special fragrance of the air, by the blue of the sky, the sun, the exhilarating ocean breeze, the spruceness and cleanness of this southland."[72] Finally Horkheimer found "nature in Southern California as more beautiful, the climate more favorable, than one could dream," while Adorno, clearly no fan of its cultural ramifications, recognized the "immensity" in the beauty of the landscape: "even the smallest of its segments is inscribed, as its expression, with the immensity of the whole country."[73]

In short, as Mann's daughter noted, "the gleaming emptiness, monotony, and hostility of the landscape" pushed our authors to exploit resources within themselves that might have lain dormant in a more predictable Europe.[74] To this extent, their creative outlook in California echoes Josiah's Royce's admiration for the speculative possibilities inherent in dwelling within California nature. Straddled between such natural clarity and inspiration on one hand and the burgeoning of the new society of mass consumption and "late capitalism" on the other, Brecht, Mann, and Adorno and Horkheimer were enabled to shape their permanently challenging oeuvres to a devastated and culpable Germany. This legacy of "Weimar on the Pacific" would prove sufficiently powerful to revise

---

70 Monica Mann, cited in Starr [1997], 379. Mann [1948b], 340, [1948a], 521. Mann's positive view did not survive the postwar Californian anti-communism in which the FBI even targeted him as a friend of communism. The chagrined Mann moved permanently to Switzerland in 1952 where he died in 1955.
71 Cf. Bertold Brecht, *Poems 1913–1956* (New York: Methuen, 1976), transl., cited in Cook [1983], 167. There is a photograph of Brecht and Laughton in the latter's Pacific Palisades garden in Brecht [1993], 360. See Chytry [2008], 60–61, for further photos of Laughton's home.
72 Mann [1961], 65. Also: "all these paradisaical scenes and colors enraptured me" (186).
73 Cited in Wiggershaus [1986], 329. Adorno, cited in Israel [1997], 95. This entire article is devoted to a study of Adorno's "gratitude" toward America, which in terms of personal living experience meant Southern California.
74 Cited in Starr [1997], 379.

and modify "Weimar modernism to meet the challenges of the period between 1933 and 1958."[75]

3.

Finally, there is an additional figure worth considering when recapitulating the Central European diaspora in its relation to California civilization. The case of Franz Werfel is significant for the degree to which he took a consciously California turn in his work that stands out in contrast to the still lingering European orientations of Adorno, Horkheimer, Mann and Brecht. In his upbringing, ethnicity, work, family and marriage ties, Werfel could consider himself at least as Central European as these peers.[76] Born in Prague of Jewish parents, attached to Czech influences like his contemporary and friend Franz Kafka, a noted figure in prewar Expressionist poetry and a momentary radical during the upheavals of 1918, Werfel embarked during the 1920s on a long and successful career as a novelist, composing novels loved respectively by Armenian-Americans (*The Forty Days of Musa Dagh*) and by American Catholics (*The Song of Bernadette*) without renouncing his Jewish roots.[77] Besides, he was the last husband of Alma Schindler Mahler, that dramatic summation of Viennese high culture whose friendships (and marriages) covered much of twentieth-century Central European high culture, among others: Gustav Klimt, Gustav Mahler, Oskar Kokoschka, and Walter Gropius.[78] It was from this Vienna swallowed up by the *Anschluss* of 1938 that the Werfels had to flee. They temporarily settled down with other prominent émigrés in Sanary-sur-Mer on the Mediterranean coast, but in 1940 the German victory over France drove most of them scurrying to the Spanish border in hopes of political asylums beyond.

After 1940 the Werfels settled comfortably in Southern California where unlike many émigrés Werfel's writings did very well on the American market. Not only was his *The Song of Bernadette* (1941/1942) a bestseller and wartime inspiration, but it was also immediately turned into a blockbuster film and winner of four Oscars in 1943. In contrast to other émigrés and even his wife who generally stayed aloof from its idiosyncratic culture styles, Werfel warmly embraced

---

75   Bahr [2007], 289.
76   Werfel's protagonist in *Star of the Unborn* (1946) identifies himself as "neither an Englishman nor an American but a Central European." Werfel [1946a], 358. To the U.S. Department of Justice, Werfel in 1941 stated: "My fatherland is Czechoslovakia, as I was born in the beautiful city of Prague." Werfel [1910–1944], Box 9, 2.
77   Details in Steiman [1985], Jungk [1987], Bartl [1996].
78   For her autobiography see either Mahler-Werfel [1960] or Werfel [1958].

California: "[California's] climate, landscape, people .... Franz loved them, I never did," recalled Alma Werfel somewhat disdainfully.[79] Werfel avidly followed the movie scene, even becoming a fan of Grade-B films, particularly the science-fiction adventures of Buck Rogers which figured prominently in his final imaginative work.[80]

Thus it is perhaps no great surprise that Werfel located his last novel *Star of the Unborn* (1946) square in his own home at 610 North Bedford Drive, Beverly Hills, California – albeit 100,000 years into the future.[81] What was perhaps more surprising is Werfel's expansion of "California" to encompass the entire globe. "Summoned" into the future by Werfel's real Prague boyhood friend, the writer Willy Haas ("B. H."), as a special gift for a wedding, Werfel's protagonist – who significantly matches Werfel's own initials of "F. W." – appears to have died in his own Californian temporal reality of April 1943.[82] Yet the future world to which he is summoned remains in an important sense "California": "Our appointment," his friend assures F. W., "is taking place in California." Since F. W. sees nothing but gray turf stretching monotonously in all directions, he immediately protests, "I know California," and brings up some characteristic features of the California with which he is familiar – "It is appropriately called a paradise" – consisting of deserts, Sierra mountains, Pacific ocean, and luxurious orchards "with a fragrance that beggars description." He even humorously describes the typical Californian as an extension of the mythical Lemurians: shadowy, actor types who might be described as "phonies" by snobs who have associated California "chiefly" with the film-making proclivities of "a famous city," presumably Werfel's Los Angeles.[83]

B. H. gently explains that everything has become one city: "California is the name of a city" that includes all settlements in one overriding system which effec-

---

79 Werfel [1958], 298. Steiman notes that Werfel "enjoyed American popular culture quite uncritically" and that "there was nothing snobbish about him." Steiman [1985], 145.

80 Werfel's attraction to science-fiction and more popular Hollywood films is clear from the evidence in the Werfel Papers housed at the University of California, Los Angeles: see Werfel [1910–1944]. Werfel saw a good deal of such films in Santa Barbara while resting from his labors on *Star of the Unborn*: he enjoyed "worthless products of the dream-factory Hollywood" and valued his friendships with actors like Edward G. Robinson. Jungk [1987], 326, 329. Also Bartl [1996], who brings in the influence of Walt Disney cartoons (56–58).

81 To be precise: 101,943 years, since the novel explicitly begins – and ends – in April 1943, around the time Werfel first conceived it. The text also makes sure to use Werfel's real age of 52 at the time (he was born on 4 September 1890). Werfel [1946a], 102, 156, 221. Werfel liked to call his home "Tusculum" in memory of the Mediterranean home of Cicero. Steiman [1985], 147.

82 F. W. explicitly refers to his "California mortician" and speculates that he is probably buried in "Forest Lawn". Werfel [1946a], 155, 218, 12.

83 Werfel [1946a], 15, 16, 17. Also: mountain lions (396).

tively allows a unique civilization called the "Astromental" to function according to individuals' capacities to move in any direction they wish by drawing a given objective toward them rather than travelling toward that objective, "mental" being understood as "every impulse of the soul, every emotion that is washed clean and therefore spiritualized by the light of consciousness."[84] Significantly, F. W.'s hosts in the Astromental world ask him questions in which their identification with California is assumed: "Do you find our California changed, Seigneur?," they politely wonder, and: "Is this your first trip to California?"[85] At the same time, there remain unkept outskirts of this Astromental civilization known as the "Jungle," which split up into discretely different and identifiable geographical entities. Under this heading there exists a more geographically precise "California" – "near the Pacific" – which F. W. expects to include "Indios and Mestizos, since we were in California," and which even includes a stereotypic filmic military center and commandante whose relief map on the wall clearly states: "Southern California Sector."[86]

By responding that his F. W. has indeed been earlier to California, namely as an "emigrant," Werfel raises the larger question of exactly what genre this idiosyncratic "California novel" is meant to constitute for its author.[87] From the start Werfel intended it to belong, in some malleable sense, to "travel" literature: a "*Reiseroman*."[88] In the text itself his protagonist regularly apologizes to his reader for the loose sense of travel writing that he is offering. Both author and protagonist are vaguely tempted by a possible analogy with Dante's *Divine Comedy*, and Werfel frequently has F. W. refer to his boyhood friend and guide as his "Ver-

---

84   Werfel [1946a], 17, 23.
85   Werfel [1496a], 48, 47. The Geodrome or "central plaza" is referred to as "the central plaza of California, or of the continent, or perhaps of the entire globe, how should I know?" (95). Werfel also refers to this "universal city" as "Panopolis" (e. g. 66, 378, 452).
86   Werfel [1946a], 383, 423, 452, 461–462.
87   The English translation – by Werfel's close family friend Gustave O. Arlt, a professor of German literature at the University of California branch of Los Angeles – reads "refugee" (Werfel [1946a]), 47, but the precise wording in the German original is "ein Emigrant" (Werfel [1946b], 56). Bartl's [1996] analysis of the novel is inspired by its function as exile or emigrant literature.
88   The earliest formulations are: "Short visit in the distant future," "Behind the back of time" (Jungk [1987]), 312. Eventually the German original would use "ein Reiseroman" as the subtitle, but it would be left out in the English translation (Werfel [1946b], 5). Werfel's notes include other possible formulations that were marked out, e. g. "Three days beyond the beyond," "Behind the bar of Time," "The furlough from Beyond," "World without end." Werfel [1910]1944], Box 14. Bartl [1996] comments that the form of the novel resembles "ein Puzzlespiel" (27). Klarmann [1046] calls it mainly "a spiritual autobiography" (385).

gil."⁸⁹ Still, Werfel is too aware of the protean quality of his own work and the eminence of the Dantean standard to push the analogy too far; after summing up Dante's achievement, he can only wryly add: "Somebody should try that today."⁹⁰

What Werfel wants to establish from the outset is that his work is not intended to be narrowly "political"; in this sense it differs sharply from the works already mentioned by Mann, Brecht, Adorno and Horkheimer. Not that Werfel was not deeply concerned with the monstrous events of 1943–1945, as his other works and speeches of the same period attest.⁹¹ But *Star of the Unborn* aimed at a more universal range, including forays into domains only later identified as a genre labeled "science fiction."⁹² Werfel quickly recognized that his novel would be – as he then told a reporter – his best and most important work, and soon it became evident that its format freed him not only to widen his net to experiment stylistically with the novel form, but also to embark on futuristic reflections relating to humanity and the cosmos as a whole while simultaneously bringing in extensive recollections of the key moments and influences within his own life: all pinioned to that precise spot on the globe – 610 North Bedford Drive, Beverly Hills – in which both author and protagonist placed themselves in April 1943.⁹³

Of equal importance, the novel came to reflect the sudden onset of the final crises of Werfel's health. After quickly writing the first parts – Werfel told his publisher in May 1943 that the novel was perhaps one-quarter completed – the author suffered a severe heart attack in September 1943, followed by a similarly serious attack in May 1944.⁹⁴ Besides marking the practical pace of his writing, both attacks understandably came to accentuate an important turn in the narrative toward matters of mortality and death. Thus the first part was written in the spring of 1943, the second part in the fall of 1944, and the third part in the spring

---

89 Werfel [1946a], 406. Werfel also evokes the original author of the *Aeneid* by referring to "Vergilian hexameters" (334).
90 Werfel [1946a], 475. F. W. stresses that he does not want to offer his readers thrilling adventures but to acquaint them "with an unknown world, with a completely blank spot on the map of the most distant future" (267).
91 E. g. Werfel's play *Jacobowsky and the Colonel* which was put on Broadway (but not following the author's original). Even in the novel itself there are references to the increasingly appalling revelations of the war, including the extermination camp Maydanek encountered by Russian troops in July 1944. Werfel [1946a], 561, also mentioning Buchenwald.
92 This same period generally marks the beginnings of such recognition through the writings especially of the young Los Angeleno Ray Bradbury. Southern California served as an important focal point for the evolution of the genre. See Starr [2002], 311–312; Starr [2005a], 270.
93 Jungk [1987], 321; Werfel [1946a], 240: "Something inside me conjectures that I re-entered life at approximately the same geographic spot where I left it" (240). For a good example of Werfel's experimentation in Joycean stream-of-consciousness, see the end to Part 1, 191–192.
94 An earlier attack had occurred in October 1938. Jungk [1987], 315, 317.

of 1945, the whole novel only being completed on 17 August 1945 in Santa Barbara a few days before Werfel's death from a final fatal attack on 26 August.[95]

Werfel's widow Alma later saw fit to stress the change in the direction of Werfel's novel as a result of these crises.[96] One aspect is no doubt the increasingly bizarre elements that Werfel added to his themes – at times he himself seemed to admit that such elements were spinning out of control – but perhaps more important was his commitment around the spring of 1944 to make central to the novel a key event in his own life.[97] With this decision Werfel grasped the deeper metaphysical implications that he wished his work to impart to posterity.

If the Astromental era forms the overall environment for the novel, Werfel is not timid about leading up to it with his own particular account of what the rest of the twentieth century will comprise, an account embedded in that final metaphysical message. The highly rationalistic twentieth-century era wedded to science and technology will culminate in a breakdown. Signs include the Germans turning from "blood and iron" to becoming "the world's pet" with humanitarianism and good will, North Americans reaching the cul de sac of consumerism and technology before becoming the home of a "new mysticism" which in its "plutophobia" turns entirely against market values, and Europe unifying but going into decline as "entirely new Eastern nations" arise. In short, the "skepticism" and "naturalism" of the 1950–2000 period will give way to a powerful new post-technological and spiritual longing.[98]

Yet Astromental civilization will only fully realize that longing after a cosmic event propelling a quantum shift in consciousness. Werfel describes it as a sudden cataclysmic moment, a "sun-catastrophe" of illumination – alternately also labeled a "rapture," a "transparency," the "Event" of a Day of Judgment – followed by the sun's greater distance from the earth and constituting, in cultural terms, the great dividing line of "history", the inauguration of a presumably entirely new relation to the cosmos and the stars.[99]

---

95 These dates follow Werfel's statement concerning his "Reiseroman" in Werfel [1910–1944], Box 16, restated in Werfel [1946b], 8, but not in Werfel [1946a]. It appears that Werfel still hoped to add an "Epilogue" as an "Apology" and was frustrated that he had not yet done so during those final days of his life. He did tell his friend Friedrich Torberg that the third part was finished, but presumably the Epilogue would have followed that third part. Following Jungk [1987], 335–337.
96 Mahler-Werfel [1960], 360.
97 Jungk [1987], 321.
98 Werfel [1946a], 185, 187–188, 181 (177–180 contains some of Werfel's most cutting humor regarding the German character).
99 Werfel [1946a], 26–33, 175, 185, 243: it was "an infinitesimally brief hesitation on the part of the sun between continued shining and flaming self-annihilation, an instant of balance, so to speak" (31–32).

Accordingly, there follows a highly refined civilization, the Astromental, which Werfel wants to present as "post-technological" for having entirely eschewed the fervors of the twentieth century, although strictly speaking it would be more correct to describe that civilization as having simply abandoned the heavy industrial facets of technology for more "aesthetic" and "aristocratic" expressions.[100] If past material history consisted of pushing technology to "the complete subjugation of nature" along with "the struggle for a little social justice," Astromental civilization has succeeded brilliantly in superseding both aims: in effect it represents "the realization of the dreams of communism, but on a strictly aristocratic basis" with its "aristocratic individualism."[101] And as F. W. is shown about this brave new world, its unique contours – as well as achievements and potential shortcomings – are made increasingly clear to him.

Basic to Astronomental civilization is the distinction between "Djebel" and "Dschungl" ("jungle").[102] Strictly speaking, Astromental civilization contains more than the Djebel, but the latter forms its crowning glory, the very epitome of mankind's deepest and most extensive strivings. Werfel runs through a variety of hierarchies upholding Astromental society, which include a Geoarchon covering the political, a Worker covering the economic, and the Grand (Catholic) Bishop covering the ecclesiastical (although the "Jew of the era" [*der Jude des Zeitalters*] has also survived to attest to Judaism's persistence despite the prior epochs of nihilistic skepticism). These all help maintain a highly refined, non-violent, gentle, and sustainable mode of life, rich in its diaphaneity with politesse and good manners. Yet the crown to the system is the Djebel for encapsulating the cosmological dimension.[103] The Djebel crystallizes – literally no less than metaphorically – the most vivid spiritual character of Astromental civilization: its new and unprecedented intimacy with the cosmos and with cosmic space and time.[104]

---

100 Twentieth-century technology "was a primitive abomination composed of mass murder, gasoline stench, electric high tension, splitting of atoms, useless, slow haste, and a mania for enervating comfort." Werfel [1946a], 21. Still, Werfel later admits that the twentieth century was also "the early and clumsy cradle of the later cosmic industry based on the utilization of stellar forces," citing such indicators as "popular scientific journals" and the splitting of the atom (638).
101 Werfel [1946a], 125, 81, 82, 188 (on "neo-communism"), 403.
102 The alliterative play is plain in the original German and constitutes the title of the second or middle part of the novel. "Djebel" means "mountain" in Arabic and the "Jungle" (in fact a variety of discrete "natural" topographies) contains the only "real" or natural mountains in an otherwise flattened world.
103 Werfel [1946a], 352.
104 An important component of Werfel's treatment of the space-time continuum is his invocation of musical analogies, particularly the theme of Harmony of the Spheres. Werfel [1946a], 288–289, 416–417. Werfel's entire life was closely associated with classical music, both instru-

The Djebel is an artificial crystalline mountain of about 4,000 feet containing various schools for "chronosophers" – Werfel pointedly compares them to Tibetan or Hindu "lamaseries" rather than western educational institutions like Harvard and Oxford – trained to embark on the most far-reaching voyages into the cosmos.[105] The three levels of accomplishment are: "Starrovers" (*Sternwanderer*), "Marvelers" (*Thaumazonts*), and "Foreign-feelers" (*Xenospasts*), culminating in the eminence of the Office of the High Floater (*Comptoir des Hochschwebenden*).[106] Each level enters more profoundly into direct exploration of the spatio-temporal mysteries of the cosmos. After being given a whirlwind instruction for the Starroving level, F. W. undergoes the joys of becoming "a beam, an almost immaterial streak of radiant energy" enabled to visit a variety of planets in emulation especially of a brilliant student called Io-Runt, "the cosmic dancing genius," and he confirms through personal experience the existence even of angels as "protomaterial, ultracorporeal beings." Such experiences directly convey to F. W. "the idea of pure meaningless play as a purpose in life" for Astromental civilization in general.[107]

Meanwhile the Marvelers represent individuals who have traveled so far as to experience a "full cosmic consciousness" in which their hearts are "ready to burst with divine amazement" at the very nature of existence, and the Foreign-feelers have penetrated to the limits of creation, returning – beyond "the state of approving ecstacy" – only to look upon the entire material universe as a place of exile. Nonetheless even these supreme voyagers are subordinate to the High Floater himself, "the most original of all." Visiting him in his Arachnodrome – composed of shining spiders and their nets which represent the entirety of the cosmic archives – F. W. is faced with a being whose very evanescence constantly lifts him to the ceiling. At this climactic moment of exploring Astromental spirituality, F. W. is permitted three questions, the main one concerning – as we shall see – the most important moment of his own life.[108]

The High Floater's answer occurs at the exact turn in the novel that leads to the imminent catastrophe of collapse of the Astromental world under the growing challenge of the Jungle. This collapse allows Werfel to underscore important weaknesses in the Astromentral achievement, such as its failure to accommodate more primeval human characteristics which threaten to break out even

---

mental and operatic. His close friends (and neighbors) in Beverly Hills included the conductor Bruno Walter with whom he had a final dinner at Romanoff's the night before his death.
105 Werfel [1946a], 337, 496. In keeping with his California orientation, Werfel compares the Djebel to Mounts Whitney and Shasta as well as to the Mount Wilson observatory (272, 273).
106 Werfel [1946], 272; Werfel [1946b], 283.
107 Werfel [1946a], 286, 318, 188.
108 Werfel [1946a], 344, 345, 347, 352, 360–372.

among its most educated and favored classes. But perhaps the most problematic shortcoming, for Werfel at least, is the Astromental confusion between even a refined materiality – as summed up in the outmost strivings of the chronosophers – and spirituality proper. This distinction is graphically demonstrated by F. W.'s "descent" in Part 3 into the "Wintergarden" where an entire civilization tries to overcome the fact of mortal death by providing an apparent "retrogenetic" solution consisting of rethreading one's life like a movie reel (another example of the Hollywood film industry's influence on Werfel's imagination).[109] Such confusion is repeatedly exposed and critiqued in the extensive discussions F. W. exchanges with the two eminent representatives of the more ancient spiritualities of Catholic Christianity and Judaism, the author's favored religions.[110] The Grand Bishop effectively articulates Werfel's own position that ultimate matters of life and death cannot be approached even through the most benign technology but require the insights of a genuine religiosity.[111]

It is true that in narrower terms Werfel leaves his reader with a hopeful closing image of Astromental and Jungle folk making their halting way toward a benign if grudging reconciliation for the future. Yet F. W. continues to prefer, "in spite of the victory of the Jungle," the Astromental's "world without economics": "It's a better world, even though man isn't any better in it." After all, man may not have improved morally, but he has "become esthetically more beautiful" and "also more intuitive."[112] Even so, there remains a much grander prize than Astromental civilization, and what that might be requires a further consideration of the specific "I" in Werfel's account, that irremediably autobiographical core to F. W.'s experience.

---

109 The plethora of references to films, pro and con, include Werfel [1946a], 411, 421, 462, 480, 577, 638. In notes dated April 1944 Werfel stated his belief that motion pictures were not yet a brand of the arts and potentially belonged more to the epic than dramatic form, perhaps even providing a new kind of hieroglyph or "ideographs for storytelling." Were motion pictures to be no longer identified with the entertainment industry under the control of businessmen but were put into the "hands of artists," they might well constitute an entirely new art. Werfel [1910–1944], Box 9.

110 From Werfel's other allusions it seems clear that important features of Buddhism, especially Tibetan Buddhism, will also have survived. An integral part of the novel is Werfel's exploitation of his boyhood friend Willy Haas' stay in Darjeeling, India, during the 1940s to study Tibetan Buddhism and its psychic feats. Werfel [1946a], 10, 11, 51, 337.

111 The Bishop is probably modeled on Werfel's good friend Father Cyril Fischer with whom the author held extensive talks during the writing of the novel. Fischer was born in Vienna. His death in May 1944 came at a grievous moment in Werfel's own life. Werfel's visits to Fischer at the Santa Barbara Mission confirm another distinctive "California" feature to the novel, since the Mission, its occupants, and its library played an important role in the evolution of the spiritual articulation of Werfel's theme. Jungk [1987], 304, 325, 426–427.

112 Werfel [1946a], 637.

For although one function of F. W. as a character is to furnish Werfel's unique glimpse into the future and the larger meanings of mankind and cosmos, *Star of the Unborn* is after all the story of Werfel himself. As noted by his translator, it is perhaps the most autobiographical of all his works, threading its way through his upbringing in Prague, involvement in Bohemias and the 1918 revolutions, life in Vienna with Alma, flight from France, and final settlement in California.[113] Throughout these wanderings both Werfel and F. W. are permanent "emigrants," exiles, and even now in the time-space of the novel his main protagonist is floating somewhere between life and non-life, perhaps dead and buried (in "Forest Lawn"), perhaps in purgatory, horribly lonely at key moments, neither fully in the California of 1943 nor of the year 100,000, eventually requiring the Grand Bishop to assure him that his account of his particular state of being does not square with the Church's insight into the stage of death and that by implication he must therefore in some important, if murky, sense still be "really" alive.[114]

Thus, beyond even Astromental and Jungle priorities there remains a deeper truth toward which Werfel was apparently working in this, his last work. Intrinsic to his protagonist's insights into reality is the primacy of the cosmos from a variety of angles. One incontestable truth he wishes to convey throughout is that the cosmos is literally alive: "*the universe breathes.*"[115] Moreover, it is both geocentric and finite, taking the shape of man, while the earth "is a woman."[116] In the end, the collapse of Astromental civilization literally exposes the fact that the Djebel is actually the "eye of Gaea," or Earth, and that its true meaning is incapsulated in an "Isochronion," a contraption which contains the secret of "cosmic simultaneity," the confirmation that the "cosmos has the shape of a man."[117]

Werfel's master starrover Io-Runt loses his life in order to retrieve the Isochronion and thus allow future generations to be attuned to the universality of this "celestial man." Thanks to his sacrifice, Astromental civilization is therefore to be succeeded by an even more advanced stage: "Isochronic civilization." Indeed Io-Runt turns out to be none other than Franz Werfel's real and only son, the sickly child born to him and Alma in 1918 who died a few months later in 1919, and this turns out to be the "most important moment" in F. W.'s – *and* Franz Werfel's – life as earlier revealed by the High Floater. It knits together the underlying philosophical threads into Werfel's closing vision, for when Werfel lauds

---

113 Gustave O. Arlt, cited in Jungk [1987], 322.
114 Werfel [1946a], 173, 240, 241, 420, 634.
115 Werfel [1946a], 109 (emphasis in original).
116 Werfel [1946a], 110,185, 525. For Werfel the interconnection of man and cosmos has already been captured in the ancient Babylonian wisdom: "Everything that is below, is also above" (209).
117 Werfel [1946a], 613, 619.

Isochronic civilization as the final goal of all true scientific endeavors over time, he ventures the additional clue that this goal is in fact coterminous with what has often been called "inspiration" or "a sudden ecstasy" akin to a "flash of lightning."[118]

Thus Werfel's final meaning may be effectively traced by following his own key "inspirations" during these final years of his work and life. Thanks to an original "inspiration" on Palm Sunday 1943, Werfel was in fact motivated to embark on the entire novel after undergoing a long memorable dream of feeling himself "bodiless." Then, at the start of the novel itself his protagonist F. W. posits an experience of "sudden enlightenment"[119] which teaches him that reincarnation is made up only of a finite number of egos accumulating "a key bouquet of incarnations" over time. F. W.'s later recognition of the greatest moment of his "life" – namely, the birth of his son who is no less an early incarnation of Io-Runt – further confirms a critical lesson from the High Floater: "the moment of greatest continuity is the most important" since it teaches the "wealth of continuity" as such. Finally, the Grand Bishop's closing assurance to F. W. that he is not really "dead" lifts him to his final "ecstasy": if, from a spiritual-religious perspective, humanity has been moving away from the "beginnings" of all things, it is also coming closer to the "end" of all things, a revelation that teaches F. W. that "alienation is nothing but a form of approach." Far from being an ultimate closure, Io-Runt's explicit acceptance of his own mortal death – in contrast to the Wintergarden proclivities of Astromental civilization and even of Io-Runt's own "parents" for that epoch – opens up higher possibilities for the human spirit (Io-Runt will be the next "High Floater") of which the Isochronion is Werfel's supreme symbol, namely, the truth of the cosmic simultaneity that is accessible to humans through their experiences and recognition of modes of reincarnation. Armed with this insight, F. W. dives into the joyful "smile of the star dancer," and this leap becomes the novel's mechanism for taking him – and Franz Werfel – all the way back to the exact corner in Beverly Hills in April 1943 from which they had originally set out.[120]

Werfel was the first to grant the strangeness of this "humoristic-cosmic-mystical world poem" that he was so assiduously weaving. His good friends such as Max Brod and Willy Haas would call it his best novel, but perhaps the most revealing comments come from Werfel's fellow-novelist in the Southland, Thomas Mann. Mann was quick to judge that the "book has a coldness which no longer belongs entirely to life and which cannot be called artistically happy." Yet the most dis-

---

118 Werfel [1946a], 373–376, 620.
119 It takes place "in a drugstore on Wilshire Boulvevard." Werfel [1946a], 12.
120 See Jungk [1987], 312. Werfel [1946a], 12–13, 376. 642, 643, 645.

turbing underworld scenes, he admitted, contained "scarcely any match in all literature as imaginative achievements." Above all, Mann saw *Star of the Unborn* as a rich continuation of the tradition of the "travel novel" in world literature even if, unlike its predecessors, "the book has no real language of its own."[121]

With what he called its "monstrous mixture of philosophy and entertainment," Werfel left his fellow Californians a unique product for speculation and introspection.[122] Given its remarkable explorations into real and imaginative California reality, human and cosmic history, and the intense spiritual reflections of a man approaching his own death, *Star of the Unborn* may alone stand out among the products of the Central European diaspora as a serious candidate for the Great California Novel.

4.

From the second to the third periods in the relationship between California civilization and European speculative thought, California's economy further advanced to the rank of a major power, thanks largely to its central role during World War II and the beginnings of the cold war. At the same time, burgeoning anti-Communism in California and the United States frightened large numbers of the Central European diaspora into permanent departures by the late 1940s. Adorno and Horkheimer settled into important academic positions in what became the Federal Republic of Germany, while Brecht preferred the new communist regime in East Germany. Mann meanwhile moved to Switzerland in 1952, where he died in 1955.

The 1950s proved a difficult period of social and political conservatism. It was therefore only thanks to the upheavals of the 1960s that a further third phase of active exchange between European speculative thought and the evolution of California civilization is worth tracing. This third phase belongs to "theory" in a sense somewhat broader than Critical Theory since it would include not only the contributions of the Critical Theory tradition proper but also poststructuralism and deconstruction. Three figures best representing this phase contributed some

---

121   Cited in Jungk [1987], 330; Mann [1961], 159, 160. Mann even "toyed" with the thought of lecturing on the novel but "never got around to that." Bartl [1996] stresses the importance of Mann's *The Magic Mountain* for Werfel's conception of his novel (58–64). Werfel was also invited to hear Mann's readings of his *Joseph the Provider* manuscript.

122   Cited in Jungk [1987], 332. It should be noted that Werfel intended the English translation of his work by Arlt to come out as quickly as the German original. Arlt was translating on a daily basis as Werfel wrote the original pages.

of the most original expressions of these three modes of critical thought to California: Herbert Marcuse, Michel Foucault, and Jacques Derrida.

With regard to Herbert Marcuse, it has already been noted that Marcuse joined his colleagues Adorno and Horkheimer in Los Angeles in 1941. Unfortunately for Marcuse, notwithstanding his earnest wish to stay and work particularly with Horkheimer on their earlier aims of a new dialectical logic (one reason for his inclusion after 1934 in the Frankfurt School), Marcuse decided to accept a position offered in Washington, DC, in 1942 when it became clear that the Frankfurt School funds were temporarily strapped, and went on to work for the Office of Strategic Services (OSS), predecessor to the future Central Intelligence Agency (CIA), as part of the U.S. government's campaign against Germany and on behalf of eventual denazification.[123] After the war, Marcuse remained on the American east coast to work and teach at Columbia and Brandeis universities where he eventually produced two important products of Critical Theory: Marcuse's own "dialectic of enlightenment" addendum, *Eros and Civilization* (1955), and the work that established Marcuse's academic and political notoriety, *One-Dimensional Man* (1964). As a result, Marcuse was offered, and accepted, a post at the San Diego campus of the University of California, moving to California by 1965 and helping to launch the speculative branch of the sixties protest movement in California and elsewhere.[124]

Marcuse's California years were marked by a body of work that both established him at the forefront of American radical thought and temporarily made him the object of a number of threats by political reactionaries in the Southland. *An Essay on Liberation* (1969), *Counterrevolution and Revolt* (1972), and Marcuse's closing aesthetics, *The Aesthetic Dimension* (titled *Die Permanenz der Kunst* in German) (1978), form only part of Marcuse's voluminous writing and lecturing both in the US and in Europe, at a time when banners in the 1968 Paris uprisings proclaimed the forthcoming age of "Marx, Mao, and Marcuse."[125] Fervently pursuing the task of formulating the concept of a new revolutionary subject that would supplant and replace the classic Marxist proletariat class, Marcuse proved the only member of the original Frankfurt School to become enthusiastically a political activist.[126] In this endeavor, Marcuse drew deeply on his new and final California home.

---

123 See Katz [1982] and Kellner [1984].
124 At San Diego, Marcuse assumed "his new role as the philosophical idol of militant youth." Hughes [1975], 181.
125 See Marcuse [2005] and [2007] for other relevant essays; also "Marcuse: Aesthetic Ethos," in Chytry [1989], 434–435.
126 Marcuse's enthusiasm is reflected in his comments on the 1968 student movement: "The radical utopian character of their demands far surpasses the hypotheses of my essay," and: "No

Perhaps the most apt evidence of the role of California in Marcuse's New Left thought is the chapter "The New Sensibility" in *An Essay on Liberation*. Building on his earlier fusion of Marx and Freud in the call for a solution to the "dialectic of civilization" through the Schillerian ideal of "the aesthetic state," Marcuse drew on the events of the California sixties, from the Free Speech Movement in Berkeley to the emergence of a counterculture and political protest against the Vietnam war, to envisage an "aesthetic ethos of socialism" in the making that, he claimed, was engaged in the praxis of a new revolutionary subject freed from the external and internal impositions of domination.[127] Undeterred by the short-term defeats of the movement in 1968–9, Marcuse went on to exhort the New Left to extend the "new sensibility" to the level of everyday life and the "long march through the institutions."[128] While the conventional struggles against dominant capitalistic institutions should continue to be part of the strategy toward the goal of an ultimate direct democracy, Marcuse insisted that repressive patterns would be repeated unless consciousness came to embody this new aesthetic ethos. Throughout the 1970s Marcuse developed his position that participatory democracy, feminism and environmentalism were key components for shaping the new working majority.[129]

To keep open this prospect, shortly before his death Marcuse completed his Marxian aesthetics. Against orthodox Marxist theory, *The Aesthetic Dimension* insisted that art and its object, beauty, invariably transcended any finite political practice and he anchored such practice in an ongoing critique of pragmatic institutions: "At the optimum, we can envisage a universe common to art and reality, but in this common universe, art would retain its transcendence."[130] For only the aesthetic imagination was capable of coping with those universal conflicts – chance, fate, tragedy, love – that surpassed every revolution.[131] Throughout these matured formulations of his postindustrial political philosophy, Marcuse both

---

matter whether their action was a revolt or an abortive revolution, it is a turning point." Marcuse [1969], 11.

127 See Marcuse [1961] for his use of Schiller. Marcuse's "aesthetic ethos" is very probably a translation of Hegel's "schöne Sittlichkeit" (Marcuse was the house Hegelian in the Frankfurt group), and his use of "aesthetic morality" is probably a reminder of Nietzsche's "ästhetische Moral."
128 Marcuse [1972], 55, 42; also 134.
129 See Balbus [1982], 353–398.
130 Marcuse [1978], 7. Even in the earlier Marcuse [1969] despite his favorable treatment of 1960s art forms, Marcuse had criticized desublimation and "abrogation of the Estrangement effect" (53). Cf. also Marcuse [1972], 121.
131 Marcuse [1978], 72. For a nuanced reading on the evolution in Marcuse's aesthetic thought, see Douglas Kellner, "Introduction: Marcuse, Art, and Liberation," in Marcuse [2007], 1–70.

learned from and contributed to the variety of experiments ongoing in California in shaping a new "counter" culture.

If Marcuse closed with recognition of the new stage of political struggle as one of decentralization and localization of efforts, it was Michel Foucault who more directly took up the project of the emancipatory individual in a postmodern context. Foucault's dazzling interpretations of a history of reason and unreason (including "madness") as well as his agentless theories of historical epistemes had already established a quixotic reputation for its author prior to the May 1968 uprisings in Paris. A late joiner to these upheavals, Foucault then became a key figure in their institutionalization through the reform of the French university system, and to a lesser extent, its prison system. Internationally recognized by the early 1970s as the most prominent voice of the new radicalism, Foucault often lectured throughout the globe.

One such stop, California, in May 1975 occasioned Foucault's first lingering taste of its "limit-experiences" and helped change the trajectory of his work. Foucault's LSD experience in Death Valley, California (including the obligatory visit to a nearby Taoist commune), recounted by companion Simeon Wade, began a major stylistic change around 1975–76, as Foucault later recounted, for his next project after *Discipline and Punish* (1975).[132] Although the first volume of this project to be called the *History of Sexuality* – the French original of the first volume is entitled *La Volonté de Savoir* (1976) – continues the characteristic Foucauldian moves of demasking and exposure of forces of domination, it proved the last of the genre. Foucault, who like Marcuse had been avidly searching for an alternative to the classic proletariat as the revolutionary class, gave up on his early 1970s expectations of the *gauche prolétarienne* and the "plebes" in favor of the new gay culture emerging between 1975 and 1980 in the Castro Street neighborhood of San Francisco, California. From this stage on, Foucault was found experimenting with its new forms of pleasure, along with the S/M fixations of nearby Folsom Street. Even if such subgroups could be found in Paris and Mediterranean cities familiar to Foucault, he regarded the California version as a far more promising candidate for the vanguard of new regimes of bodies and pleasure that could also serve the wider heterosexual community.[133]

Around 1977–78 Foucault was finding it increasingly difficult to pursue his Collège de France lectures in the conventional Foucauldian mould. The problematic of a "biopolitics," as he had previously framed it, was over. Specific political events – from the revelations of the Gulag archipelago to the plight of Vietnamese

---

132 Simeon Wade, "Foucault in California," a manuscript of 121 pages, summarized in Miller [1993], 246–253, 437–438. Unfortunately I have been unable to secure a copy of this manuscript.
133 On the *Gauche Prolétarienne* and Foucault, see Macey [1995], 217–219 and ff.

refugees and the struggle of Czech dissidents to the revolutionary fervor in Iran – encouraged Foucault to contemplate more positive readings in the direction of a "*transcendens* pure and simple."[134] Foucault's Howisohn lecture at the University of California, Berkeley, in October 1980 marks the watershed toward a new reading of his history of sexuality project in which "techniques of the self" increasingly replace the former fixation on domination and repression. It is perhaps not surprising that this turn was accompanied by Foucault's willingness to become more "Californian" – even apparently to preferring its club sandwiches to haute cuisine – and tighten his links both with the gay scene in San Francisco and with Californian academic life. Foucault seems to have been in the midst of negotiations to make permanent his academic presence either at Berkeley or Stanford at the time of his unexpected death due to AIDS in June 1984.[135]

Publication of the second and third volumes of Foucault's *History of Sexuality* shortly after his death – a fourth, almost complete volume was never published – reveals a dramatically different Foucault, one which disappointed a great many of his admirers who expected more of the standard Foucault. Even to the point of style, these works – *The Use of Pleasure* and *Care of the Self* – are reserved, classical in tone, and committed to what Foucault increasingly called "an aesthetics of existence." In effect, the entire *History of Sexuality* project was transformed into a "history of the techniques of the self" in which Foucault concentrated on modes of "subjectivization" *(mode d'assujettisement)* leading to a reinstatement of the Hellenic aesthetics of existence and stylistics of the self, but on the new levels achieved through a subsequent dialectic of bodies and pleasures.[136] Even though Foucault, on one occasion at least, insisted that his new object was not the "Californian cult of the self,"[137] it is clear that California was the appropriate site for further experimentations along this trajectory – certainly for Foucault.

Foucault's new account established three major stages in the process of the creation of a new aesthetics of existence. The first one, the classic-Hellenic, had been centered on the "aphrodisia," an ethical substance capable of interrelating acts, desires, and pleasures, even if these were primarily on behalf of a ruling male hierarchy.[138] Increasingly, however, "care of the self" began to reflect concerns in

---

134 Miller [1993], 299, 305.
135 See "Zen and California," in Eribon [1991], 309–316. Eribon's prose tries to capture a Foucault "happy in the pleasures of the flesh," as around 1983 he looked ahead to "moving to the United States. He dreamed aloud of living in the Californian paradise. Sunny, magnificent ..." (316).
136 Foucault [1985], 27.
137 See Foucault's disclaimer in a 1983 interview. Foucault [2003], 118. Foucault held that this "Californian cult of the self" was premised on the effort "to discover one's true self" and to this extent differed sharply from the "ancient cult of the self." Note also his interviewer's emphasis on the "Berkeley" (California) attempt to "perfect all aspects of everyday life" (109).
138 Foucault [1985], 38ff.

the subsequent Hellenistic-Roman period of bodily and ethical excess that needed to be domesticated and disciplined.[139] Such "care of the self" remained a subcategory of the "aphrodisia," but it was beginning to problematize concerns about protecting the self that could be seen as transitions to a very different perspective. This perspective, Foucault believed, was one obsessed with the "flesh" as the site for temptations that needed to be simultaneously confessed and repressed.[140] Having reached this epochal turn toward the Christian suspicion of the body and its "libido," Foucault appears to have been aiming at completing the circle to his earlier works on "sex" as a mode of disciplinary discourse emerging in the nineteenth-century society of disciplinary "knowledge." Notwithstanding Foucault's premature death, his account of a basic history of the body from (1) the classical *aphrodisia* (an aesthetics of existence turning into care of the self), through (2) the late antiquity-early Christian confessions of the flesh, to (3) the modern discursivity of sex and sexuality remains clear.[141]

By 1978 California had taught Foucault to sponsor the emancipatory aspects implicit in this account as a possible "extraordinary falsification of pleasure" in which the body might become "a place for the production of extraordinarily polymorphic pleasures, while simultaneously detaching it from a valorization of the genitalia and particularly of the male genitalia," in short, a "general economy of pleasure not based on sexual norms."[142] Freed from the characteristic orgasmic goals of the penis or vagina, such "limit-experiences" opened up an anarchy within the body that promised a "nondisciplinary eroticism." Through experiments in which a non-disciplinary theatricality of S/M was to be primary, Foucault foresaw a domain of pulsation and oscillation that could resemble the intensities of traditional mystical and meditative experience, or for that matter the intensities offered by psychedelic experience. The gay life (*vie gay*) could play the vanguard role in such explorations, since it offered the possibility of a creative life (*vie creatrice*) that hovered beyond the disciplinary limitations of "sex" and sexual discursivities.[143] If Marcuse had found California inspiring for suggesting the goal of an "aesthetic ethos of socialism," Foucault thus came to draw from California this closing image of a technique of the self that gave rise to his new "aesthetics of existence."[144]

---

139 Foucault [1986].
140 See especially "The Battle for Chastity [1982] in Foucault [1988], 227–241. Also Foucault [1978], 18–21, 156.
141 The best brief account by Foucault is Foucault [1985], 11–13.
142 Foucault, cited in Miller [1993], 269.
143 See Miller [1993], 262–284. Also Macey [1995], 365–377.
144 Besides the introduction of the "aesthetics of existence" theme in his second volume of *The History of Sexuality* (*The Use of Pleasure*), the most relevant text is Foucault's 1983 interview in Foucault [2003], 102–125.

For Jacques Derrida meanwhile, the value of California remains to be fully clarified. French postmodern writers often associated with Derrida had already singled out the importance of California prior to Derrida's intervention. In 1975 Jean François Lyotard claimed that the postmodern had been localized in California.[145] In 1986 Jean Baudrillard regarded California as the quintessence of western civilization where history, the modern, and humanity approached its end.[146] It was also argued that since the 1960s California had become the "site in which the conflicts of the modern and postmodern" were played out. The heterogeneous body of critical thinking that came to be known simply as "theory" (generally following Jonathan Culler's designation) even encouraged the suggestion that "California" represented the "flipped-out side" of "Germany,"[147] or to put it bluntly: "the scene [*Schauplatz*] of *Theory* ... is California."[148]

Given the fact of his recent death in 2004, Derrida's enormous output is only now the subject of an effective overview.[149] That career cannot be adequately assessed without taking into account Derrida's turn to California. After his noted participation in a conference at Johns Hopkins University in 1966, Derrida in the 1970s was brought to the United States through allies and sympathizers at such academic centers as Yale University, and through J. Hillis Miller made a connection with the Irvine campus of the University of California by the early 1980s. Derrida's Irvine Wellek lectures in 1984 on his friend, the recently deceased and lately controversial literary theorist Paul de Man, belong to a new phase in the response of deconstruction (augmented by Derrida's slightly later work on Heidegger) to charges of its ethical and political emptiness.

Derrida scholars like John D. Caputo regard the subsequent period of Derrida's writings as one that makes increasingly plain his "religion without religion," a "hoping in a certain messianic promise of the impossible," an "ethico-political turn" in deconstruction.[150] Of course, Derrida would strenuously deny that deconstruction had ever been "empty" in this sense – let alone implicitly anti-progressive – but his writings of the 1990s do reflect a new seriousness in grappling with

---

145 From Lyotard, *Le mur du Pacifique* (1975), cited in Kniesche [1995], 14.
146 Baudrillard [1986], 245: "la puissance mythique de la Californie est dans ce mixte d'une extrême déconnection et d'une mobilité vertigineuse prise dans le site, le scénario hyperréel des déserts, des *freeways*, de l'océan et du soleil" (emphasis in original).
147 Rickels [1991], 7. "If postmodernity is postmarked ... 'made in Germany' ..., then California is its address and technofuture" (11). I follow in general the helpful introduction by Kniesche in Kniesche [1995], 11–17.
148 Kniesche [1995], 12.
149 See a first complete biography by Powell [2006], followed by Peeters [2012]; also Bennington & Derrida [1993].
150 Caputo [1997]. xix.

conventional issues of ethics and politics. This seriousness went hand-in-hand with Derrida's assumption of a professorship of philosophy, French, and comparative literature at Irvine in 1986 (at the same time as his colleague J. Hillis Miller), a position he held to his death, and the creation between 1990 and 1995 of the Derrida Archives on the Irvine campus. Without questioning that Derrida remained throughout a distinctly French thinker, it is worth asking how these new commitments to California – even to entrusting his precious manuscripts to its archives – are reflected in Derrida's writings of the 1990s, particularly such substantive works as *Specters of Marx* (1994), *Gift of Death* (1995), and *Politics of Friendship* (1997).

Once professionally connected with California, Derrida began to offer appreciative comments on his new base. Shortly after his Irvine appointment, Derrida participated in an imposing colloquium of "theory" scholars at Irvine in 1987 where, claiming to have misunderstood the theme of the colloquium to be "the state of theory" (rather than: "the states of 'theory'"), Derrida reflected:

> "And I thought that the answer to this question – What is the state of theory today? – was then self-evident, it was obvious, hic et nunc. The state of theory, *now and from now on*, isn't it *California*? And even Southern California?"[151]

Immediately forestalling the temptation to take his words "as a play on words or as a way of avoiding the issue," Derrida added that "this answer may be more serious, more realistic, more historical, and 'historian' than it seems." Why indeed, he wondered pointedly, was this colloquium "*happening* in California?"[152]

According to one interpreter, this pregnant passage suggests that Derrida was pinpointing California as the very "institutionalization of deconstruction in America" and that he was underscoring "the ambivalent potential of this state or state of mind."[153] Looking upon the "state of 'theory'," Derrida was buoyed up by the "taxonomic disorder" of "theory" in its double sense as "political organization" and "as report, assessment, account = *statement*." Deliberately classifying "California" under the former – that is, under "political organization" or "institutional fortifications" – Derrida saw "increasingly flexible, mobile" conditions for this "state" as he added:

---

151 Derrida [1990]. 63 (emphasis added). Formally the colloquium was intended to initiate the Critical Theory Institute at Irvine.
152 Derrida [1990], 63 (emphasis added).
153 See Sarah Roff's review of Kniesche [1995] in Roff [1997], 487, and Kniesche [1995], 13. Kniesche also draws the connection with the U.S. president's annual "state of the union" speech (13 [note 6]).

"the state of California is once more exemplary in that respect, *we* are used to theoretical earthquakes here, and institutional architectures are erected to respond to the seisms or seismisms of all the new *isms* which might shake the structures, both post and new structures."[154]

"California" also meant for Derrida the infusion of "theory" into such burgeoning academic movements as the New Marxism and the New Historicism, the latter which Derrida associated with "Northern California" after "transplants" from "French vineyards." These two apparent challenges to the putative a-historicism of deconstruction were welcomed by Derrida – indeed he claimed that he "would be very happy to contribute to this development"[155] – insofar as they in effect matured from being mere reactions to "a deconstructionist poststructuralism" which was little more than a "caricatural myth," and embraced the degree to which deconstruction was itself not a "theory," nor a "manifesto," but a summation of this entire outflow of ideas and original thinking called "theory." Put provocatively: "deconstruction is the case," it was not a theory "but the opening of a space," encouraging that "something happen, that's what's better, that's all." Preceding all ethics, politics, aesthetics, historical and social reality, "it is what happens, what is happening today."[156]

Derrida felt justified in absorbing all these more apparently historically-oriented approaches into the ecumenism of deconstruction by reminding his audience that ultimately the double game of deconstruction "*starts* by tackling logocentrism," thus already containing the kind of concern for the "political-juridical-sociohistorical" that the New Marxists and New Historians were presumably pushing. Hence Derrida's punchline: deconstruction "isn't essentially theoretical, thetic, or thematic because it is *also ethical-political.*"[157] With this injection of the pivotal phrase "ethical-political," Derrida wedded the direction of his later works to the goal of a "happening" that had been building up "for twenty years" (1966–1986) in no less a "state" than the "state of California" where New Historians were prospering in Northern California (e. g. the University of California, Santa Cruz) and the non-"theory" of deconstruction was securing supporters in locations as varied as the Santa Barbara and Berkeley campuses of the University of California. Doing his best semiotically to discourage deconstruction from itself freezing into an institutionalized theorizing, Derrida pressed the language of "happening" – clearly derived from the Heideggerian concept of history-as-happening *(die Geschichte geschieht)* – for his vision of what might well

---

154 Derrida [1990], 87–88 (emphasis added). Note Derrida's use of the collective "we" in this passage.
155 Derrida emphasizes: "I very sincerely wish that they develop even more." Derrida [1990], 90.
156 Derrida [1990], 80, 82, 85.
157 This language also means "reality, history, society, law, politics" according to Derrida. Derrida [1990], 91 (emphasis in original), 87 (emphasis added).

unfold for both "California" and "deconstruction" as the paradigmatic "state of theory," his pointed answer to the original question of why such a colloquium was "*happening* in California."

Derrida's substantial efforts to articulate the "ethical-political" dimension of deconstruction permeates his major works of the 1990s across a wide spectrum of topics from justice, religion, and mourning to politics and friendship. With California as its "state of theory" for "the opening of a space" in which something "happened," deconstruction became increasingly "messianic" in the straightforward sense of exploiting the double movement of expecting a "coming" that remained simultaneously eternally deferred. Precisely this deferment saved such ultimate standards from hardening into the kind of conceptuality that deconstruction eschewed as remnants of logocentric western thinking.

Thus in the 1989–1990 lectures later published as "Force of Law" (1994), Derrida approached the "idea of justice" as an always coming, a to-come (*a-venir*, French for "future"): "The future loses the openness, the coming of the other (who comes), without which there is no justice;" indeed, "perhaps justice is another kind of mysticism." As for "God," it is "the Wholly Other, as always," "the name of the absolute metonymy."[158] Similar moves marked the later Derrida's most narratively coherent text on the ethical-political proper. In *Politics of Friendship* (1997) Derrida presented a compelling image of a (future) Democracy in which the very concept of friendship, and such interrelated terms of fraternity, comradeship, hospitality, and even perhaps love, were deconstructed from their bounded historical implications – along with the latter's complicitous relationship to dialectic movements of friendship and hostility – to emerge reconstructed without the confining baggage of past interpretations:

> "For democracy remains to come; this is its essence in so far as it remains: not only will it remain indefinitely perfectible, hence always insufficient and future, but, belonging to the time of the promise, it will always remain, in each of its future times, to come: even where there is a democracy, it never exists, it is never present, it remains the theme of a non-presentable concept."[159]

---

158 "Force of Law" originally consisted of two separate talks, the second one given at the University of California, Los Angeles. Derrida [2002], 256, 254, 293.
159 Derrida [1997], 306. Notwithstanding the connections between Derrida's image of the "state of California" and such ideas, his biographer notes that in his final years Derrida became less interested in America and more reoriented toward Europe. Powell [2006].

5.

"California is very important ... because nowhere else has the upheaval most shamelessly caused by capitalist centralization taken place with such speed."

Karl Marx [1880][160]

Where, finally, do we stand today in terms of the interchange between Californian civilization and European speculative thought? Although there is no reason to doubt that productive dialogue will continue indefinitely, it is highly probable that the great age of interchange is over for the following reasons.

First, the three stages clearly record the story of a young civilization gradually but unmistakably catching up with an older civilization. Thus the *first* stage is highlighted by a native Californian, Josiah Royce, seeking out superior European wisdom, both cultural and speculative, in German university centers that reflected the rise to prominence of modern German culture and power in the heart of Europe. The *second* stage is the story of a major intellectual diaspora, the Central European emigration from an increasingly totalitarian Europe to more clement Californian shores, where Californian asylum helped support at least three major contributions to European speculation: Bertolt Brecht's second version of *Galileo*, Thomas Mann's *Doktor Faustus*, and Max Horkheimer and Theodor W. Adorno's *Dialectic of Enlightenment*; and perhaps one major California Novel: Franz Werfel's *Star of the Unborn*. By the *third* stage the European contributors were coming to California not only for the fiscal largesse of its thriving universities but also for the stimulation of new social and cultural patterns to be embedded in the variety of concepts – an aesthetic ethos of socialism, an aesthetics of existence, a politics of friendship and (impossible) Democracy – developed by three major thinkers in the postwar European radical tradition of thought: Herbert Marcuse, Michel Foucault, and Jacques Derrida. Thus, by the third stage, it could be fairly claimed that Europeans were also learning from California, and this meant that as of the twenty-first century California and Californians had in effect more than caught up, in their own self-images and self-confidence, with the phenomenon known as "Europe." From now on "Europe" need no longer function as the necessary great Fount.

Second, the great European speculative tradition itself is probably fading. This is due to a variety of factors, not least to the growth and expansion of a globalizing European "union" that has increasingly had the same dampening effects on speculation that the American continental republic had on earlier centers of American speculation – something Josiah Royce himself lamented as an undermining of

---

160 Marx & Engels [1975-], 34: 478 (5 xi 1880).

"provincial" cultures by the hegemonic center.[161] While it is evident that Europe continues to produce its throngs of first-rate scholars and critics who, like thinkers at other cultural centers, will have their influence on a continually expanding Californian intellectual life, no monumental name in speculation has appeared to follow the stature of the last wave associated primarily with the names of Jürgen Habermas (successor to Horkheimer in running the reconstituted Frankfurt Institute of Social Research in Frankfurt, Germany), Michel Foucault and Jacques Derrida.

Last, the Californian demographic future of cultural diversity with its growing plurality of Western Hemispheric Hispanic speakers and increasing prominence of Asian-Americans (primarily Chinese Mandarin-speaking in origin, but also Japanese and Korean) at academic and research centers leaves increasingly less room for anything like a common interest in a source known as "Europe" – let alone the latter's speculative tradition. If it is probable that by 2050, a population of 60 million Californians will divide into 52 percent Hispanic speakers, 26 percent non-Hispanic white speakers and 13 percent Asian speakers, it seems clear that such general trends away from exclusive concern with Europe not only will continue but will become increasingly accentuated in the broad future.[162]

Still, as this chapter recounts, the fact of significant interchange has indeed taken place. Whatever the character of speculative thought in California's future, Californians can ill afford to ignore the fruits of the three stages we have traced and delineated – from Royce's vision of a Goethean-Hellenic civilization all the way to Derrida's baroque defense of a Democracy "never-to-be". To this extent European speculation must be henceforth reckoned a vibrant element in the unfolding story of a California civilization.

---

161   In his call for a "Higher Provincialism," Royce critiques these tendencies of centralization that undermine variety. "Provincialism," in Royce [1908], 74–76. This essay is closely tied to Royce's own "provincialism to which I, as a native Californian, personally owe most" (vi).
162   Following projections in State of California [2007].

Chapter 4
A Golden Age?
The California Fifties as Watershed[1]

California in the Fifties – for many observers this was the spectacular, the "golden" moment of California "civilization." As never before, California seemed to have found the secret to the "good life," and increasingly the rest of America, as well as the world, began to pay serious attention to what was "going on" in California.

All the more significant then is the appearance of Kevin Starr's appropriately titled *Golden Dreams: California in an Age of Abundance 1950–1963* (2009), the book that fans of his epic venture *Americans and the California Dream* have long awaited.[2] As far back as 1973 Starr came out with the highly regarded *Americans and the California Dream* which covered the period 1850–1915 in Californian history. For the occasional reader, there was no clear indication at that time that it was to be the start of a long narrative road. Even what became the second volume in the series, *Inventing the Dream* (1985), which shifted to the California Southland for roughly the same period, seemed more by way of rounding out Starr's account for both parts of California, North and South. However, with *Material Dreams* (1990), which extended the theme to 1920s Southern California, Starr was off and running, eventually demarcating the distant 1950–1963 period as his final arrival point for the celebration of a California that, as underscored by its permanent ascension around 1962 to the most populous state of the Union, had become a great power in its own right, a "mega-state" of massive economic and cultural proportions—serving, according to the preface to the present volume, as the "epicenter" for "the single greatest arc of rising prosperity in American history and, quite generally, in all of history" (x, xi).[3]

As Starr's project has deepened over nine volumes,[4] so too have his resources and commitment to increasingly exact investigations into minutiae that are ele-

---

1 Originally published as "California Irredenta," *History and Theory*, 50:2 (May 2011), 270–284.
2 Starr [2009]. All page references in the text are to this volume.
3 In a 2007 interview after publication of his work on 1990–2003 California, Starr declared he would "leave it to future historians to deal with the mid- and late 1960s, the 1970s, even the 1980s." Robinson [2007], 24.
4 Formally there are eight volumes to the series so far, with a further volume for 1964–1980 (*Smoked Dreams*?) being contemplated, according to a recent interview. I also however include Starr [2005] for an understanding of the overall trajectory of Starr's reading of California civilization.

gantly guided through a taut blend of scholarly and colloquial locutions. Starr has also shrewdly deployed a variety of organizational strategies to structure his project for the different periods—more or less decades—by which he scaled his way to the 1950–1963 period. Yet there has also been an interesting chronological hiccup in the meantime. After reaching 1950 through the account in *Embattled Dreams* (2002), Starr jumped forward into contemporaneity (thanks apparently to his relations with a different publisher) to carve out *Coast of Dreams* (2004) from the 1990–2003 period, extending his narrative all the way to the inauguration of Starr's favored governor Arnold Schwarzenegger.[5] Stressing in that volume that it was meant less as history than as a series of investigative impressions ("a collection of snapshots and sketches"), Starr provided his followers with a set of problematic concerns about a diverse and increasingly atomistic California at the millennium. Then, almost as if he needed to take one last deep breath before embarking on the completion of the present volume, Starr produced an excellent terse introduction to the whole history of California, *California: A History* (2005), which, while repeating more briefly some of his prior accounts, also included for the first time his version of California history to its origins, something that the first volumes, starting as they did for the most part with American statehood in 1850, had underplayed.

Particularly the existence of the opinions expressed in *Coast of Dreams* must influence any reading of *Golden Dreams*. It is as if a postmortem to Starr's "golden" period has been deliberately slipped in to tint any final triumphant texture to this latter volume. But the temptation to draw such an inference is somewhat countered by Starr's admonishment in a more recent interview that "the Golden Age of California is *now*," thanks to greater equity, diversification, and globalization.[6] This latest opinion seems in tune with Starr's simultaneous endorsement of a recent publication exhorting more globalizing stances recommended for California and Californians.[7]

Of course, any work as nuanced as *Golden Dreams* is not to be taken simply as another boosterist salvo. As with all his volumes, Starr's narrative works carefully out of an immediately preceding past into an inevitably oncoming future. 1950s California stands indeed for a certain level of achievement—one which then became a magnet for the large immigration figures of the following decade—but it was a delicate, and perhaps unsustainable, achievement. Congratulations certainly go out to an impressive body of political leaders, starting with Earl

---

5 Modestly claiming that "I know him a bit," Starr [2005b] goes on to present his case for "the raw intelligence and honed intellect" of the then new governor. Schwarzenegger returned the compliment by publicly bringing up Starr's work on California.
6 Los Angeles Times (2009) (emphasis added).
7 "Foreword" to Lowenthal [2009], ix-xi.

Warren (1942–1953) and continuing on through Goodwin J. Knight (1953–1958) and Edmund "Pat" Brown (1958–1966), a Republican-Democratic governors' synthesis best highlighted by Warren's nomination in 1946 by *both* the Republican and Democratic parties (Warren regarding himself as representing "the Party of California" (193)). This synthesis—which covers the entire period of Starr's present volume—remained unalterably progressive in its continued commitment to social services and infrastructure—as well as, it must be admitted, to somewhat unreflective growth policies. Even so, Starr points out the justifiable reasons for the emergence of a more politically-tilted party system in the 1950s, as both Democrats and Republicans developed their adversarial stances leading in time to the far more fractious party struggles of the ensuing Ronald Reagan and Jerry Brown periods of the later 1960s and 1970s (191–216). The best step to take then in reading *Golden Dreams* is perhaps to grant that it describes one of those rare arrival periods in the course of a political entity, the details of which are worth clarifying, without simultaneously lamenting the inevitable disintegration to follow its imposing synthesis.

1.

For this instalment Starr utilizes a five-fold arrangement highlighting Suburbs, Urban Development, Politics, Cultural Life, and Dissent, generally following a chronological line and thus conveniently ending his Fifties (which extend to 1963, and even 1965 and 1969[8]) with increasing mention of those adversarial forces which foretell the Protesting Sixties. Starr's narrative rounds out with a "cool" Californian self-image (which turns out to be not so "cool" after all), implying a vector of sorts that begins with the astonishingly rapid colonization of, above all, the San Fernando Valley in the late 1940s. This classic case of suburbanization by which a fundamentally agricultural valley is transformed into a sprawling network of real-estate projects will morph over the next decade into some of the most compelling images of the California Dream, from modernist functional homes and networks of mobility for a generation committed to early marriage (unprecedented according to available records[9]) to the efflorescence of surfing

---

[8] Thus, for his account of the less attractive side to the growth of fifties Los Angeles, Starr sees fit to carry his narrative through the Watts riots ("a civil insurrection of historic proportions") of 1965 (185); for his account of Clark Kerr and the founding of the Santa Cruz campus of the University of California, Starr goes as far as 1969 (243–244).

[9] Starr cites William Strauss and Neil Howe's study of the Silent Generation (356).

subcultures highlighted by the feel-good beat of the Beach Boys, even to the partial domestication of the rebellious Beats as media "Beat-niks" (378).[10]

Behind these shining surface images, however, the unceasing hard work of constructing a genuine economic behemoth is lovingly detailed by Starr. In the prior volumes, this side to Starr's larger narrative had already focused readers' attention to the miraculous, if often problematic, projects of water systems, highways, and real estate expansion—not to mention the infrastructural reality behind the Hollywood film and media industry—making up the literal formation of "California" during the 1910s and 1920s, followed by even more epic constructions of dams, roads, bridges (such as the fabled Golden Gate Bridge)[11] and Federal art projects during the otherwise blighted Depression years of the 1930s. Now, however, thanks largely to the momentous shove generated by wartime Federal largesse that fast-forwards the Californian economy of the early 1940s, the scale shifts exponentially.

So far as cities are concerned, San Diego emerges as "the Boston of the Pacific Coast, a city keyed to science, technology, and biotech," out of the quasi-sleepy naval center of an earlier epoch (82). Meanwhile Los Angeles soars to the status of "Supercity" from having been a mere "regional capital" (131). Giant civic figures crowd its cityscape: from Archbishop James Francis McIntyre and L. A. Police Department chief William Henry Parker, to L. A. baseball Dodger owner Walter O'Malley and cultural missionary Dorothy Chandler. By the time they are through, Los Angeles is bejeweled with a constellation of civic spotlights—and police protection—worthy of global admiration.[12] Even San Francisco, albeit constricted by its beautiful bay location, takes on a strikingly new identity as "Baghdad by the Bay," thanks to its most famous journalistic booster Herb Caen and the fame of the city's increasingly liberal life for a bevy of fascinating urban dwellers, facilitating its transition from a partly blue-collar city to the tourist hub of the future (88–99).

Of course, very little of this progress could have been carried through without the blessings of "the Party of California," a rare period—worthy of nostalgia—of party harmony when a trinity of progressivist governors—Earl Warren, Goodwin J. Knight, and Pat Brown—stride the political landscape like veritable colossi. In light of today's governance dysfunctionality, it is naturally easy to overstate their combined effectiveness, and in any case the equal and growing presence of the highly partisan Richard M. Nixon, ballooning throughout the decade as the most nationally important political figure from California—although Earl Warren's

---

10 The name coined by San Francisco's own columnist Herb Caen.
11 For the Golden Gate project, see, more recently, Starr [2010].
12 The popular television series Dragnet, with its famous image of the L. A. City Center building, was a showcase for the LAPD and was monitored by police chief Parker (142).

nomination as Chief Justice of the Supreme Court in 1953 merits, and receives, almost equal treatment for his extension of California liberalism into future epochal legal precedents (203–207)—reminds us no less of the new turn in state and national politics reflective of Southern Californian plutocrats, media-driven campaigns, and the rise of the New Right: the controversial John Birch Society is founded in Southern California in 1959 just shortly after the Democrats' landslide victory of 1958 (201).

Still, it is surely thanks to this temporary lull in partisanship that at least three momentous California legislative acts come to fruition and generate historic advances in transportation, water supply, and education. Proposition 1 in 1960, which Starr rhapsodically describes as "the most ambitious water distribution system in the history of the human race" (267),[13] realizes some eighty years of the most expansive ideas and projects to form a coherent water supply system for the entire California—propelling, as did the earlier Owens Valley system of 1913 for Greater Los Angeles, the dizzying growth of Southern California later in the century (280). Similarly, the California Freeway System of 1958 integrates state and federal freeway plans to forge, between 1956 and 1972, the most automobile-oriented transportation system on the planet (245, 248, 254).[14] Finally, the 1960s Donohoe Higher Education Act sponsors the most extensive (tuition-free) public higher education system in the world for California residents, capped by the world status of the University of California campuses at Berkeley and Los Angeles (218). Indeed, this most directly ideological of the three plans unfolds the cultural vision of the "multiversity" ("Ideopolis") as propounded by University of California President Clark Kerr in his liberal attempts to redefine society away from the Cold War campus toward the ideals shaping his favored "city of intellect."[15]

The critic might rightly counter that these accomplishments bore counter elements which only needed time to emerge. The University of California system, as well as other great California institutions such as Stanford, the University of Southern California, and the California Institute of Technology, were after all sustained in large degree by federal funds supporting military and defense research (217–237). Water supplies and highways generated environmental vices

---

13   Or: the "biggest single water project in world history" (281).
14   Starr provides additional details on the care taken to create aesthetic designs for the landscaping of the motorways and effectively articulated signs to guide motorists (256).
15   Perhaps the high point was the Berkeley campus chancellorship of Nobel-Prize winner Glenn Seaborg (1958–1961), Kerr later regretting that the highly effective Seaborg had not been in charge during the Berkeley protests of the Sixties (240). Probably, however, the high point for Kerr himself was the inauguration of the Oxford-style campus at Santa Cruz in 1965 (241–244).

against which the anti-growth movements of the Sierra Club and David Brower were to brew, to which might be attached the successful anti-freeway resistance by San Franciscans in the late 1950s as well as the struggle to save the San Francisco Bay itself in the early 1960s (403–435). And of course Kerr's Multiversity was to be directly and violently challenged by dissenting Berkeley students by the early 1960s, followed by, among others, Santa Cruz students in the late 1960s.

To Starr's credit all these dissenting movements receive ample coverage, particularly in the final two parts of his narrative, "Art and Life" and "Dissenting Opinions." The first part, "Art and Life," panoramically recounts cultural forces in process which play out the middle ground with a tilt toward dissent. Chapter 11, covering the 1950s so-called San Francisco "literary renaissance," categorizes these forces under three headings: the generally conservative "Provincials," the liberal "Baghdaders," and the rebellious "Beats." Its climax, the famous reading of Allen Ginsberg's poem *Howl* in a San Francisco gallery in 1955, followed by a highly public censorship trial on its publication in 1957 by local City Light bookstore owner and poet Lawrence Ferlinghetti, is really an indication that the first two forces will evaporate before the increasing influence of the Beats as San Francisco and dissent move toward the Sixties hippies and radicals with some Beats, including Ginsberg himself, happily joining the fray (311–313).

Starr also looks to the emergence of Big Sur as symptomatic of a new spirituality, often associated with terms like New Age and Human Potential, for his fuller picture of California high culture during the Fifties. Although extending back to the poet Robinson Jeffers and the somewhat manic author Henry Miller, this Big Sur phenomenon grows significantly during the Fifties and early Sixties to give birth to such portentous centers as Esalen—as well as more sedate Catholic and Zen monasteries—which over time, and in tandem with comparable movements in the Southland associated with names like Aldous Huxley, Christopher Isherwood and Gerald Heard, will also tilt over into dimensions turning visibly "psychedelic" (314–351).

To these trends Starr however provides a balance with two remarkably crafted chapters on the cultural middle path unfolded by the "Silent Generation" and the triumph of a California culture of "cool" jazz largely shaped by the popular success of Californian musician Dave Brubeck. Utilizing among his sources high school yearbooks, Starr traces the markers of California high school life at its Ozzie & Harriet premium, punctuating his account with pocket biographies of such selected representatives as Richard Serra, future California governor Jerry Brown, Richard Rodriguez, Natalie Wood, and—of course—(Ozzie and Harriet's son) Ricky Nelson, teen TV star and rock-and-roll singing celebrity (361). Starr's choice case remains Joan Didion making her cautious way eventually to Berkeley, the voice who will judge California in her later works, and whose judgment, thanks to a reflective, almost mournful fluency, has had lasting impact (370–371). Meanwhile Starr also affectionately details the musical scene of the late 1940s from which jazz made its move toward "cool," thanks perhaps paradoxically to Darius Milhaud, the French composer teaching at Mills College in Oakland, whose combining of classical compositional knowledge with an openness to the possibilities of popular jazz directly influenced the young Brubeck toward a quintessentially Silent Generation blend of improvisation "governed by law" (395). Brubeck's sound proved perfectly attuned particularly to college audiences, and California jazz acquired its national patina—as well as, coming from the East Coast, a degree of opprobrium (406–408).

Finally, "Dissenting Opinions" all the more directly examines dissent, political and cultural. It narrates the emergence of the California environmental movement against the growth policies of the Party of California and, backed by a broader historical account of suppressions of minority rights during the century, follows more precisely the undulations of the Fifties struggle over Jim Crow laws. Starr's chronicle comes to a head with the impact of civil rights legislation in the early 1960s as Berkeley assemblyman Byron Rumford pushes through the Rumford Fair Housing Act in 1963, which however is overturned by the initiative Proposition 14 in 1964, before the latter is itself overturned by the California Supreme Court in 1966 (462–465).

Starr thus reaches his general conclusions for the entire period, which must be necessarily rather transitory. He tries the nomenclature "coolness"—"this stylized restraint, this coolness, this distance and reserve"—to account for a "modernism, California style" (466) that might describe a California ethos by the turn of the decade. With very limited effectiveness, however, because Starr's narrative tempo seems already eager to switch to the "uncool" side that the latter two parts of *Golden Dreams* have increasingly underscored. The book concludes with snapshot accounts of a former Marxist Harry Hay making his way toward articulating an explicitly gay civil rights position, harbinger of the gay and lesbian Seventies (469–471); meanwhile outrage over the execution of convicted rapist Caryl Chessman merges with vociferous protests against HUAC subcommittee hearings in San Francisco in 1960 (472–480) to intimate the forthcoming Berkeley salvos of the Sixties.

For Starr, historian of the specific and picayune, this is all to the good since it galvanizes his and our interest to get on to the next installment of the California Dream. But perhaps, notwithstanding the signal contribution of *Golden Dreams* toward a detailed understanding of the Fifties, there might be another kind of History that also needs consideration at this historic nexus.

2.

From his lifelong duel with political romanticism, Isaiah Berlin once surmised that its core was the doctrine of nationalism, a dogma toward which Berlin, notwithstanding occasional sympathy for those aspects of romanticism that helped brew the pluralistic thought dear to Berlin himself, expressed some disdain and worry.[16] For Berlin nationalism historically began as a German invention ("the first true nationalists") in the late eighteenth century, originating in the spheres of aesthetics and criticism where a reaction against French cultural dominance over German life and society was intended to serve the needs of displaced intellectuals seeking a new dignified social and spiritual role in their relation to the "people." Ultimately their demands for "free expression," ideally represented by the Artist of genius, presumed the priority of "the creations of the collective genius of peoples," and this notion of a "creative faculty" pumping through individuals and societies stressed the vitality of diversity, "of the world as a garden" of unique human plants and formations.[17]

It might be argued that the ultimate product of this larger trend in German culture would be the grand project of the *Gesamtkunstwerk* inaugurated by Richard Wagner, both in terms of his massive theatrical creations (from the *Ring* cycle to individual music dramas such as *Lohengrin* and *Die Meistersinger*) and of his formation of a literal site, Bayreuth, for their performances in adulatory festival form. Even if Wagner ended up controlling most aspects of these ventures, in principle his originating idea had been a common enterprise freely arising from the spirit of the people, the *Volk*, more or less akin to, as he saw it, ancient Athenian political and theatrical practices.[18]

Loosely playing out this hint, if there is a California roughly corresponding to these objectives, it would surely be found in the phenomenon known as Hollywood—and of "classical" Hollywood (1929–1945) at that.[19] To be sure, "classical" Hollywood is no less a classic case of the vertically-integrated firm organization operating sectorially through an oligopoly of five—or eight—members. Already in the 1920s the Business (as it came to be known) had begun to blow

---

16 This remained, to my understanding, the crux of Berlin's position in my last extended conversation with him at his home in Headington House, Oxfordshire, on 7 April 1997, a few months before his death.
17 Berlin [1979], 350, 348.
18 Bernbach [1994], esp, 146–167; Chytry [2007].
19 For the designation and dating of "classical" Hollywood as 1929–1945, I follow Jewell [2007]. The date could be extended to 1948 when the success of governmental antitrust litigation began the formal breakup of the classical studio system. This is also the rough dating for the rise of television, the culmination of union struggles in Hollywood, and the anti-communist blacklisting of Hollywood screenwriters and actors.

away international competition from similarly developing film operations in Italy, Germany, and Britain; by the 1930s it had welded together the production, distribution, and exhibition arms of the film industry to achieve world dominance in all aspects of the film-making economy. Notwithstanding the collapse of the "classic" system due to a variety of factors that included successful government antitrust litigation by 1948, it has since morphed into the present-day media conglomerates of which the film aspect remains a central piston of productivity and profit.[20]

This picture is hardly an image attractive to Isaiah Berlin's German political romantics—but then neither, in time, was Wagner's Bayreuth with its concessions to a primarily entrepreneurial mode of functionality. In any case such an objection overlooks the remarkable fact of Hollywood as perhaps the most important cultural event of the twentieth century, unfolding, it needs to be underscored, *in a society, the Californian*, which had adjusted and in important ways itself corresponded to the premises that made the birth and success of a Hollywood at all possible. In his final novel, *Star of the Unborn*, completed just before his death in 1945, the Prague-born author Franz Werfel placed his protagonist square in his own real home in Beverly Hills (610 North "Bedford Drive") to identify the essence of the Californian as that of *Schauspieler* or "actor," or—to invoke Americanese—a "phony."[21] This identification, exactly the same designation—*Schauspieler*—applied by Friedrich Nietzsche to the Wagner of Bayreuth,[22] speaks to the transmutability of the Californian character by the mid-1940s such that Hollywood had grown into not so much one of most important industries in California, as that it had become the major expression of the latter's secular mission to absorb and disgorge all past narratives within the physical and organizational properties of its major studio cities. Each of these proto-civic ensembles brought together, if not the *Volk*, at the very least (in addition to their private arms of fire, police, sanitation, hospital, classrooms, and other necessary services) a vast number and range of professionals extending from the directing and the acting areas to those infrastructural elements of stage, lighting, design and fashion, without which no three-dimensional reality can, absent animation, be effectively transmitted onto the two-dimensional "silver" screen.

Historians of this Hollywood have had to concede that no narrowly *auteur*-driven reading (centered on directors) of its higher products can accurately account for the panoply of factors and decisions at play that sustained and

---

20 For the details, see Epstein [2005]; also Scott [2005].
21 Werfel [1946a], 16; Werfel [1946b], 24. Werfel meant this designation sympathetically. Note also the significant subtitle to Steiman [1985].
22 "Der Fall Wagner," in Nietzsche [1966], ii, 920, 921.

expanded these entrepreneurial worlds.[23] But just when words like "industry" and "factory" seem most appropriate to describe the large-scale, reiterative elements behind the Hollywood enterprise, it has been necessary to recall that the product, however "Grade-B" in so many cases, had to be somehow inimitable, a creation of sorts, drawing on exemplary performers, if it hoped to attract the needed audience: hence the cognomens of "dream factory," "glamour factory," "entertainment industry," and the core of its products as the "star system."[24]

Although driven by generally cynical attitudes toward Hollywood, a largely Europeanized body of critiques has had to concede the outsized effects of this Hollywood culture and its "values" on the rest of the world by 1945–1950—along with, of course, Coca-Cola, jeans, and fast-food cuisine. But for historians of California civilization the greater implication of this influence is its global ubiquity well beyond the obvious functions of some ideological message. Throughout the classical period—as well as earlier[25]—the studio system with its massive lots and countryside annexes generally ignored distant location shooting to exploit the technical and communal advantages of the studio lot for its themes and tales. As a result, Hollywood's cinematic reproduction of California reality, from the latter's skies, seas and mountains to the growing extension of the super-city that was to be Los Angeles—including the "fast talk" embodied in its modern lifestyle—, fashioned and exported an "existential" cultural world far more real than anything available to the formal Existentialists who at that time crowded the cafes of an overly erudite Paris cityscape.[26] Strictly speaking, after all, the burning "Atlanta" of Civil War vintage was actually in Culver City, "Shangri-La" was not really in Tibet but in the Ojai Valley, "Casablanca" was in Van Nuys rather than Morocco, just as that "Streetcar Named Desire" headed for its end-stop not in New Orleans but in Burbank.[27]

---

23 See especially the corrective by Shatz [1988]; also Gabler [1988].
24 This point is already noted in the early extended studies of Hollywood. See Rosten [1941], Powdermaker [1950]; also Davis [1993], Jewell [2007].
25 In an earlier volume Starr points to the striking case of early silent comedies seductively showing American audiences through their backgrounds the rapidly growing and compelling civic reality and model known as Los Angeles and Southern California. Starr [1985], 294.
26 For that matter, it is claimed that leading existentialists were inspired by California novels of the 1930s. Jean-Paul Sartre was said to have regarded Horace McCoy's *They Shoot Horses, Don't They?* (1935) as the first great existentialist novel, according to Starr [1997], 307, and Albert Camus was said to have been inspired by James M. Cain's *The Postman Always Rings Twice* (1934).
27 For location-filming purposes, Paramount studios actually made a map of California on which were superimposed suggested fictional or historical locales from elsewhere for moviemaking purposes. Thus, e.g. the Carmel Valley was suggested for "New England coast" and Big Sur for "Africa." See the reproduction in Brown [2002], 35.

What then would be the grand upshot of this presumed Hollywood refashioning of all Humanity? Perhaps that "we"—not just "Hollywood" or "Californians"—are now all "phonies" (with a confirming glance at present-day media, the net, and the exponentially expanding world of texting); or, put less unkindly, that we are now all "playactors" (*Schauspieler*), role-players, wearers of mask after mask,[28] constantly transmuting, constantly expected to be somehow—however feebly defined—"creative," "innovative," "entrepreneurial:" in any case part of what every presumably forward-thinking entrepreneur, managerial theorist, firm organizer, and culture critic applauds as our "aesthetic age" where, it is strongly urged, "anything goes."[29]

3.

Indeed, the roots of this "Hollywood" formally begin much earlier. In the mind's eye of Horace and Daeida Wilcox visiting the Cahuenga Valley in 1887, it meant the prospect of a "dry" Protestant real-estate development, eventually to be given (thanks to Mrs. Wilcox's attraction to the English holly bush) its historic name. But even before that, in this very same valley the Treaty (or "Capitulation") of Cahuenga was signed in January 1847 whereby the indigenous Californian forces formally surrendered to the United States, beginning a fateful process of transfer of sovereignty.[30] This site is now a state historic park and is located exactly across the freeway from Universal City, the first true Hollywood studio city constructed in 1915 to handle some 15,000 employees.[31]

These are fortuitous connections no doubt—still, what true German Romantic could ignore them? We, while admittedly no Romantics, are nonetheless driven by such errant coincidences back to Starr's narrative of the California Fifties and

---

28 Including of course Wagner's great critic Nietzsche. See Avital Ronell's reference to Nietzsche's own "unquestionably Californian invention of lifestyle." Ronell [2008], 303.

29 For an extensive example of the argument that we are in an "aesthetic age," see Postrel [2003], xiv, 164, as well as my critical review in Chytry [2009], 146–148.

30 The treaty, supplanted by the Treaty of Guadalupe Hidalgo between the United States and Mexico ending the larger war, was formally signed between representatives of the "United States" and "Californians." Andres Pico was referred to as "Commander-in-Chief of the California forces under the Mexican flag." The Cahuenga Pass was also the site of an important victory in 1845 by the rebellious Californian forces led by Pio Pico and José Castro over then-governor Micheltorena which ousted the latter and Mexican military presence from California. See the account in Pico [1973], 107–112.

31 Universal owner Carl Laemmle explicitly recognized and expressed pride in the physical proximity of his founding film city to such History. See, more generally, "Universal City," Drinkwater [1931], 181–187.

the story he deliberately left out when deciding that the "entertainment" component was being sufficiently treated in other studies.[32]

What do "history" and its scribes, the "historians," have to offer with respect to a special birth, the "birth" of a "nation"? And to what extent are they morally responsible if they help to "abort" that moment of birth—through their indifference, disbelief, even hostility? All understandable responses perhaps, since in this case anyway, to envisage a "birth" of this order concerns that potentially most treasonable of speculations: making plain the actual birth of a "nation-state" called California ("*Viva* California, free, sovereign, and independent!"[33]) that was incubating sometime in the 1950s at the economic-political heart of what had recently become a hegemonic "super"-power, the United States of America. Putting the matter this exaggerated way necessarily provokes the predictable gasp: can such a prospect be remotely entertained by the "historian" as, however improbably, a viable thought in the interpretation of the history of that particular political entity?

The great historians of the Canon have made it a commonplace in their writings that nations come and nations go, regions rebel, a few succeed, the vast majority are crushed. In any account of overall world history, about which Hegel once moodily ruminated: "Full many an innocent flower must be trampled," the very thought of secession of this order seems a violation of the one underlying substance to the endless transmutations of "history." True, like all political constructs, this substance, the United States of America, once came into being, and at some future date may no longer exercise the global dominance it still enjoys today, at least militarily and geopolitically; but is it really conceivable that just as the highly successful eighteenth-century oceanic empire of Britain gave rise to those same United States from former Atlantic coastal colonies, so too in the evolution of superior political experimentation a California "free, sovereign, and independent" might have been already brooded in the midcentury American womb?

If we take such a hypothesis with some seriousness, Starr's expressed puzzlement toward the presumed hyperbolic developments recorded for the much later 1990–2003 period begins to make more sense, since the Fifties would have defined the period in which these questions might have first materialized. Unfortunately,

---

32   Occasionally Starr does mention cinematic figures (360–361), but he provides no sustained account of post-classical Hollywood and the newer media system of the Fifties, a period which gave rise to the first of many "New" Hollywoods. For postwar Hollywood see Casper [2007].

33   As apparently uttered by a member of the *Californio* elite in an 1846 discussion contemplating the different prospects for California at that moment, which included possible absorption by Britain, France, the United States—or direct independence from Mexico. See Miller [1998], 116.

as in the case of his previous volumes, Starr himself furnishes little by way of the necessary overview: the preface is slender, nor is there an extensive conclusion, the last chapter mainly serving to prepare the stage for the onrushing Sixties. Yet this is the kind of deeper reflection that Starr's own assiduous researches into the Fifties, even more than in his prior volume where California scrambled onto the world stage in the World War II- and postwar years (1940–1950), provoke.[34] In place of a mixed agricultural, real estate, media and oil economy, California came out of that war as, in the eyes of the powerful Eastern establishment, a true industrial power, and the Fifties mark the makings of an American society in which the California Dream, formerly somewhat realized in the California Thirties, had become, thanks in large part to the movies and now television, the content for the American Dream.[35]

Starr's prose consistently, and perhaps patriotically, insists that all this must be kept within a larger "American" story.[36] Yet his boosterist vocabulary breaks through at key stages of his overall account. Thus, by 1930, thanks to the prodigious growth of Southern California,[37] Starr's California can contemplate "a golden age of California as a *regional American civilization.*"[38] Then, by the post-World War II period, California has become, according to Starr, a "megastate" (268, 279, 280), "a world commonwealth."[39] After further developments Starr is forced to adopt even more encompassing terminology: California as indeed "an emergent nation-state," eventually as today "a *nation-state or global commonwealth.*"[40]

---

34   Culturally the 1940s also saw California hosting some of the major European works of the century as detailed in Chapter 3 above. It also included the composition of Eugene O'Neill's greatest plays, *The Iceman Cometh* and *Long Day's Journey into Night*, composed above Danville, California. See Bahr [2007] and Chytry [2008].
35   As Starr notes, prior to 1940 the self-image of California "had been relatively modest," whereas "no one by 1950 was envisioning California as a modest agricultural state." Starr [2002], x. By the 1970s, according to Kotkin & Grabowicz [1982], people in the U.S. "are becoming slowly, but perceptibly 'Californians'" (263).
36   In a 2007 interview Starr insists that while calling California a "commonwealth" (or "an ecumenical world culture"), he keeps it "within the legal and political framework of the constitution of the United States and the constitution of the state of California," or: "a sovereign entity within the larger sovereignty of the nation"—a somewhat confusing set of statements in its mixture of the political concepts of commonwealth, state, and nation. Similar disclaimers are expressed by Lowenthal [2009], 13.
37   Starr [1990].
38   Starr [1990], 393 (emphasis added).
39   Starr [2002], 183.
40   Starr [2005a], 244, 343 (emphasis added). In the present volume Starr also refers to California as "a modernist Commonwealth" (269).

119

What exactly is the purport to the crescendo in such heady language—especially when it is parroted by California's own former governor? In his 2007 State of the State address (possibly influenced by his reading of Starr), Arnold Schwarzenegger celebrated California as "this nation-state": "*I call California a nation-state* because of the diversity of our people, the power of our economy and the reach of our dream."[41] No doubt such language is largely the harmless rhetoric of a politician, yet it is less easily dismissible when similarly employed by California's leading historian. If therefore Starr has admitted to moments of depression when contemplating the 1980s and early 1990s "that California had gone seriously awry," his more assuring conclusion that perhaps 1990–2003 may simply represent the end of one California and the beginning of another could prove, historically anyway, too schematic a reading.[42] It may be that in fact it is all one historic evolution of what Starr himself eventually admits to being, in the fullest sense, a genuine "nation-state."

In this respect the general closing date of 1963–1964 for Starr's Fifties carries a deeper significance than simply the onset of the dramatic protests of the Sixties (starting with the 1964 Free Speech Movement in Berkeley). For that year also marks the workings of U.S. Congressional legislation that culminated in the 1965 Immigration Act eliminating national quotas and opening up California in particular to the range and diversity of non-U.S. immigrants who have since ended the white Protestant demographic dominance of the golden years of Starr's account with a trend that, while heavily favoring Latinos and to a lesser extent east Asians, has also included substantial minorities from other areas—earning California one of its more recent titles as the first "Third World" state in the Union.[43]

These demographic changes have been the stimulus for one set of secessionist declarations which espouse an "Aztlan" or "MexiAmerica" reuniting California to its old homeland of Mexico, and which have been pilloried by Samuel Huntington with his post-"clash of civilization" warnings against such challenges to a common Anglo-Protestant cultural unity for the United States. For their part these demands seem in any case disingenuous for overlooking the highly chequered history of Mexican California (1821–1845) in the course of which the new State of Mexico entirely bungled its California mission for a variety of reasons that culminated in two successful Californian independence revolts, 1836 and 1844–45, the latter permanently driving out the Mexican governor and the

---

41   Los Angeles Times [2007] (emphasis added).
42   Starr [2004], xi., xiii.
43   See the relevant tables and figures in Hayes-Bautista [2004], 2, 17, 19, 30; also the projections in State of California [2007].

Mexican military *prior* to American involvement and future U.S. annexation.[44] Meanwhile, from an entirely different quarter a 1980s publication, impishly titled *California, Inc.* to cover the further prodigious growth of California's economy in the 1970s, utilized for the first time (at least to the knowledge of this reviewer) the notion of California as "the nation-state of the emergent Sunbelt,"[45] and brought up secessionist thoughts in the "West" at a time when leaders from the Western U.S. states apparently saw their economies surge sufficiently ahead of the presumably declining Eastern centers to justify talk of a "Western nation" and encourage "virtually a secessionist movement in the West."[46]

Neither of these prospects merits further serious comment, but they may be taken at least as tokens of a more substantive set of historical concerns. After Starr's Fifties and the Seventies of "California, Inc.", California went on to further demographic and economic advances, overcoming the deleterious effects of the end of the Cold War (1989–1991) on its post-1950 defense-oriented economy, largely creating the global dotcom miracle of the 1990s,[47] and apparently setting itself up to take advantage of the newest prospects in biotech and green technology.[48] Possibly the statistical highpoint of this surge is California peaking as the fifth economic power in the world as recently as 2000–2001.[49] The counter to this benign account is of course the familiar media litany over the dysfunctional elements in California governance and the varied problems attendant to becoming the first Third World U.S. state. Yet such dysfunctionality, best symbolized perhaps by its antiquated Constitution of 1879 with its excessive length, attests to the massive discrepancy between the power of a society which is already a world civilization and the confining strictures of its political sovereignty.[50]

---

44 See Chapter 2 above.
45 In a 1969 cover article on California, "California: A State of Excitement" (November 7, 1969), Time Magazine already referred to California as "a nation-state." Time [1969].
46 Kotkin & Grabowicz [1982], 3, 252.
47 During this recovery period California established, among other "foreign relations" ventures, the Technology, Trade, and Commerce Agency (1992) and set up thirteen trade offices on three continents; the Agency was discontinued in 2003, along with the trade offices. Details in Lowenthal [2009], 38–44. An early call for a California "foreign policy" in the influential journal *Foreign Affairs* is Goldsborough [1993]. For California foreign trade, besides Lowenthal, see also Bardhan, Jaffee & Kroll [2004].
48 See the cover article on California in Time [2009].
49 See Chapter 1 above.
50 See "California's Constitution" in Wilson & Ebbert [2000], 7–21, and "Constitution of the State of California," in Encyclopedia of California [1984], 525–618. The California constitution is said to be longer than any constitution other than the constitutions for the U.S. state of Louisiana and for the State of India. A relevant indicator for the growing concern on governance dysfunctionality is the present debate on the need for a California constitutional convention.

So long as California's political fate is not entirely its own, perhaps key ingredients of its operations, which reflect its expanding role both within the United States and globally, cannot be fully addressed.[51] This does not automatically imply addressing them in some politically radical fashion, but for the historian it does raise the importance of rereading twentieth-century California—particularly once it had arrived at the synthesis of 1950–1963 so ably recounted by Starr in this volume—in light of these constrictions. Fallout from such constrictions might well be inevitable in principle once California had surpassed a certain index of global economic and cultural power without acquiring full sovereign control over its resources, and such fallout may be the price that a politically constricted, albeit "mega-state" may have to be prepared to pay into the indefinite future.

4.

Starr himself rarely admits to this breadth of historical context. He will however occasionally mention "California's existence in modern times—under the jurisdiction of Spain, of Mexico, and of the United States," itself a good start toward a serious reexamination since it acknowledges an entity, California, in principle separable from such jurisdictions.[52] What then is still needed is a far more inclusive panorama. The very word "California," it may be recalled, originally emerged as the validation of a mythical line extending all the way back to the survivors of ancient Troy, perhaps the most pedigreed patrimony in the Western genealogical arsenal. In usage and in application it carried implications of a magical island, in more ways than one, the real political boundaries of which came in time to comprise, as *California* or as *Las Californias*, a Greater California markedly larger than the present U.S. state boundaries.[53]

Whether or not California has in the long run realized the implications of its myth and historical geographic possibilities may be left to more precise evalua-

---

51   In a section aptly called "Stakes without Standing," Lowenthal [2009] cautions that his book "does not offer a full-blown foreign policy for California, a notion that makes no sense in the U.S. federal system" (13) and "California is faced with a structural gap between its high stakes in the realm of international policy and the modest scope for authorized direct action" (125). In addition, he warns: "because they have global links without sovereign power or international standing, Californians are ever more vulnerable to globalization" (125).
52   Starr [2005b], 344.
53   For details see Chapter 2 above.

tions of the concrete results to date.⁵⁴ At this stage what seems worth granting at least is that the particular game being played out as "California" merits more than regional cultural demarcations. Kevin Starr's project of some forty years may not wish to frame his questions in such terms, but the monumental body of works that makes up his *Americans and the California Dream* series—a veritable treasure-house for understanding California—and that comes to a timely head in *Golden Dreams* encourages taking on this far more overarching reading of California: Past, Present, and—(a California specialty) Future.

---

54 A good start would be to assess in macroeconomic detail the extent of California's continued economic and cultural clout throughout the former parts of Greater California, Baja California included. See Chapter 6 below.

Chapter 5
California Political Economy: The Emotional Environments of Walt Disney[1]

In his 1920 ur-handbook on the art of animation, E. G. Lutz provides a handy list of the necessary qualities for the successful cartoonist or "animator."[2] These include such obvious traits as a sense for form and hard "courageous" work. But they also include a further requirement that may not be all that obvious: "skill as a manager" in planning the whole work through "expedients and tricks" and "economy of labor" in getting as much action as possible through as few drawings as possible.

In 1920 Walter Elias Disney, arguably the most significant figure in the twentieth-century affair with animation, read Lutz's book as he made a crucial turn in his own development from producing art, drawing and film to producing animation proper. Although Disney later deprecated the standard of Lutz's work and while Lutz's reference to management skills clearly refers to the animator's control over his own resources, it is perhaps not an exaggeration to suggest that this third trait would be expanded soon enough by Disney into his most enduring contribution to the field and activity of animation, namely, the creation of the "emotional environments" of the first fully animation studio and, in time, application of what he learned through that creation into a series of innovative projects that in effect created the modern theme park (Disneyland), the modern *Gesamtkunstwerk* art school (the California Institute of the Arts), and hoped, at the time of his premature death, to advance into the realms of city planning and urban community proper (EPCOT, or the Experimental Prototype Community of Tomorrow).

Above all it might be said that Walt Disney and California came together in the very myth of something called "Disneyland":

---

[1] This version is a revision of a paper presented at the Max Planck Institute for Human Development International Workshop "Emotional Styles – Communities and Spaces" in Berlin on 23 July 2010 and subsequently published as "Walt Disney and the Creation of Emotional Environments: Interpreting Walt Disney's Oeuvre from the Disney Studios to Disneyland, CalArts, and the Experimental Prototype Community of Tomorrow (EPCOT)," *Rethinking History*, 16:2 (June 2012), 257–278, as well as in a shorter and slightly different version as "Disney's Design: Imagineering Main Street," *Boom: A Journal of California*, 2:1 (Spring 2012), 33–44. My thanks to Benno Gammerl and the workshop participants for their very helpful comments and stimulation. I am also thankful for comments from Richard Benefield, Founding Executive Director of the Walt Disney Memorial Museum, San Francisco.

[2] Lutz [1998], 58–59.

"There is a way in which all Californians believe all California should feel like Disney's vision, and a way in which it does. There is a way in which California called Disneyland into being, and in which Disneyland only reflects back the light of its own place."[3]

1.

This chapter explores Walt Disney's overall oeuvre as a key contribution to a characteristically Californian mode of political economy. It approaches its subject through two connected motifs, one derived from historical scholarship, the other from management analysis. Through the notions, respectively, of "emotional environment" drawn from the subfield of the history of emotions and of the "experience economy" drawn from contemporary firm and management studies, it intends to clarify Disney's contribution to a distinctly Californian political economy.

Walt Disney as primarily creator of "experience" spaces or environments has seldom been given the understanding he merits, partly it must be said because of the denigration of the label "Disney" by a critical body of analysts (probably strongly influenced by Disney's political conservatism during and after the ideological 1940s), notwithstanding the historical fact that up to the early 1940s Disney had been congratulated by the political left for his collectivist approach to art ("The Communalistic Art of Walt Disney") and was feted as a kind of "folk artist" on a par with Charlie Chaplin.[4] Even if more recent favorable comments by architectural theorists on the positive role of Disney in urban and communitarian thinking and at least one argument that Disney may have helped "invent" the counterculture of the 1960s have somewhat softened this attitude, the full import of Disney's efforts has still been generally underappreciated.[5]

Fortunately a field of study more sympathetic to the Disney project has emerged in the newly growing areas of organization and management which are concerned with organizational aesthetics, "experience economies" and "experience environments." Recent scholarship has labeled this area "the artful firm"

---

3   Greil Marcus, "Forty Years of Overstatement: Criticism and the Disney Theme Parks," in Marling [1997], 207.
4   The Communist journal *Daily Worker* actually saw the dwarfs in *Snow White and the Seven Dwarfs* (1937) as a "miniature communist society." Citations in Gabler [2006], xvi-xviii, 141, 273, 441.
5   Favorable architectural commentators include Robert Venturi, Charles Moore, and even (an earlier critic) Vincent Scully. See Dunlop [1996], 7–10. For Disney and the counterculture see Brode [2004].

where it exploits such organizational principles as "ensemble."[6] Ensemble is a notion largely utilized by theatrical and dramaturgical groupings, but also more recently by management scholars, to argue the importance of place, site and openness for the localization of those ventures and enterprises which carry a strong orientation toward the aesthetic primacy of theatricality in a variety of communal expressions.[7] The thrust behind such research is to argue the case for a concept of the future firm called the "aesthetic firm"[8] as requiring a competitive edge which makes full use of the human and emotional content among its members for operations that are less oriented toward conventional profit motivations than toward more general standards of "value-creation" that make full use of human satisfaction and collective cooperation.

Central to such research is the notion of "immersive environments" associated with "experience economies." Experience economies are not simply concerned with consumption of goods and services but with the offer of a total experience: "a series of memorable events that a company stages – as in a theatrical play – to engage the consumer (the "guest") in a personal way."[9] Key to such experiences is the degree to which they are "memorable" through individuals' immersion and interactive participation. Such experience economies include not only an entertainment component, but also education, escapism and explicitly aesthetic rewards. Examples include theme parks, ecological cafes, and forms of healing, exercise and long-term educational systems. They can also entail applying theatrical methods to the "performance" of a given firm through the application of dramaturgical methods such as Release, Collaboration, Ensemble and Play.[10]

This complex of institutional practices and theory is what this chapter focuses upon through the term "emotional environments."

---

6 See "The Artful Firm," in Chytry [2009], 125–220. The term is borrowed from Pierre Guillet de Monthoux's concept of the "art firm" (Guillet de Monthoux [2004]) and Rob Austin & Lee Devin's concept of "artful making" (Austin & Devin [2003]).

7 Contributors include Rob Austin & Lee Devin; John Dobson; Pierre Guillet de Monthoux; Anna Klingmann; Joseph Pine & James Gilmore; Virginia Postrel; Bernd Schmitt, David Rogers & Karen Vrotsos; and Antonio Strati. See also the important new scholarly journal issued by The Aesthetic Project through the University of Essex: *Aesthesis: International Journal of Art and Aesthetics in Management and Organizational Life* (2007–2010).

8 "Aesthetic firm" is a term coined by John Dobson [1999] to draw a contrast with the conventional "technical firm" of vertical integration as well as with the "moral firm" which simply aspires to add an ethical edge to the technical firm.

9 Pine & Gilmore [1999]; also Schmitt, Rogers & Vrotsos [2004].

10 Austin & Devin [2003].

2.

One of the more influential examples of an experience economy is the classic Hollywood studio system. Historically it made up the infrastructure of the equivalent of a small city devoted to the construction of literal social and natural spaces for the enacting of narratives displaced onto the two-dimensional surface of the film. Likened to the factory, it remained a mode of operation that, unlike the typical industrial factory, aimed ideally at creating new and inimitable products ("the dream factory").[11] Over time the Hollywood system developed five major oligopolistic studio lots – MGM, Paramount, Warner Brothers, Twentieth-Century Fox, and RKO (or eight if Universal, Columbia, and United Artists are included).[12] According to Carey McWilliams, these studios were not primarily a factory, firm, or company town, but were "more in the nature of a community, a beehive, or, as Otis Ferguson said, *'fairy-land on a production line'*."[13] The importance of this system has been emphasized by architect and city historian Peter Hall according to whom the future for communal spaces will be ruled by a combination of "artistic and intellectual creativity with technological innovativeness, *on the model first created in Hollywood between 1915 and 1940.*"[14]

This studio city system also reflected larger patterns of early Californian civic development corresponding to the meteoric growth of Californian society and economy during the late nineteenth and early twentieth centuries. Southern Californian towns and colonies which had been originally planned out by a range of ethnic and religious colonies and already contained a highly urbanized character were absorbed into the new and highly profitable citrus industry. Such civic entities became citrus-belt towns with all the hallmark institutions of small cities, from drugstores and churches to colleges, and were "beautifully laid out."[15] Similar patterns may be also found elsewhere in California during this period. Indeed the classic prototype of the American small town in the Pulitzer Prize-winning play *Our Town* was conceived by the writer Thornton Wilder who, although choosing to fictionalize his town in New Hampshire, grew up in the carefully designed Californian neighborhood of Elmwood in the university city

---

11 See Rosten [1941], Powdermaker [1950], Davis [1993], and Jewell [2007].
12 See Epstein [2005] and Scott [2005].
13 McWilliams [1973], 336–337 (emphasis added).
14 Hall [1998], 961 (emphasis added). As Aida Hozic notes with regard to the Hollywood studio, "competitors around the world recognized the studio – the physical plant – as the key to American superiority." Hozic [2001], 58.
15 McWilliams [1973], 217, particularly citing the example of Redlands, California.

of Berkeley and was a graduate of its high school.[16] This play, John Hench has pointed out, strongly appealed to Walt Disney for his concept of Main Street, USA (although, as will be noted, the key "small town" for Disneyland was to be Marceline, Missouri).[17]

In the second place, the construction boom cycle typical of the exponential growth of Los Angeles itself in the early twentieth century encouraged the production of instant towns, synthetic communities of an artificial kind which invariably included the required shop, church, soda fountain, filling station, school, and movie theatre laid out overnight in quasi-theatrical fashion.[18] Even more relevant for the Hollywood connection, Southern California was the site for several ambitious projects to create a utopian or spiritual city or community. Most imposing perhaps was the theosophical city of Point Loma, San Diego, around 1900 which became nothing less than "a templed" or "white city" composed of almost all the functional facilities of a real city and which prospered until the Great Depression.[19] Meanwhile the theosophical rivals of Point Loma attempted their own alternate city which they called "Krotona" – named for the ancient Pythagorean polis in Magna Graecia – and constructed in Hollywood proper.[20] Although Hollywood's emergence as the world's film capital around 1915–1925 forced Krotona to move to the nearby Valley of Ojai, the Hollywood arising in this era retained some of Krotona's spiritualist aspirations as a perfect example of the "universal city" – "a truly cosmopolitan, polyglot town" – with the latest "muse," film, promising to become "a new art form for a new civilization." This civilization was to be right in the heart of a California seen as "a kind of paradise" by occultists and alternate cults. Their spiritualist standards proved sufficiently influential that certain early film celebrities claimed them as inspirations for their own careers.[21] Perhaps then it is not all that surprising that future observers of

---

16   Wilder attended the Emerson Grammar School in 1906–1909 and later Berkeley High School in 1913–1915 from which he graduated in 1915. Harrison [1983], 19–22, 30–36.
17   In the course of designing for the 1964–1965 New York World's Fair, Imagineer John Hench mentions being "inspired by" seeing a production of *Our Town* on Broadway and notes that Disney saw the play in Los Angeles "and liked it too." Hench [2008], 10.
18   McWilliams [1973], 233–234.
19   Greenwalt [1978], 47. Greenwalt recounts its ambitious projects in music, dance, drama, literature, philosophy, agriculture, and education. Its Greek Theatre and a couple of buildings remain on the site today.
20   A good summary of the surviving buildings of the Krotona colony in Hollywood is Ross [2004], Appendix, 1–22. See also more generally Ross [1989].
21   Brown [2002], 50, 58. Brown provides a detailed account of these Hollywood celebrities, including Natacha Rambova, Alla Nazimova, and Rudolph Valentino.

the California scene such as British author Aldous Huxley invariably noticed the overall resemblance of Southern California to a motion picture set.[22]

3.

No sooner did Walt Disney, having failed to sustain animation companies in Kansas City, arrive in Hollywood in 1923 to try out his prospects than he became instantly enthralled by the concrete reality of these studio cities, spending as much time as he could in the original studio lot Universal City, as well as visiting other studio lots such as Paramount and Vitigraph. Indeed, the very fact that he would choose Hollywood over New York, at that time the center of the animation industry, indicates the degree to which Disney's affair with animation actually formed part of broader goals intimately connected with Hollywood as this "most flourishing factory of popular mythology since the Greeks."[23]

What those goals were to be may have been unclear to Disney himself at the outset; they only became attached to animation proper after Disney was disabused of his hopes of entering into live-action filmmaking proper. What does become steadily clearer is that Disney was mainly concerned to create a unique organization: not just the first truly animation studio in Hollywood, but also one that would flourish as an environment markedly different from the typical mogul-driven vertically-integrated structures of the great studios.[24]

Who, or what, was "Walt Disney"? Since between 1946 and 1956 Disney became a "brand" and since it is commonplace to refer – especially after "Disneyland" (both park and television series) – to the expanding enterprises spawned by his more business-oriented brother Roy as "Disney," it is here emphasized that this chapter is solely concerned with the historical figure "Walter Elias Disney".[25] However, as that figure has been variously described – with reason – as an artisan, an artist, an entertainer, a manager, a strategist, an entrepreneur, finally "a visionary planner," it must be admitted that the task of focusing on his master aims becomes only somewhat more coherent.[26]

---

22 McWilliams [1973], 344.
23 Alistair Cooke, cited by Gabler [2006], 76–77; also 77–78. Allan [1999], 15.
24 Colonel William Selig had already recognized that by working entirely inside the studio, filmmakers were not simply protected from rain and inclement climatic conditions but were allowed to reproduce reality in any way they saw fit. Hozic [2001], 57.
25 See Thomas [1998].
26 Gabler [2006], 57. As educator when contemplating his radical school of the arts in the future California Institute of the Arts, Disney, perhaps half-seriously, saw himself teaching as a "sto-

At the outset one can broadly distinguish between two projects – the animation itself and the organization to provide that animation – but since they would eventually converge as the former was effectively swallowed up into the latter, the distinction is only apparent. If only then for expository purposes, we shall consider first the "organizational" Disney.

From his professional entrepreneurial start with the varied group of animators he brought together for his Laugh-O-grams in Kansas City in the early 1920s, through his cultivation of the first animation studio on Hyperion Avenue in Los Angeles after 1925, to (thanks to the blockbuster success *of Snow White and the Seven Dwarfs* in 1938) his meticulous planning and active design of the brand-new Disney Burbank Studio between 1938 and 1940, Disney was clearly committed toward a new kind of emotional environment for artists, or at least animators, a space compared by contemporaries to a college campus or a Renaissance *bottega*. Over the 1920s and 1930s this Hyperion Studio stood out as an exceptional communitarian space. Disney stressed informality and "a sense of fraternity;" the atmosphere was casual but prevented from degenerating through Disney's intense commitment to excellence. During the highly political Hollywood 1930s, his employees found their community in "the artistic enclave of Hyperion" with Disney himself calling his studio "a sacred space."[27] Consistently unconcerned with money (a burden he left to his brother Roy), incessantly raising the level of animation quality that he expected, Disney brought in regular art classes after 1932[28] and he methodically expanded the civic space of the studio, decorating it with bright colors, appropriately informal furniture, even a gossip paper, along with sports and parties to maintain the college campus parallel.[29]

By this stage Disney was himself uninvolved in the actual animation work; when later asked what his contribution had been, the most common employee response was his "storytelling," Disney's remarkable capacity to act out the roles he wanted to have animated as well as to project his unerring sense for the animation narrative and musical environment he had in mind.[30] Often enough the Disney studio was described as "a cult" led by a "messianic figure" drawing a group of devoted acolytes who felt they were "disciples on a mission."[31]

---

ryman." John Hench emphasizes Disney's "innate talent for storytelling and his understanding of human nature." Hench [2008], 138.
27 Cited in Gabler [2006], 161.
28 This early cooperation with the Chouinard School of the Arts would later morph into the Disney project of a City of the Arts.
29 Gabler [2006], 238.
30 Allan [1999], 36–37. Interestingly, this is a talent that Disney shared with Richard Wagner.
31 Gabler [2006], 212.

It is true that what continually fascinated Disney about animation was its fusion of drawing *and* technology. Yet, if the technology component later led Disney to his experiments in robotics and Audio-Animatronics, it still remained anchored in the priority that the artist Disney gave to "personality" for narrative exposition. In a minimal sense animation is about the movement of figures against a background, but for Disney such movement was the lesser aspect of the more primordial significance of movement from the inanimate to the animate ("anima"), which, it has been argued, is the true core to something like a religiosity driving Disney.[32] Disney furiously experimented with such bare features to advance animation experiences to the level of what *Motion Picture News* at the time hailed as the first effective simulations of the "gestures and expressions of human beings."[33] Once this level was reached, Disney called upon every available device, theatrical as well as technological, to advance animation from the simple gag and concomitant emotion of shock to something like persuasive narratives, stories that might produce the equivalent – and more – of live-action film. Finally, he focused on the narrative most conducive to the unique potential in animation, its capacity toward realizing the ultimate wish-fulfillment: "Happiness."

Sigmund Freud's biographer Ernest Jones once quoted Freud's definition of happiness as: "the subsequent fulfillment of a prehistoric wish."[34] While "prehistoric" in the context of Jones' text could also mean such "faraway" realms as the ancient Minoans and Egyptians whom Freud greatly admired,[35] the primary focus is no doubt early childhood. That Disney's master theme was increasingly characterized as "happiness" is therefore no accident, given his preoccupation with not just the realms of childhood but those of maturation over archetypal odds within natural environments replete with memories of Disney's own nostalgic attachment to turn-of-the-century small-town America and fairy-tale Europe.[36]

---

32 Disney seems never to have shown interest in any institutional religious affiliation.
33 Gabler [2006], 103. See also Hench [2008], 88.
34 If we recall as well the French writer Stendhal's definition of "beauty" as "the promise of happiness" *(la promesse du bonheur)* – a definition greatly admired by Nietzsche – then we might telescope the two definitions accordingly: beauty as "the promise of the subsequent fulfillment of a prehistoric wish." Jones [1953], I, 330–331. Herbert Marcuse singled out this definition as one of Freud's "most advanced formulations." Marcuse [1961], 186.
35 Perhaps one explanation for the exploitation of such realms in the later Disney theme parks.
36 Disney often stressed that his works were not meant merely for children: "When we make a movie, we try to please ourselves instead of some composite, imaginary child." Cited in Miller [1957], 246. Allan notes that seven out of Disney's first eight films were based on European fairy tales or folk tales. Allan [1999], 17. Later at Disneyland Disney stressed the importance of providing such spaces for adult play; according to chief Imagineer John Hench, "Ultimately, we give them a place to play, something Walt believed adults need as much as children." Hench [2008], 2.

What remains striking is the degree to which both the organization of his studio and the choice, in theme as well as in technological stylistics, of his first full-length feature animation film *Snow White and the Seven Dwarfs* have the same motivation of realizing "happiness." The *Snow White* project, rightly called "the most deliberated-upon movie in the history of film," took at least four years in which Disney risked everything on what was considered the impossible task of holding an audience to an animated feature film of some ninety minutes.[37] At its height the project required some 700 animators along with a vast supportive staff in a precise production of designs and colors that began to approach serious landscaping and figurative art. Nor could Disney be sure of the success of his gamble ("Disney's Folly," in the parlance of the trade papers) until he could witness that the test case of the closing "Bier Scene" at the 1937 premiere generated genuine tears and empathy for what were after all mere cartoon figures given the illusion of "life" and "aliveness." Disney's overall innovation was that he had done whatever was necessary, at great financial cost, to ensure that both his organization of creators, the Hyperion Studio, and the core emotion of their work were wedded through the realization of wish-fulfillment or "happiness": "In the very organization of the studio and in the manner of production, he was creating an environment, the establishment of which was in its way every bit as important a mission for him as the cartoon feature itself. Put simply, *the studio would replicate the cartoon*."[38]

In turn, Disney's new Burbank studio was intended to extend this success to the new levels of "an animation utopia" (or "a workers' paradise").[39] Although Disney brought in Kem Weber for his architecture (in fact Weber was a designer who had done sets at Paramount), he alone controlled the entire process. Once again Disney was congratulated for his "physical utopia" with its comforts to encourage work stemming from joy rather than obligation: in color, palette, and variety of space patterns and with its greenery and abounding animal life, the Disney Studio meticulously avoided any suggestion of an industrial plant.[40] Meals were taken democratically and only employee housing was lacking. Once again, the most apt parallel was an Ivy League college campus. Artistically Disney used the new studio to launch his boldest effort at turning animation into a serious art form beyond gags and even narrative.[41] *Fantasia* (1940) (originally called *The*

---

37 Gabler [2006], 274.
38 Gabler [2006], 240 (emphasis added).
39 Gabler [2006], 288.
40 Gabler [2006], 322.
41 Asking himself what abstract art was, Disney answered: "It's what you feel when you see something. It's an impression you get, it's the shape an observed incident takes in your own mind." Cited in Miller [1957], 243.

Concert Feature) was meant "as an entirely new kind of theatrical experience," transforming his choices of classical composition into audience experiences of pure form and sound, even to the extent of introducing a new sound technology called Fantasound to envelop the audience.[42]

Although the audience and critical response (outside the musical critics) to *Fantasia* was generally favorable and although Disney had further ideas for a sequel, practical disappointment in securing the proper performance venues and declining ticket sales discouraged Disney from continuing along this trajectory.[43] Meanwhile *Snow White* proved too expensive to repeat, given the exorbitant time and cost such a level of animation presupposed.[44] Moreover, the Burbank studio was increasingly being turned into an efficient business operation, while unionization attempts in 1941 awakened the wrath of the anti-Communist Disney and permanently severed the earlier studio family ethos. Finally, world war and the requisitioning of the studio for military-propaganda purposes inaugurated a lengthy period of struggle and sub-par work. Once the studio had to install the time clock (something detested by Disney since his Kansas City days) and hire business managers while being forced to put the studio under the control of banks, his dreams of an "animation utopia" were, certainly by 1946, the nadir year for the studio, over.[45]

4.

The contours of a Disney animation style, roughly called "realism" for its soft linings, chiaroscuro effects, deep dimensionality, and detailed landscape and figure background had proved too expensive for a self-sustaining studio, and indeed for any animation studio.[46] In any case it was soon displaced not only within Disney animation proper but also by rival animators pushing flat, minimalist lines in conscious evocation of a more "moderne" look. Disney's innovations of the late 1940s were therefore more in the areas of introducing the first thematic live-ac-

---

42 Gabler [2006], 309. Disney made sure to call upon the most talented contributors from the musical and art worlds. As an example: for the piece "Toccata and Fugue" by Bach, Disney brought in Oskar Fischinger, possibly the boldest experimenter at the time in pure cinematic sound, form and color.
43 Allan [1999], 104.
44 Disney later averred that it was not possible to make a better animation film than *Snow White*. Gabler [2006], 653.
45 As Disney wryly put it, "My wife used to accuse me of running a Communist outfit, well, all that is over now." Cited in Gabler [2006], 377.
46 A key figure for this aesthetic was the German-born illustrator and artist Albert Hurter.

tion nature film *(Seal Island*, 1948) and a mainly live-action replication of the American turn-of-the-century golden age reminiscent of Disney's recollections of his boyhood in Marceline, Missouri *(So Dear to My Heart*, 1948).

In fact the first significant signs of an important new stage in Disney's interests that would eventually lead to the Disneyland theme project were to be found elsewhere. In the late 1940s Disney became fascinated with trains, building a miniature version in his office and subsequently a real train on which he himself engaged in precise craft detail work. Around the same time he began collecting miniatures and attending miniature shows. These two interests coalesced into a series of ideas: creating "a sort of Lilliputian Marceline" miniature show with which he might tour the entire country – the exhibition would be called *Disneylandia* – and transforming the idea of a tour of the Burbank studio into a train ride circumnavigating the studio, the route of which would be landscaped with a "village" that included an opera house and movie theatre.[47] By 1952 Disney formed WED Enterprises to exploit the idiom and sets of motion picture studios for his park idea, which was still restricted to the studio grounds. Eventually, partly because of Burbank city authorities' hostility to the idea, Disney radically expanded the theme park idea and selected a far more massive site in Anaheim, California.[48] Disneyland in effect would be "essentially a giant movie set" with each feature on the grounds designed to awaken emotional or archetypal responses common to everyone. Disneyland, the new name for the project, would be Disney's consummate act of wish-fulfillment.[49]

Most important, Disney's former aims of dimensionality and his dream of "providing a new world onscreen" were permanently transferred to the Disneyland idea.[50] Unlike animation proper, Disneyland would be "a live breathing thing" provoking continual change and evolution. It would be located, in Disney's own words, "in cinematic time," a "cute movie set."[51] Visiting Disneyland would be "like a theatrical experience – in a word, a *show*."[52] Accordingly the staff came to be known as "Imagineers" – fusing engineering and imagination – and at the Walt Disney University they were coached to treat the park as movie sets and stagings, in which "guests" (the formal name for the paying customers) would

---

47 Gabler [2006], 484–485. See an early plan in Marling [1997], 39. My thanks to Richard Benefield for this reference.
48 Disney's intuition was excellent: as Charles Phoenix notes, "If ever there was a perfect time and place to create an entirely new concept of family entertainment, it was Southern California in the 1950s." Phoenix [2001], 149.
49 Gabler [2006], 497, 499.
50 Gabler [2006], 561.
51 Disney, cited by Gabler [2006], 564, 533.
52 Hench [2008], 2 (emphasis in original).

be drawn into the typical Disney storytelling experiences, enjoying the feeling of watching a film as each main attraction represented key frames in the extremes of an action.[53]

In practical terms the entry to the park was substantively separated from outside reality so that once "guests" came into "Main Street, USA" – another invention of Disney's – they were ready for "happiness."[54] The main avenue then culminated in the magic castle, originally identified as that of Snow White and eventually of Sleeping Beauty, in front of which an Italian-like piazza radiated out to four corners or "lands." Two were concerned with pure imagination partly wedded to technology: Fantasyland and Tomorrowland; while the other two recapitulated Disney's unique version of the past: Frontierland and Adventureland.[55] The "Present" was either non-existent or manifested as the emotional experiences of the "guests."

Once again, Disney took part in every minuscule detail of Disneyland's construction to achieve the requisite effects, even acting out for his Imagineers the potential reactions he anticipated from his guests. The scale was meant to remain strictly human as pedestrian paths and their interweavings were carefully calibrated to produce a sense of overall unity; in 1959 the first monorail in America was inaugurated in Disneyland to maximize this preponderance of human ambulation.

Throughout, the Disney staff was required to use theatrical terminology to suggest that a park visit was like witnessing a performance; according to John Hench, "we thought of the park as if it were a three-dimensional film."[56] Besides customers being referred to as "guests," park employees were labeled "cast members." "Onstage" referred to areas open to guests; "Backstage," to those closed to them. Any large group of guests was "an audience"; "cast members" were "costumers," helping to provide the "show." Overseers were "stage managers" and cast members in charge of a team had a "lead role" as they followed a "script."[57]

The upshot of these effects would be to ideally engender the "almost religious aura of feeling 'alive'"; in this sense it was Disney's boldest theatrics to induce "happiness."[58] John Hench describes its aim as "an overall feeling of optimism,

---

53 Gabler [2006], 435. John Hench, the key Imagineer, compared the stages designed to sequences of scenes in animation. Dunlop [1996], 29.
54 The first space to be experienced was an idealized Town Square (railroad station, city hall, opera house, bank, and firehouse). Dunlop [1996], 29.
55 Gabler [2006], 29, 499.
56 Hench [2008], 23.
57 Disneyland Park (Anaheim) [2009]; Hench [2008], 29.
58 Gabler [2006], 535. At the same time, Disney in "The Disneyland Story," a 1954 60-minute infomercial on the new TV series Disneyland and the future Anaheim Disneyland, described Disneyland as a place of *"knowledge* and happiness" (emphasis added).

threaded with adventure, romance, thrill, and fantasy."[59] Guests would acquire a feeling of "owning" the events at the park through the variety of stories they underwent and through the intensified stimuli utilized for enhancing their sense of reality.[60] At the same time, the overall emphasis on the play dimension as central to children and adults was meant to create a "ceremonial" or "ritual" aspect constituted by the park as "a special dedicated play space."[61] In terms of these aims the variety of "guest" responses since the 1955 opening suggests a very high rate of effectiveness and success among visitors. Certainly the striking financial gains from Disneyland were the key factor in helping to secure the Disney Studio and inaugurate the Disney organization's leadership in forming the kind of multi-media conglomerate into which all the classical Hollywood studios which have survived eventually had to morph.[62]

Yet for Disney himself, Disneyland was merely the beginning. At best it was "just a prototype" for what Disney now wanted to design: "an entire city."[63]

5.

In 1958 Disney began talks with his WED staff on a new target he called "a City of the Arts," or "the Seven Arts City."[64] At its core was Disney's ambition to turn the Chouinard Art Institution, with which he had maintained close personal and professional relations since the 1920s and 1930s and which during the 1950s was undergoing severe financial strains, into "the broadest possible creative education."[65] Already Disney had deployed WED executives to help run the school. Envisioning a new site to bring together a host of other educational institutions, including the Pasadena Playhouse and the Los Angeles Conservatory of Music, Disney found a site on a hill in the heart of West Los Angeles to form a striking cultural ensemble in Disney's take on the Bauhaus ideal. In fact when Chouinard and the LA Conservatory merged in 1961 thanks to Disney, it was Disney who gave the merger its name as the California Institute of the Arts ("CalArts") and

---

59 Hench [2008], 56. Hench can only think of the artist Salvador Dali as someone who could match Disney's optimism (besides, of course, Disney's creation Mickey Mouse!) (138).
60 For details, see Hench [2008], 56–57.
61 Hench [2008], 65. For his part Hench takes the position (similar to that taken by German poet Friedrich Schiller in his *Letters on the Aesthetic Education of Man* (1794–1795)) that "play may precede human culture. I believe it is vital to our survival as human beings."
62 Epstein [2005].
63 Gabler [2006], 573.
64 Gabler [2006], 573.
65 Gabler [2006], 592.

the land on which that Institute was eventually developed after 1969 in Valencia, California.

Originally Disney contemplated a city of shopping and dining around a complex of art programs. By the early 1960s he had given up the idea of the city as too costly, but still pursued his goal of a school.[66] Even in his later vision Disney saw the school as multidimensional, realizing, according to CalArts official statements, Richard Wagner's *Gesamtkunstwerk* vision. At the very least Disney expected to bring together all the major arts under one roof with full use of the latest technological communication tools, and to turn out professionals who had learned all facets of filmmaking as Disney himself generously understood it. Disney even had a model of CalArts set up to publicize his efforts at winning support and financial contributions.[67]

Still, Disney's ambitions of creating an actual city and not just "a faux utopia" like Disneyland lingered.[68] When Disney turned to the task of a Disney World in Florida, his aims were not simply to reproduce a more splendid Disneyland on the East Coast. Rather, he saw Disney World as his opportunity to build his utopian city adjacent to the theme park.[69] In effect, Disney took his former City of the Arts project and injected it into his version of Disney World.[70]

Disney's final project, the "Experimental Prototype City of Tomorrow" (EPCOT), proved his boldest vision to move beyond theme and resort park to a real community, presumably truly focusing "on the public need and happiness of people."[71] For this endeavor Disney drew on a variety of sources, some of which represented his own managing experience over the Disneyland project, but two authorities stood out. One was Ebenezer Howard's *Garden Cities of Tomorrow* (1902) that had been recently reissued (1965) with an introduction by Lewis Mumford, the influential city historian and contemporary admirer of Howard.

---

66   Gabler [2006], 592.
67   California Institute of the Arts [2005–2009] provides a film version of the original grand plans for CalArts as conceived by Disney. The original site in Los Angeles proved too ambitious and CalArt was later developed north of Los Angeles in the community of Valencia. After Walt's death in 1966, his brother Roy persisted in pushing the project, although the late 1960s and early 1970s were a very difficult period of clashes between his and the students' personal ethics. See Thomas [1998], 321–326.
68   Gabler [2006], 574.
69   As Gabler notes, this was "the only real appeal to him" of constructing a Disney World in Florida. Gabler [2006], 608. This perspective might be contrasted to the subsequent proliferation of Disneylands throughout the world by the multi-media conglomerate developed after Disney's death in 1966 by his practical brother Roy.
70   Gabler [2006], 604.
71   One of the explicitly stated primary goals of EPCOT. Mannheim [2002], 6. See also the useful EPCOT Chronology (185–189).

The other was *The Heart of Our Cities* (1964) by Victor Gruen, often regarded as the father of the modern supermall.[72]

Howard brought back to city planning what Mumford termed "the ancient Greek concept of the natural limit to the growth of any organism or organization, and restored the human measure to the new image of the city."[73] Howard stressed the need for communities to be fully equipped with all essential urban functions and he had it protected, not with the ancient wall of the Greek polis, but with an agricultural green belt. Although the familiar term "garden city" stems from this latter component, Mumford clarifies that it was its "urbanity," not its "horticulture," that was Howard's distinctive contribution to re-establishing the human city at a size of around 32,000 inhabitants and which was somewhat realized in the town of Letchworth, England.[74] Meanwhile Gruen's work encouraged a Metropolis of Tomorrow vision based on a set of cellular clusters starting at the neighborhood level of 900 persons and expanding through community, town, and city, to the level of metropolis, shaped in accordance with the "petal" principle of organic planning.[75]

Disney was taken by both plans, especially Howard's radial system which corresponded perfectly with his own lifelong penchant for the Circle (including indeed his choice of the shaping of the original Mickey Mouse figure!) which he thought gave people a sense of orientation ("they know where they are at all times") and thus induced the important human quality of reassurance which had been such a central component in the envisioning of Disneyland.[76] Gruen encouraged him to conceive of EPCOT in terms of a City of Tomorrow cultivating a continual state of becoming.

The experience of Anaheim had taught Disney that any such ambitious design required a far more extensive purchase of land than he had secured for the original Disneyland where the theme park had been soon surrounded by unsightly growth of parasitical enterprises he could not control. Accordingly Disney made sure that the Florida project would encompass some 27, 000 acres (in contrast to the original 160 acres in Anaheim). This vast property, extending over two Florida counties, was then first sketched out in the Disney Seventh Preliminary Master Plot Plan of 1966, a rare case of an actual drawing by Disney himself, rather than his illustrators, to diagram his overall project. The sketch reveals a vast amount of green space with EPCOT at the center and the

---

72 Howard [1951]; Gruen [1964].
73 Mumford [1961], 586.
74 Mumford [1961], 590–591.
75 Gruen in fact greatly admired Howard's work, noting that the only difference between their respective plans was intervening technological and social changes. Mannheim [2002], 25.
76 Mannheim [2002], 11. On Mickey Mouse and the Circle, see Hench [2008], 87.

"Magic Kingdom" – the Disneyland theme park recapitulation – relegated to the north while other features, such as an industrial park and airport, were located to the south.[77] EPCOT would consist of two cities, one of "Yesterday" and one of "Tomorrow." Four zones shaped by a radial plan would start with the inner central commercial zone and work outward through the high-rise apartment ring, the greenbelt and recreation area, and the outlying low-density residential area, all linked by monorail, the whole unit further linked to an outlying satellite community and industrial park.

The town center of fifty acres would be designed for some 20,000 residents – compared to Howard's Garden City of 32,000 inhabitants (although sometimes the projected figure rose to 60,000, or even 100,000 by 1980).[78] Its themed shopping mall would include a landmark hotel and convention center at its core, along with international-themed retail areas, theatres, restaurants, nightlife attractions, both for the residents and for the anticipated millions of visitors. It would be enclosed from the humid heat of Florida weather by a bubble and it would have a motion picture set design somewhat similar to the more recently added New Orleans Square in Disneyland. South of EPCOT an industrial park covering some 1,000 acres would be developed along the lines of the Stanford Industrial Park of 1951, the kind of Silicon Valley industrial parks that have proliferated since the onset of the digital age.

Given that EPCOT would be a real community connected with a theme park, a central area of concern consisted of questions of legality of property and control. Disney was able to secure Florida state legislation that established a multifunction, multicity and multicounty special district with many financial rights passed on to The Reedy Creek Improvement District.[79] In effect the legislation removed the project from control by Orlando voters and officials, but it certainly did not settle the question of what would happen when EPCOT became inhabited.[80] To describe the result as a "Vatican City of leisure and entertainment" simply raises a number of issues related to Disney's understanding of what "community" proper entailed for a structure combining residents and visitors.[81]

---

77 See Figure 1.1. in Mannheim [2002], 4.
78 Gabler [2006], 609. Compare the figures for the ideal polis of some 50,000 suggested by Aristotle and also around 50,000 by Plato (based on some 5,000 "citizens").
79 For a thorough study of the collusion between Florida's Orlando area governments and the Disney Corporation over time, see Foglesong [2001].
80 Gabler [2006], 609 (note *); Mannheim [2002], 106.
81 Mannheim {2002], 107. Ironically, although EPCOT was never built, it was the idea of EPCOT that finally won over the Florida legislature to provide for a special district, allowing for the erection of Walt Disney World. See Thomas [1998], 306–308.

What does seem clear is that Disney continued to view EPCOT as made up of a community of tenants. Obviously he wanted to retain full control, but that weakened his vision of a community in a continued state of becoming and also raised the question of lack of stakeholder commitment. In any case, legally Disney could not control voting, a right reasserted by the US Supreme Court, whatever the residential permanency of his residents. Moreover, if, as has been suggested, his expectation was that residency would be limited to one or one-and-a-half years, it seems difficult to imagine much sense of community stability, one of the stated aims of his grand plan. At best, one can merely record Disney's plan as a two-tier system of government with developers retaining authority over town planning matters while democratic control over other civil features was to be left in the hands of residents.[82]

Remaining questions touch on the nature of the inner life of the community. Since EPCOT was both a "showcase" and a community, how would residents be expected to comport themselves? In an environment designed to be neighborhood- and pedestrian-friendly, were residents expected to "dress up" for visitors every time they ambled to the local store? How would the almost rustic flavor of daily life fit in with Disney's expectations of a state of continued technological transformation that he was equally seeking? How clear were the parameters for limiting growth? Since Disney envisaged a satellite community for senior citizens, would that not limit the community mixture? Finally, how would community functions be kept separate from those of a "model-city" attraction?[83]

The best response is probably that Disney was just getting started on the implementation of his grand vision and that, as in the case of his other enterprises, further important adjustments could have been expected from his agile imagination. Certainly EPCOT remained Disney's last and most intense obsession right to his death: in October 1966 he appeared in a film pushing EPCOT and he was still thinking of EPCOT as "the overriding passion of his life" at the time of his death in December 1966.[84]

Disney's EPCOT did not survive that death. Eventually an EPCOT became part of Disney World, but more as an international fair than as Disney's City of Tomorrow.[85] Although his brother Roy did later look at a more developed scheme for EPCOT championed by Imagineers, Disney's vision was dropped as financially and legally too difficult. No doubt, however, the major reason for abandon-

---

82 Mannheim [2002], 114.
83 These concerns are raised in Mannheim [2002}, 9, 113, 123. The more recent construction of the residency Celebration does not fit the EPCOT community concept.
84 Gabler [2006], 621.
85 Gabler [2006], 631 (note *).

ment of EPCOT was the permanent loss of the charismatic Disney presence in driving that vision.[86]

6.

In their announcement of the advent of the "experience economy," Joseph Pine and James Gilmore leave no doubt about the founder of the whole phenomenon: "We trace the beginnings of this experience expansion to one man and the company he founded: Walt Disney." For Pine and Gilmore, Disney was the first to create "a living, immersive cartoon world."[87] He taught through the exemplar of Disneyland that if entertainment, education, escapism and explicitly aesthetic rewards were brought together into a single setting, any plain space could be turned into a space appropriate for "staging an experience." Full immersion and interactive participation gave "guests" the freedom to be fully in the experience, thus undergoing that personalized intensity which makes experience "memorable."[88] Similar arguments are made by Bernd Schmitt, David Rogers and Karen Vrotsos in their promotion of an "experience culture" in such cases as cooking, the art business, and the civic phenomenon of Las Vegas.[89] From these observations it is a relatively easy step to focus on the "show" or "theatrical" nature of such immersions and to propose the injection of theatrical practices into the organizational firm or enterprise as such.[90]

These speculations carry a further provocative thought: contemporary societal structures and economies are headed increasingly in this direction for a variety of reasons, not least the critical characteristics of the new information world or "internet galaxy."[91] If these speculations are on the right track, then Disney was indeed a seer with his vision for Disneyland as a "theme" and not simply "amusement" park, and his occasionally idiosyncratic gyrations between the technological ubiquities of Tomorrowland and the emotional reassurances of Main Street USA and the Magic Castle are actually quite prescient with regard to the presently unfolding social realities, whatever the evaluative judgments made concerning them.

---

86 Following Mannheim [2002], xviii.
87 Pine & Gilmore [1999], 2, 3.
88 Pine & Gilmore [1999], 42, 2, 5, 31–40. As John Hench notes, the Disney theme parks were meant to be as real as a story film through connecting visitors' experience "to their own emotions and memories." Hench [2008], 124.
89 Schmitt, Rogers & Vrotsos [2004], 239.
90 The best account remains Austin & Devin [2003].
91 Castells [2001].

Yet although Disney certainly was not oblivious to the entrepreneurial moment – which is what draws these management scholars to his oeuvre – the preceding narrative has also shown a distinction between Disney's intentions and what others have made of the "Disney" phenomenon since his death. Perhaps it makes more sense therefore to look to parallels with another art-cultural entrepreneurial phenomenon where the "art," however "managerial" a venture, still wins out over the entrepreneurial as such.

As already noted, Richard Wagner's *Gesamtkunstwerk* project has been officially invoked by the California Institute of the Arts as a main inspiration for Disney's aims at CalArts. Indeed earlier Disney critics have noted the parallels between Wagner's dream of a union of the arts and Disney's animated films synthesizing music, drama, comedy, drawing and dialogue into an aesthetic whole.[92] Nor is it difficult to detect the striking resemblance between the Disneyland Castle and Neuschwanstein Castle erected by Wagner's greatest admirer and supporter, Ludwig II of Bavaria.[93] Neuschwanstein, the true name of which was Neue Hohenschwangau (it was changed after Ludwig's death), had been erected as a homage to Richard Wagner; it was meant to invoke both the medieval Bavarian order of the Knights of Schwangau and Wagner's Swann King Lohengrin, and it was designed not by an architect but by a theatrical set designer Christian Jank. Besides its opulent medievality the castle served Ludwig – who with his technological side resembled Disney – to function as patron of such modern inventions as electricity. Wagner's *Lohengrin* (1848) had first drawn Ludwig to the Wagnerite Cause, and in later days when Ludwig's patronage saved the Wagner enterprise, it was not uncommon for Wagner to hail his patron as Lohengrin or the "Swan King."[94]

Lohengrin was also Wagner's last composition in the conventional operatic medium of his day. From that stage on Wagner was resolved on an entirely new project into emotional realms that could only be realized through what he termed "music drama." Bringing together all the major arts in a public setting had been, according to Wagner, the ancient Greeks' greatest accomplishment in the dramaturgical form known as tragedy (with comedy later added) because it had produced a collective experience (*Gemeinsam-Kunstwerk*) in shared pathos and catharsis. Wagner thought that with the technical and emotive advantages of the modern symphonic form, his version could better the Greeks by plumbing more deeply into moods and feelings not otherwise approachable through prose

---

92 See Watts [1997], 124. For the color and music components, see especially Hench [2008].
93 As John Hench makes clear, Disney's Castle "was inspired by the royal castle of Neuschwanstein in Bavaria." And as he adds, it "set a pattern" for all the other Magic Kingdoms in the Disney parks. Hench [2008], 53.
94 Details in Chytry [1989], 274–317; also Guillet de Monthoux [2004], 110–121.

or even poetry. In effect, music would allow the natural "tonal cry" of primordial humanity ("the purely human") to be rediscovered and articulated after millennia of presumed suppression. And like the Greeks – with Ludwig's indispensable support – Wagner in effect created a site of pilgrimage and temple to his art where this experience could be separated from everyday reality. The Bayreuth Festival, Wagner's "Gralsburg der Kunst," became the most important such site since the Theatre of Dionysos in ancient Athens, and it was accompanied by Wagner's grand plans for his "sanctuary" which included a supportive journal, societies of patrons, musical school to develop training in naturalness of voice and gesture, fan clubs, spa atmosphere, unique auditorium and educational seminars.[95]

For these reasons Pierre Guillet de Monthoux has persuasively argued that Richard Wagner launched the very idea of an "art firm" in European society and management. With his Bayreuth temple to art, Wagner became "the pioneer of the modern art enterprise."[96] Notwithstanding the claims of its champions, Guillet de Monthoux's nomenclature furnishes a helpful distinction between mere enterprise – or even an "experience economy"– and the "art firm," the former remaining primarily imbedded in entertainment while the latter discharges aesthetic surplus into even the entrepreneurial character which sustains it.[97]

It may be conceded that Wagnerian standards are too elevated to be compared to the Disney oeuvre. Yet the presence of a category like the "art firm" undermines any premature tendency to grant the "experience-economy" managerial scholars their exclusive claims on the significance of Disney's oeuvre – in contrast to what has since evolved as the multi-media Disney conglomerate. Where Wagner had looked to opera – the standing performance medium of his day – for his redemptive domain to regain the "purely human," Disney committed himself to motion pictures, the key medium of the twentieth century, to develop a form within filmmaking, animation, that could maximize the display of human and natural emotions. If Wagner's metaphysic ultimately rests on the primordial tonal cry, Disney's goes back to the realms of childhood and its maturation. A recent study concentrating on the first five years of childhood has noted that infant brains are mainly ruled by the occipital cortex (concerned with the visual world) and the parietal cortex (adjusting to new events). Both cortices apparently light up also in adults while they are engrossed *in watching a movie*.[98] To this degree Disney may have been the most astute exploiter of these characteristics both in children and in adults when he formed narratives that both highlighted the perils such a brain underwent in reality and furnished

---

95   Chytry [1989], 301–305.
96   Guillet de Monthoux [2004], 121.
97   Guillet de Monthoux [2004], 118.
98   See the recent study by Gopnik [2009].

ultimate reassurances of not just satisfactory but happy – i.e. primordially wish-fulfilling – endings.

Nonetheless it is not enough to highlight the medium of motion pictures (and animation within it) as the key toward Disney's oeuvre. Equally important is Disney's lifelong fixation on the physical and emotional environment or site, the motion-picture studio, in which motion pictures were actually made. As we have briefly traced, from the moment that Disney arrived in Hollywood he felt at home because he intuitively grasped that the studio was the necessary incubator for his deepest fantasies, as well as those of his fellow animators and the audience. We have shown Disney's increasingly sophisticated rendition of such emotional environments through the Hyperion and Burbank studio periods, but the same standard drove him no less toward creating Disneyland as well as the City of the Arts and the Experimental Prototype City of Tomorrow. At such levels his closest collaborators, such as head Imagineer John Hench, claim a "ceremonial" or "ritual" core to the emotional environments that resulted. In all such cases Disney's standard remained the *movie experience* of defined sets, unfolding narratives, clusters of actors, and eudaimonic arrivals.[99]

Most importantly, "animation" furnished the criterion throughout. As Ken Peterson, a Disney animator, has underscored, the key to this criterion is not just movement, but life, liveliness, aliveness – something driving Disney throughout his career.[100] It is certainly possible to critique particulars of Disney's later projects: Disney's "technocratic populism," as it has been described, may be too technocratic, corporate, business-oriented, even perhaps potentially authoritarian toward genuine possibilities of community, but the judicious critic should still grant strong residues of the humane in the "populism" component attaching to this formula.[101]

7.

In his *Symposion* Plato offers one compelling definition of *poeisis* (ποίησίς): "Any action which is responsible for something emerging from non-being (μὴ ὄντος) to being (τὸ ὄν)."[102] This is not exactly the equivalent of the meaning of animation as the "movement from the inanimate to the animate"; but it is close. Disney reveled in the experience of the aliveness that motion-picture films promised, and often

---

99   Hench [2008] is particularly useful in detailing the manner in which the film experience is imbedded in the Disneyland experience.
100 Cited in Gabler [2006], 176.
101 See the balanced account in Watts [1997], 442–445.
102 Plato, *Symposion* 205b.

enough delivered. Throughout his life Disney tried to induce, provoke, encourage its manifestations at both the "production" (the studio) and the "performative" (theatre, theme park, art university, experimental city) levels: at times he even hoped to fuse them, as in Disneyland. If his palette was limited to certain childhood and maturation themes as well as to narrower American midwest tastes, it still intuitively recognized an important stage of human emotion that merited cultivation and deserved ultimate reassurance.

It has been suggested that the heightened states of absorption enjoyed by children allow for greater plasticity and a more highly attuned capacity to take in new information – with obvious evolutionary advantages. These experiences prepare humans to a later appreciation and creation of art; philosophically they often result in something like a vitalist view of the universe akin to the Chinese concept of *chi* (*qi*).[103] This is the area in which Disney ultimately thought that he was making humane contributions by furnishing appropriate works as well as sites for their nurturance, both in the children themselves and in adults who would benefit from a rekindling of emotional memories tied to this period of childhood maturation. Even if the details of Disney's own trajectory into these realms could be sometimes problematic, his oeuvre still merits careful and sympathetic scrutiny.

Disney created special "emotional environments" by drawing richly on the literal spaces and sitings of the Hollywood movie studio, the purpose of which was to bring together the bevy of contributors making possible the production of a film. Disney originally exploited this site in its own terms to produce the emotional experiences of the animated film, but he then turned it into the literal three-dimensional reality of a theme park in which the model of the film experience continued to serve for the fabrication of a literal spatio-temporal reality intensifying the film experience.

What were the added advantages of doing so? This chapter has suggested that one set of relevant explanations, properly qualified, stems from contemporary management theories of the "experience economy" which valorize the collective memories extractable from such experiences. Memories that become "genuine" for whole families and visitors immersing themselves in such theme parks – and the structure of which can be expanded, as Disney went on to undertake, even to educational institutions and urban developments – indicate the degree to which historians of emotion have added grounds in our age of advanced media technologies to argue the case for the highly cultured orderings of "prime" or "hard-wired" emotions – as well as political issues related to such facilitations of fabrication.

---

103 See Gopnik [2009] for more empirical details.

Drawing on such language, this chapter has sought to clarify the historical importance of the Disney oeuvre as it fashioned a distinctively Californian innovation to political economy. Over the next half-century Disney's contributions to California civilization would exercise a marked influence over entrepreneurial ventures and their cultural ramifications throughout the world.

Chapter 6
Metaglobal California: California Irredenta

Which leads to the closing question:

Just how powerful is California?

The previous chapters have entertained philological, historical, cultural, even management readings of California civilization. Some of the conclusions may be informative, perhaps edifying, but notwithstanding occasional references to strength on a global scale which draws grudging respect, little in this volume has so far systematically brought together the rock-bottom power of California.

Fortunately Abraham Lowenthal's recent summation of California's presence in a globalizing setting, *Global California* (2009), furnishes as effective an account as is needed.[104] In a work in which much of the text is devoted to extensive documentary confirmation of the depth and range of California's competitiveness in the world market, Lowenthal's study is an indispensable starting-point for further reflection. At the same time *Global California* is committed to a specific mission: the laudable one of ensuring that optimal use be made by Californians of California's global features and tendencies.[105] While this is all to the good, it is no less important to secure a vantage-point even beyond Lowenthal's global California: to grasp, so to speak, a "meta"-global California which is not just expanding globally but also consolidating itself upon its own soil.

1.

Before developing this issue, it is first worth cataloguing the scope and depth of California's economic clout as narrated by Lowenthal and other sources. Overall, as earlier noted, California ranks eighth or ninth in the world in GDP rankings (see Figure 1).

---

104 Lowenthal [2009].
105 The purpose of Lowenthal's book is to suggest "what Californians can do, within constitutional constraints, to identify and advance our international interests." Lowenthal [2009], 13. Bardhan, Jaffee & Kroll [2004] have already pointed out that "each of the fifty United States faces a much more restricted set of policy options than a country of similar size" (147).

First, as Lowenthal points out, California agriculture is one of the most powerful in the world, its exports even exceeding those of developing countries which are dependent on such exports: California's Central Valley is "one of the main agricultural centers of the world."[106] Not only is the Central Valley the most important agricultural producer for the United States, but it has also increasingly become involved in international agricultural trade to East Asia, Europe, and Canada. The Valley is also an important source for oil and natural gas. In general California has been ranked as the world's fifth largest supplier of food and agricultural commodities. It dominates American productivity in fruit, vegetables, dairy and wine production.

Second, California is a major manufacturing center. Admittedly, the kind of manufacturing in which it used to excel, including motor and tire industries and aerospace, no longer plays a dominant role, certainly not since the end of the Cold War.[107] However, accepting NAICS classifications for high-tech manufacturing, California is a major player both in high-tech hardware – computers and semi-conductors – and high-tech services – software publishing and information services, computer systems design, and data processing.[108] Such preeminence stems of course from California's just claim to be creator of one of the most imposing industrial innovations of the twentieth century: "Silicon Valley." Repeatedly this original homeland of the computer revolution has spawned unprecedented new products for the world market, from the PC phenomena of the 1970s to the internet "galaxy" of the 1990s. Moreover, despite troughs in its evolving fortunes, Silicon Valley is again showing signs of new thrusts into yet uncharted worlds of digital convergence.[109] Of equal importance is the newer feature that despite the continued creation of new Silicon Valleys throughout the rest of the world, particularly India and China, Silicon Valley's export of technical talent brings with it the recurring centrality of Silicon Valley proper for continued exchange of ideas with such "new Argonauts." These "face-to-face encounters," far superior to videoconferencing, increase the likelihood of new breakthroughs that would serve California: "often these breakthroughs occur in high-spirited meetings between passionate people," and their nerve-center remains, more often than not, the original Silicon Valley: "Silicon Valley is still the best location in the world for the definition of new system architectures, high-level design, management of cross-cultural projects, and basic as well as first-generation engineering research."[110]

---

106 Lowenthal [2009], 2, 74.
107 See Table 2–6 in Bardhan, Jaffee & Kroll [2004], 36.
108 Bardhan, Jaffee & Kroll [2004], 38.
109 Silicon Valley's GDP growth in 2010 "exploded" at 13.4% according to Brown [2011].
110 Saxenian [2006], 338.

Third, an even more dominant feature within the general category of services, California is also the world center for motion pictures, television and the music industry as well as newly emergent multi-media industries, thanks to another distinctive California creation: "Hollywood" in its broader sense as the nucleate agglomerate to global media industries. Even with increasing outside competition, Hollywood generally dominates 80% of the entire industry, maintaining "virtually absolute mastery of global film and television markets."[111]

Fourth, as reflected in world university surveys, California is a leading player among the world's top university and research centers. Characteristically, according to (London) Times Higher Education and Shanghai Jiao Tong University surveys, its major universities – Stanford University, University of California, Berkeley, California Institute of Technology, and University of California, Los Angeles – occupy three of the top six or eight slots, or four of the top ten or eleven slots. In other words, at the very crown of such respected rating systems, California consistently matches world competition from the entire rest of the United States, the United Kingdom, and, for that matter, China. California also ranks among the leaders in the number of Nobel Prize winners among its residents and academics.

Such strength naturally carries over, fifth, into California's eminence as a major site for research and information organizations. As Lowenthal points out, a number of leading research laboratories make their home in California. Californians lead the U.S. states in patents granted and California institutions invest more in research and development than any other nation outside of the rest of the United States, Japan, and Germany.[112]

It can be countered that California's superiority in these areas is, and will be, increasingly challenged by domestic and foreign competition, particularly from emerging economies. Yet it should be equally recognized that challenges of this order have been successfully met in the past by Californian ingenuity. Moreover, economic theory has had to make room increasingly for the competitive advantages accruing to established cluster agglomerates and regional concentrations ("asset specificity," "firm-specific assets") which uphold economies of scale that new entrants have great difficulties in overcoming.[113] Finally, convergence patterns in high-tech and multi-media ventures promise new clusters which the higher-educated sectors of the Californian population can be reasonably expected to exploit.

---

111 See Scott [2005], 159, for a full account and such statistical details as Table 9.1 (160).
112 Lowenthal [2009], 3–4. In addition, it should be noted that beyond these five factors Lowenthal brings in others, such as California philanthropy, as part of Calfiornia's overall clout.
113 See, e. g., Teece [2009] on these and related concepts such as "dynamic capabilities."

Indeed, if future economic trends favor such industries as green technology, biotechnology and pharmaceuticals, California is uniquely well placed to take advantage of such trends. With its abundant solar, coal and geothermal resources, California is positioned to develop a fully effective high-tech green economy, its efforts so far having placed it at "the forefront of green technology" through its recent cutting edge of "carbon usage."[114] In biotechnology, California, "the birthplace of the U.S. biotech industry," leads the field by housing 40% of all U.S. public biotech companies and 40% of all employment in the area.[115] As if these factors were not enough, there are, finally, firm signs that California could become the next "oil boom state," thanks to its massive amounts of shale oil.[116]

More generally, thanks to its location California occupies a favored position in the continually expanding Pacific Rim; among the top ten world economies only China and Japan (besides the rest of the United States) can make a comparable claim. Of additional advantage is the astonishing ethnic variety of California's population which compares favorably to all its economic rivals, including the rest of the United States. Such diversity should help considerably in Californians' affiliations with an increasingly globalizing world economy.

Finally, California's size and population provides optimistic comparisons for the future. More or less equal in size (163,000 square miles) to Japan (145,000 square miles) and France (210,000 square miles), California's population of 37 million is far smaller than that of France (65 million) or Japan (127 million). Accordingly, an increase to 60 million by 2050 (as conventionally predicted) should make California all the more competitive in the future: even today with its far smaller population it is able to compete among the top ten economies in a world with rivals containing hundreds of millions or even billions of residents.

It will be granted that there are present concerns attached to the economic downside of California's struggling state budgets, uneducated lower classes, dysfunctional political and constitutional structures, and problematic features in its secondary education system. No doubt these are serious handicaps that Californian policymakers and citizens must be expected to confront, but such concerns are not necessarily endemic to California and do not constitute an automatic barrier to the ranks that California's industries have so far scaled. What remains worth recording is the spread of California's economic strength over the past half-century precisely into areas that are exemplary for characteristically twenty-first century sovereign states: from the (Physiocratic) celebration of the primacy of agriculture and natural resources for a nation's wealth, through

---

114 San Francisco Chronicle [2010], 1.
115 Zhang & Patel [2005], v.
116 CNNMoney [2013].

the high-tech and multi-media industries that drive innovation within contemporary globalization, to intellectuals' focus on the institutions of higher education, research, and formalized interchanges of original and creative thinking inseparable from standards that are conventionally assumed necessary to "civilization."

2.

Lowenthal's encomium to California's potentialities is therefore fully merited. More problematic is the unnecessarily narrow orientation of his global and globalizing proposals. Lowenthal asks us to skip over, in effect, one of the more imposing periods for Californian success and prosperity, the 1950s and 1960s, by criticizing its "relatively homogeneous and provincial character," and to recall instead the presumably more original and encompassing trajectory of an international California since its Spanish-Mexican origins. From this perspective he sees California's explicit passage into "global California" since the 1970s as more in tune with its overall history than that intermediate period in which "California was largely self-sufficient and regionally focused" with "too much focus" on local issues holding it to "provincial" priorities and turning Californians into "inward-looking" citizens.[117] Thanks to changes in the 1970s and 1980s, California, according to Lowenthal's happy tale, is no longer a "remote hinterland" but "a recognized heartland."[118]

Lowenthal's objectives are undoubtedly worthy but his either/or approach raises concerns. It is certainly true, as he notes, that the California of 1930–1970 in which 95% of its prodigious population growth came from California and the rest of the United States differs from a California which since the 1970s has reflected a 49% growth rate from foreign-born immigrants (as well as a net *outflow* of U.S.-born citizens), culminating in the ubiquity of international immigration in the 1990s *even as* the outflow from California continued: "California has reverted to its original DNA as a profoundly international place."[119] Clearly policymakers must adjust to such momentous shifts in the California population body. But tempting as it is to utilize such factors to promote a "globalizing" California that upholds a "global mindset," there are several reasons not to exaggerate in this direction.

First, there is something intrinsically mistaken about dismissing as "provincial" perhaps the greatest period of Californian prosperity of the 1950s and 1960s.

---

117 Lowenthal [2009], 26.
118 Lowenthal [2009], 31.
119 Lowenthal [2009], 33, 44.

As already noted, this was precisely the period in which California surged to the forefront of American and international admiration – and envy. Something must have been done right by Californian policymakers and citizens in their putative condition of "provincialism" to produce such states of wealth and well-being.[120] Josiah Royce's earlier warnings about the undermining of California's "provincial" culture by American centralization during the latter's nineteenth-century ascension to world industrial ranks serves as a timely reminder not to unthinkingly ignore the benignly consolidatory role of the "provincial" in any civilization worth its name. Granted that world history can be seen in part as ongoing migrations by human groupings, it still remains true that consolidation, autochthony (however relatively defined) and solidification are crucial moments for genuine culture and civilization. Besides, as Lowenthal himself has occasion to concede, "Californians are ever more vulnerable to globalization."[121] It is not clear that exclusively globalizing policies moderate such vulnerability.

Lowenthal understandably laments the closures of a number of state agencies by 2002 that had been founded to push California's international interests. Yet this "turn inward in the early twenty-first century" may also suggest benign consequences.[122] "Turning inward," presumably also a characteristic of the 1950s and 1960s, can solidify modes of collective identity and reassurance which exaggerated participation in globalizing trends might overlook to the detriment paradoxically of successfully exploiting such trends.

Naturally one cannot return to the particular Anglo predominance of the 1950s-1960s period, nor should one wish to. Rather, what ought to be encouraged for the sake of further cultivation of "California civilization" is some comparable "provincialism" which reflects the new California citizenry of the early twenty-first century. Fortunately there is heartening evidence of favorable trends in this direction. Patterns that have been described as "a sea change in the state's history" focus on a new "homegrown majority" emerging in present-day California.[123]

As California changes from having been a "migration magnet" toward becoming "a more self-contained society that depends on its present members," the outdated image of a ceaselessly migratory California population will have to be replaced.[124] Whereas in 1990 53.2% of those aged 15–24 were born and resided in California, in 2007 that figure had shot up to over 70%. Indeed, the figures

---

120 See Chapter 4 above.
121 Lowenthal [2009], 125.
122 Lowenthal [2009], 44.
123 Myers, Pitkin & Ramirez [2009], 1
124 See the article "Native-born Californians regain majority status," in Los Angeles Times [2010].

for Latinos and Asians-Pacificans are even more impressive at 82.6% and 82.5% respectively. Generally such "homegrown" factors sustain high support for higher taxes regarding public services and form clear signs of "the maturation of a state," particularly where, as in this case, the figures also support continued commitment to residency in California.[125]

It is therefore precisely at this time of major change in the Californian citizen body that a serious error would be committed if "provincial" concerns were underplayed. In any event, the concept of a fully globalizing society is inherently incoherent, since any authentic player on the world stage must constitute in some critically self-identificatory manner the appurtenances of a "sovereign state", "culture", "civilization". In sum, Lowenthal's important recommendations of a "global California" are to be applauded, but they also need augmentation by a policy that is not only "global" in its ambitions but also at the same time "provincial" in its concrete grounding in order to realize in due course what might be labeled a "meta-global" California.

3.

Such a goal requires in turn one final area to consider regarding California's economic power: its continued impact over those territories that once made up parts of *California* or *Las Californias*.

During the 1870s the term "irredenta" became topical thanks mainly to Italian "Irredentists" loudly campaigning to retrieve what they considered to be authentic parts of Italy not yet incorporated into the newly founded Kingdom of Italy after 1860. The term, itself meaning "unredeemed, unrecovered" in Italian, has been subsequently applied more widely to analogous political movements concerned to bring together into one political state parts of a nation that have been scattered across different sovereignties. Characteristically such applications have been accompanied by the prefix "Greater" to refer to those larger areas being claimed by the irredentists of the particular state or political entity they were sponsoring.

Thus "California Irredenta" carries the potent meaning "California Unredeemed," and the application of "Greater" to "California" to form "Greater California" serves as reminder of the much wider geographic ambit of California than

---

[125] Myers, Pitkin & Ramirez [2009], 3, 5, 6, 17, 18. Given the historical significance of Oaxaca for the story of the myth of California (see Chapter 2 above), it is also worth noting the more recent increases of Mixtec and Zapotec migrants from Oaxaca to Southern California. See Pez & Runsten [2003] and Poole [2004].

the present U.S. state of California. As we earlier detailed, it means the California originally baptized by the Spanish, whether in the singular *California* or as *Las Californias* covering alta and baja California, a vast area comprising not only the present U.S. state of California but also Nevada, Utah, Arizona, and Mexican Baja California (ignoring the slivers passed on to Colorado and Wyoming).

Unlike characteristic irredentisms, however, this particular "irredenta" is not intended to instigate demands for "lost" territories. On the contrary, it is meant to emphasize the greater responsibilities for Californians if they wish to embark on a path toward world-historical greatness. Rather than regard such territories as objects for annexation, direct or indirect, Californians should acknowledge and appreciate the extent of their continuing economic and cultural weight over these same territories, and responsibly pursue policies in line with those considerations.

For this educational process, a first step is some sort of generalized roundup of California's centrality for the economies of the rest of Greater California. Ever since the U.S. state of California, thanks to the Gold Rush and succeeding economic and industrial growth surges, sprang into prominence to dominate the U.S. West, it has served as a kind of catalyst for this Greater California. Prior to American annexation, these territories were generally unoccupied, but Mexican sovereignty was formally recognized, thus implicitly acknowledging their location in an entity called *Las Californias*. So far as the vast expanse of the Great Basin was concerned, it lacked settlers and the few who occasionally wandered through, such as Jedediah Smith in the 1820s, had to deal with Mexican authorities' concern over violations to their sovereign claims over the land.[126] When later Brigham Young brought his Mormons into the Great Salt Lake area, he was in effect entering "not yet Utah, but rather 'eastern California'."[127]

Indeed, even with American federal absorption of *Las Californias* in 1848 pressure remained strong on the American side to retain a single "California" for most of the territories newly annexed from Mexico. U.S. president Zachary Taylor sent representatives to the areas calling for the creation of two new states: New Mexico and California, with "California" covering all the territory excepting New Mexico.[128] At the Monterey convention that debated the creation of California's territorial boundaries in 1849, delegate William Gwin joined up with delegate Henry Wager Halleck to call for a California boundary that even included substantial chunks of future states Wyoming, Colorado, and New Mexico (see

---

126 Bowers [2006], 2.
127 Pomeroy [1968], 35. As Bowers [2006] notes, the Great Salt Lake area was "still within the sovereignty of Mexico" (5).
128 Following Johnson [1992], 132–133.

Map 9).[129] This extended boundary was actually approved by committee before being rejected in the final vote by only two votes. It lost because the *californio* delegates changed their minds, probably because they did not want the issue of Californian statehood to get muddied up in larger questions of slave states and inclusion of Mormons: "The Californios' shift was decisive: they essentially set the new state's boundary" at the Sierra Nevada.[130]

In any event California would become the key player for what followed: "California looms large in any story of the Far West, however conceived." The neighboring states were "in large part" what they were because California "served as catalyst, banker, and base of operations: much of what it was depended on the tribute they paid."[131] As late as 1890 observers such as John S. Hittell continued to remark on the beauties and resources of the state of California compared to which "much of her *tributary territory* is miserably poor. Nevada, Utah, and Arizona, look as if they had been impoverished for the purpose of enriching her."[132]

It will be conceded that the single most important institution in affecting the overall economy of the U.S. West in the twentieth century remained the U.S. federal government. Whereas the U.S. approached its territories in the nineteenth century as a "colonial economy," twentieth-century federal policy, especially during and after the second world war, was massive in driving the economies of California, Nevada, Utah, and Arizona, as well as other western U.S. states, in the direction of "a pacesetting technologically advanced economy."[133] In that respect the twentieth-century Western economy may be fairly described as "the creature of the federal government."[134]

At the same time it is no less worth recording the central economic presence of California in those units making up Greater California. Of these, *Nevada* retained the closest association with California. Emerging from the "Utah Territory" estab-

---

129 In 1849 Illinois senator Stephen Douglas placed a bill that called for a California to extend, excepting New Mexico, from the Pacific to the Rockies by using an 1848 (Preuss) map "which indicates that under Mexican rule this region composed California." Johnson [1992], 420 (note 125), also 133 on Douglas' efforts while William Gwinn was in Washington, D. C.
130 Johnson [1992], 130–133. Gwin and Halleck did expect that eventually this extended California would break up into smaller states, but from the outset their vision reflects the strong sense of a Greater California over these same territories.
131 Pomeroy [1968], vi. In his foreword to Pomeroy [2008], Howard R. Lamar points out that for Pomeroy "California was one of the keys of modern western history – both because the state was the largest and most powerful in the Far West and also because it had dominated the economies of Nevada, Utah, Arizona, and Alaska *in their formative stages*" (viii, emphasis added).
132 Cited in Pomeroy [1968], 344 (emphasis added). As recently as 1982 Kotkin & Grabowicz [1982] have used similar language regarding a Californian "colonialism" and "imperial designs" over these territories (248, 250).
133 Nash [1999], 145.
134 Following in general Nash [1999].

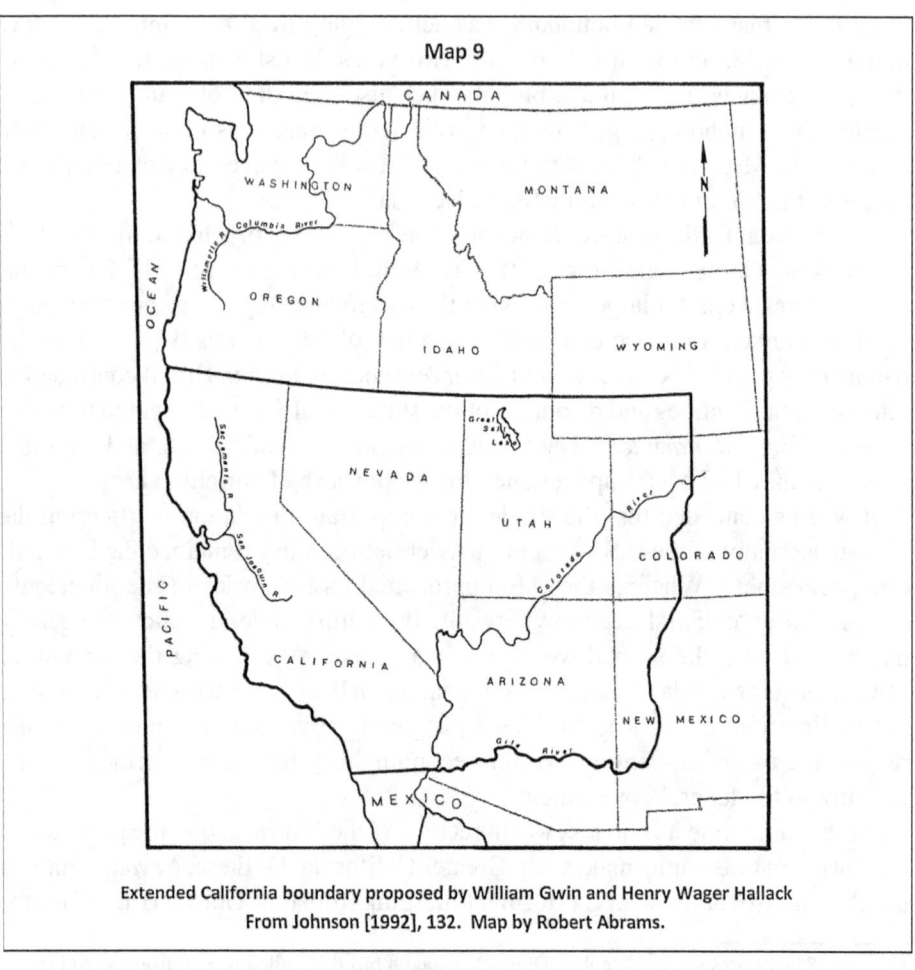

Extended California boundary proposed by William Gwin and Henry Wager Hallack
From Johnson [1992], 132. Map by Robert Abrams.

lished by the U.S. Congress which trumped the Mormons' claim in 1849 for an independent state of "Deseret" (the latter including, in part, southern California), Nevada originally stood for the "Western Utah territory" that consisted of little more than trading posts in Carson Valley adjoining California. Carson Valley settlers forcefully campaigned to be freed of the Mormon-controlled centers of Utah located some 500 miles to their east under Governor Brigham Young. In 1853 and 1855 the settlers even petitioned the California legislature to be annexed by the state of California. After the so-called "Utah War" of 1857–1858 when U.S. troops were sent into Salt Lake City – a "war" which had the practical effect of permanently drawing Mormon settlers in locations like Carson Valley, Las Vegas, and southern California back to the Mormon capital – Carson Valley settlers succeeded in 1859 in producing a territorial constitution based on that of California and adopted the name "Nevada." Their stance received formal Congressional support in 1861, splitting the original Territory of Utah into "Utah" and "Nevada."[135] An 1863 constitutional convention, to which all but five of 39 delegates were from California and the president of which was former California governor J. Neely Johnson, eventually produced a constitution based on those of California and New York and led to congressional acceptance of Nevada as a U.S. state in 1864.[136] As a local Virginia City newspaper put it, "the interests of no parent country and colony could possibly be more closely united than those of California and Nevada."[137]

Much of the quickening in the movement toward Nevada statehood reflected the 1859 discovery of the Comstock Lode and the burst of economic activity that immediately followed, bringing large numbers of Californians to the scene and reflecting Californian control through newly emergent mining companies.[138] In effect, capital from California took over, and even when Nevada's mining economy declined, the newly instituted Bank of California in 1864 became the economic powerhouse in the state: "Indeed, with the coming of the Bank of California began an era of concentrated corporate control and rapid industrialization that shaped the state to the end of the nineteenth century."[139]

For twentieth-century Nevada, perhaps the two most important economic and demographic steps were the establishment of Harold's Club in Reno in 1935 by San Franciscans Harold and Raymond Smith and the initiation of casino development in Las Vegas by Thomas Hull, a Californian developer of San Francisco and Los Angeles who hoped to create a similar desert resort area with his El Rancho.[140] While it is true that Las Vegas had already begun its road to prosperity in 1911–1918 and received a further boost with federal spending after 1930 that accompanied development of the Boulder or Hoover Dam, it was Hull "who launched a movement that would transform the town" by recognizing the value

---

135 According to Johnson [1992], it was the senators from California who introduced the bill to establish the Territory of Nevada (77). The name "Nevada" comes from the "Sierra Nevada" mountains between California and Nevada.
136 For J. Neely Johnson, see Johnson [1992], 97, 199–202.
137 Cited in Bowers [2006], 22, and 6–17. Bowers notes that San Francisco came to be known as the "city Nevada built" (22). See also Johnson [1992], 80.
138 In 1863 Nevada was described as "the land for the old Californians," making up "what once constituted the hey-day of the glory of California." Johnson [1992], 77.
139 Johnson [1992], 318.
140 In Moehring's list of the major contributors to Las Vegas' overall development in the twentieth century – Thomas Hull, Bugsy Siegel, Del Webb, Howard Hughes, Kirk Kerkorian, Steve Wynn – the contribution of Californians stands out. Moehring [2000], 290–291.

in 1941 of "a California hotel chain" in Las Vegas.[141] Hull was soon followed by gangster Bugsy Siegel who, coming to the Los Angeles area in the 1930s, decided to create with mobster backing the Flamingo hotel and casino in 1946–1947 which further transformed Las Vegas "from a recreational to a full-fledged resort city," as Hollywood celebrities increasingly flocked to the boomtown of the late 1940s.[142]

Although from this stage on Las Vegas first developed a reputation as a town run by "gamblers and hoods," the expansion of its airport in 1963 opened up a "market beyond California drivers" and initiated its further prodigious growth; by 2000 Las Vegas was better known as "a town devoted to entertaining and funded by Wall Street, providing everyone with any experience they need."[143] Such growth required Nevada to agree to the Allen-Warner Valley plan which included the Allen plant near Las Vegas, Nevada Power remaining a project in which only 20% of power distribution went to Nevada Power while 80% went to California utilities for southern California. These energy links between Nevada and California raised old Nevada worries of their dependency on the California economy but did not significantly change that dependency.[144] Given the increased need for water for the Las Vegas area, California and Nevada came to an agreement in January 2001 allowing surplus water to go to California in return for California's commitment to conserve water by promising to annually decrease the amount it took over fifteen years. The benefits ensured that Southern Nevada would not be deprived of water needs during the immediate future.[145]

As Las Vegas continues to expand "to the California border and beyond," the role of California migrants to its population increase remains major. After the post-Cold War collapse of the Californian aerospace industry, Californians spilled over into adjoining states and particularly into the Las Vegas region where during the 1990s they comprised some two-thirds of newcomers. Although Californians in Nevada "were no more popular in the Silver State than they are in any other place where California's influence reached" (indeed they were sometimes mocked as "Californicators"), Nevada scholars have conceded that they are "pivotal" to the state through the values they bring for creating "change": "They are catalysts for the rapid transformation that has made Las Vegas a true

---

141 Moehring [2000], 13, 16, 43. Gambling was legalized in the state in 1931.
142 Moehring [2000], 49. By combining Monte Carlo with Miami-style resort amenities, the Flamingo opened the floodgates for the future "diversity of images" characteristic of Las Vegas (49).
143 Rothman [2002], 319.
144 See Wiley & Gottlieb [1982], 192–194, 213.
145 Details from Rothman [2002], 211–217.

twenty-first-century frontier town."[146] After all, the claim that 2000 Las Vegas is really just a kind of adult Disneyland simply confirms the continuing California impress on the city's and region's entire self-image.[147]

Meanwhile the evolution of the future U.S. state of *Utah* stands out for representing the core of the founding of the Church of Jesus Christ of Latter-day Saints, or Mormons, in the Great Salt Lake area under Brigham Young in 1847. In this case as well the importance of the California connection is notable from the outset, significantly from both sides.

On the Mormon side it might be justifiably claimed that Young's vision of a State of Deseret is the first active effort to conceive some sort of future unity to the former California territories under Mexico: Young's State would have covered all of Alta California excepting northern California.[148] Mormon presence was even directly established in southern California with the founding of San Bernardino in 1851. The remarkable progress of the Mormon community in San Bernardino exercised a strong positive influence over adjoining economic and civic planning ventures in the area, at least until they left it in 1857.[149]

From the California side, it can be argued that the practical effects of the California Gold Rush of 1848–1849 effectively saved the Mormon project in the Greater Salt Lake region from its rocky start: as a "result of the discovery of gold in California the Mormons were able to provide themselves with a convenient circulating medium, and in addition, they were able to acquire the wherewithal with which to launch" their overall program of development for "their projected Kingdom."[150] Whereas prior to this turn they had been barely surviving on "roots, work cattle, and a small ration of cracked grain," the "miracle" of 1849 transformed Salt Lake City by amply providing the Church with all the necessities and even some luxuries. Around 10,000–15,000 gold seekers came through the area both in 1849 and in 1850, bringing provisions and providing a persistent demand

---

146 Rothman [2002], 322, 212, 296.
147 "If it sounds like Disneyland, it is." Rothman [2002], 319. More generally Abbott [1993] argues that "Nevada's historic status as *a California colony*" remains "well documented": from the Comstock Lode "to the rise of Reno and Las Vegas as weekend suburbs of coastal cities" (155, emphasis added).
148 See the maps in Arrington [1958], 22, 85, which show the Mormon Trail and Mormon Battalion Trail linking the entire region of the former Alta California. As Arrington argues, since the territory into which the Mormons arrived was "Mexican territory at the time," it has been erroneously assumed that the State of Deseret was meant to constitute an independent nation: the greater evidence shows that "the Saints fully intended to claim the area for the United States and petition for statehood" (41).
149 See Starr [1973], who describes the "cooperative venture" as "the model for all such efforts in the semi-arid Far West" (200). The Mormon residents left in 1857 to support the Salt Lake Mormons in the 1857 "war" against the Federal government.
150 Arrington [1958], 64.

for Mormon goods and labor, effectively promoting improved transportation and leaving a windfall of commodities in the wake of their somewhat disheveled through passage. Finally, the abundance of California gold allowed for sufficient coinage circulation in the area to ease concerns by Mormon leaders, thus encouraging them to plan "a mammoth (to them) program of expansion."[151]

It is often assumed that this Mormon "Great Basin Empire," as it has been fairly labeled, came to an end with the completion of the transcontinental railway system in 1869 which, by connecting the Salt Lake City area with the rest of the United States once and for all, would bring in outside cultural influences that undermined Mormon separateness as well as East Coast investors avid to profit from the imposing natural resources of the territory. The evidence however reflects relative Mormon success in at least slowing the rate of attrition.[152] It was only in the next two decades that increasing demands through individuals, groups and congressional representatives, ostensibly worried about Mormon bigamy but probably no less dismayed by the success of Mormon cooperative economics, led to the final concessions by the Church which led to acceptance of Utah as a U.S. state as late as 1896. By that point the Mormon presence, however much modified, had been permanently established as a fixture of Utah reality.[153]

Still, twentieth-century Utah proved a significantly different operation as Utah's natural resources, especially in shale oil, drew investors and diggers.[154] Integrated into the larger national and world economy, Utah suffered the pangs of an economic downturn between 1920 and 1950 which was marked by an alarming exodus of population. Utah was only gradually able to recover thanks largely to major federal investment during the second world war and postwar periods in military manufacturing and missiles.[155]

Starting in the 1960s a new wave of Californian investments in the state attracted growth officials in Utah. Although Utah sided with Arizona against California in their extended conflict over rights to Colorado River waters, Utah's need for capital led to several major projects dependent on California

---

151 Following the excellent account (with quotes from primary sources) in Arrington [1958], 64–77.
152 Arrington [1958], 235–257.
153 The Mormon "cooperative movement" is dated 1868–1884. See Arrington [1958], 293; also 356, 379–380, 411–412; more recently, see Lyman [1985].
154 Earlier, the distance between Utah and the Pacific coast had made Utah mining "uneconomic." For 1868–1872 most of the rich deposits were owned by non-Mormons and had been opened up by the Third California Volunteers, veterans from the California and Nevada gold fields. Arrington [1958], 201–202, 242.
155 According to Wiley & Gottlieb [1982], Utah's economic output in 1950 was less than that for 1920 (143).

institutions. Attracted to the rich deposits of low sulfur oil, California utilities like Southern California Edison originally supported the aborted Kaiparowits state project of the early 1970s; their decision to withdraw "highlighted the crucial role of the Californian utilities and the California market in the Utah energy situation."[156] The Intermountain Power Project drew California utilities led by the Los Angeles Department of Water and Power to furnish most of the financing in exchange for 58% of the power supply, and the proposed coal-fired Warner Valley plant was no less dependent on the California participation of Pacific Gas & Electric and Southern California Edison. Admittedly, as in the case of Nevada, such participation led to Utahn fears of dependency on California and a new emphasis for Utah itself as the energy broker. Still, even though control over energy passed to the Utah Power and Light company, the latter needed to continue to draw Californian investors, and a member of the California Energy Commission remained comfortable about bluntly expressing California's hovering interest over Utah resources as: "Utah looks good to us."[157]

If Nevada and Utah were extracted from the larger Utah Territory derived entirely from Mexican *California* (or *Las Californias*), the case of *Arizona* is somewhat different. Although the future Arizona had been part of *California*, after 1848 it was attached to the new U.S. Territory of New Mexico which represented a combination of the future Arizona part of *California* and the separate Mexican territories of "Nuevo Mexico." Still, from the outset the Arizona portion of this New Mexico Territory was no less closely attached to California: during the Mexican-American war of 1846–1848 it was an American contingent of Mormon volunteers under Colonel Philip St. George Cooke who took over the one Arizona town of Tucson before marching on to San Diego, California. Indeed Cooke used his contingent to build a wagon road all the way to San Diego which soon served as a better route than the Oregon Trail for reaching the Pacific coast, particularly after the discovery of California gold drew large numbers of gold seekers, changing the main directions through these lands from north-south to east-west.[158]

As a major stopover at Tucson for the route to California, Arizona also became in due course "a convenient and favored residence for many who failed in California."[159] With California's rapid development over the succeeding decades, speedier transports were then constructed through Arizona for easier

---

156 Wiley & Gottlieb [1982], 161.
157 Cited in Kotkin & Grabowicz [1982], 249; also 249–250; and Wiley & Gottlieb [1982], 151–152.
158 Fireman [1982], 81–84
159 Fireman [1982], 88.

access to and from California. In the 1860s Arizona became the "westernmost battleground of the Civil War" when confederate supporters temporarily created a Territory of Arizona as part of the Confederate States of America. In response, collecting a Column from California composed of volunteers from northern Californian towns and mining camps, Colonel James H. Carleton succeeded in taking Tucson in 1862 and becoming military governor of Arizona.[160] Since already by that time Arizona settlers and their Anglo-American leadership showed strong resentment toward Hispanic control from the Santa Fe government of the Territory of New Mexico, it proved relatively easy to formalize the new conditions when U.S. President Abraham Lincoln declared Arizona a separate territory in 1863.[161]

Territorial Arizona continued to function in close attachment to the California economy and politics. Fort Yuma on the California side served as an important supply point for travelers in both directions.[162] An 1863 Arizona gold rush drew large numbers of California gold seekers to the territory, and General George Stoneman who headed the military Department of Arizona in 1870 later became governor of California.[163]

After Arizona (along with New Mexico) became a U.S. state in 1912, new forces began its transformation from "a desert wasteland on the route to California" to a desirable desert state in itself. Developers encouraging a strong turn to tourism in the 1920s began to draw on "California as the model for what they wanted Arizona to become," and helped initiate the momentous urban expansion of the cities of Phoenix and Tucson in the twentieth century.[164] Ironically, however, such demographic changes also fed a long acrimonious relationship between California and Arizona particularly with regard to lower-basin water rights to the Colorado River, a battle that was only formally settled many decades later as a result of the U.S. Supreme Court decision *Arizona v. California* in 1963 (see Map 10).

---

160 Carleton was no less responsible for the cruel treatment of exile or extermination toward the Navajos and Mescalero Apaches. See Sheridan [1995], 69–70.
161 Fireman [1982], 92, 97. 100–103, 110. See the succeeding maps of "Arizona Boundaries" (89) showing the evolution of the original 1850 Territory of New Mexico into the Arizona Territory of 1863 as well as the loss of a northwest section to Nevada Territory in 1866.
162 Although the present city of Yuma is in Arizona, Fort Yuma was originally registered in San Diego, California, for tax-collection purposes, clearly indicating that Yuma's location on both banks of the Colorado River was regarded as within the jurisdiction of the U.S. state of California.
163 Fireman [1982], 139, 151, 127.
164 Sheridan [1995], 355, 240.

Map 10

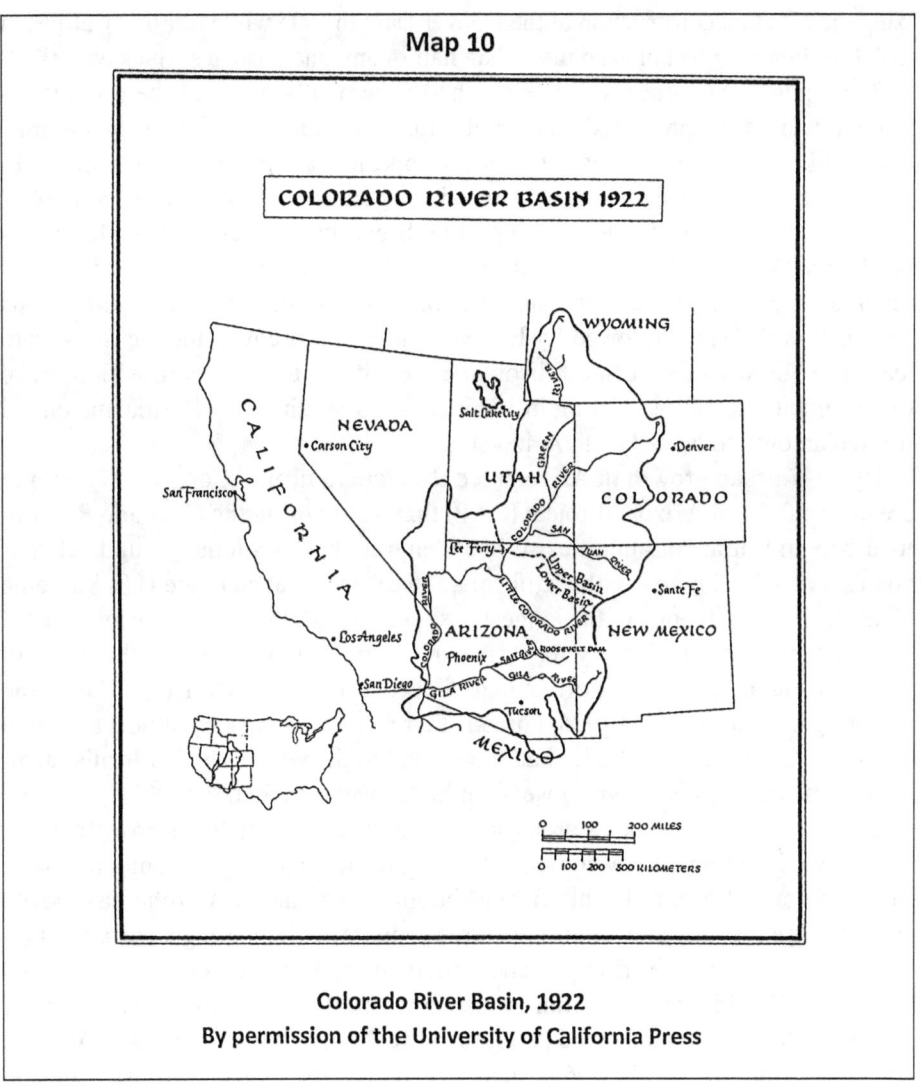

Colorado River Basin, 1922
By permission of the University of California Press

During the 1920s California had used the growing clout of its Southern Californian expansion to push for major congressional legislation to substantially increase its water supplies to the region. At first a 1922 bill seemed to give California everything it wanted with regard to exploiting the water resources of the Colorado River, but objections from Colorado Basin states led to a modified Boulder Canyon Bill authorizing the eventual construction of the Hoover Dam in 1935 while limiting California to 4.4 million acre-feet plus no more than half of any unallocated surplus water.[165]

Throughout this process Arizonans had vehemently opposed the bill, claiming that it simply represented "the whole situation from a California standpoint," and unlike the other six basin states Arizona never signed the agreement. In fact, it was true that the Hoover Dam with its enormous hydroelectric supplies was geared toward California through the direct involvement of the Metropolitan Water District of Southern California and the direction given by the newly renamed U.S. Bureau of Reclamation led, in succession, by two Californians Arthur Powell Davis followed by Elmwood Mead. Moreover, the facilities were leased to Southern California Edison and the City of Los Angeles, with most of the resultant electricity, starting in 1936, going to Southern California and only a limited amount to Nevada and Arizona.[166]

By 1947 urban growth in Arizona led the state to turn to Congress for help in creating a Central Arizona Project (CAP) that would bring the Colorado River to its urban and rural communities. When Congress balked on the grounds of Arizona's unresolved issues with California, the case was taken to the U.S. Supreme Court in 1952. After one of the longest cases on record, the court decision of 1963 proved "a tremendous victory for Arizona" by granting the state all the water of its own tributaries plus 2.8 million acre-feet from the Colorado River, California retaining the allotments of 1928. Forced as a result to cut back by almost a million acre-feet, California eventually had to respond to the worries of California farmers by embarking on its own subsequent State Water Project.[167]

Since the 1960s Arizona's prodigious demographic growth has brought about a society of "perpetual newcomers," the largest percentage of whom have come in fact from California. In this further boom environment, Arizona has moved from being a farming and natural resource economy to becoming an urban center with a strong manufacturing presence, particularly in high-tech electronics and aerospace. Yet this transformation owes a great deal to its location next to the far larger Californian economy and patterns of life. New risk-taking types of Arizona financiers emerging in the 1960s such as David Murdock came from California while the most notorious case, Charles Keating, owed his start to purchase of

---

165 Hundley [2001], 211–214.
166 Hundley [2001], 215–227.
167 Hundley [2001], 305–307; Sheridan [1995], 341–342. Both authors agree that it was a victory for Arizona, but the Arizonan Sheridan sees that victory as far more muted than the Californian Hundley.

the Californian thrift Lincoln Savings and Loan as he embarked on his Phoenix empire with grand plans "to recreate southern California in the Sonora Desert."[168]

Such enterprises did indeed represent in part the flight of people and jobs in the late twentieth century from the Los Angeles area to locations like Nevada, Utah, and Arizona, but flight of this order could also be taken as an index of the expansion of the California economy into a new cheap zone of the Pacific economy. In the last two decades official Arizona has tried to take advantage of such tendencies by luring companies from California, but the general sense is that the results have been mixed. Notwithstanding some spectacular cases of company transfer, Arizona officials now generally concede that typically California moves do not constitute relocation of headquarters but rather transfer of back-office jobs to Arizona: "California companies have proven loyal." Indeed economic and political problems in present-day Arizona have slowed down even this moderate rate of transfers. In the meantime southeastern California has become far more competitive in terms of rentals in comparison with, for example, the high rental costs in west Phoenix. It is difficult to avoid the impression that Arizona continues to dwell under the larger shadow of the "colossus" that is the southern California economy next door.[169]

Finally, the case of *Baja California* is inherently different from those of Nevada, Utah, and Arizona, given that it encompasses territory belonging to the foreign sovereign state of Mexico. This feature means that from the outset California's relation to Baja California has been fraught with problems pertaining to final national borders. Since Mexican *California* had encompassed not only Alta but also Baja California, it was not surprising that for the treaty negotiations of 1848 U.S. President James K. Polk directed his commissioner Nicholas P. Trist to demand the cession of not only Alta but also Baja California, as reflected in a draft treaty drawn up in April 1847. However, U.S. Secretary of State James Buchanan subsequently instructed Trist not to press for Baja California if the Mexicans proved obdurate. Having intercepted these instructions, Mexican diplomats sensibly decided to stand firm against ceding Baja California.[170]

The terms of the Treaty of Guadalupe Hidalgo of 1848 ending the Mexican-American War were not the final word on the border, however, since there soon followed the Gadsden Purchase of 1853 in which the United States bought land extending its Territory of New Mexico further to the south as well as gain-

---

168 Sheridan [1995], 317, 319, 330–331. Sheridan describes "modern Arizona society" as "a fragile and volatile creation – one that can never renew itself" (361).
169 Sheridan [1995], 362, and more recently Beard [2010]. The term "colossus" is used by Hundley [2001], 544.
170 Griswold del Castillo [1990], 23–24, 30–31. As Griswold del Castillo notes, Trist should therefore not have been blamed for not securing Baja California in the subsequent negotiations.

ing additional concessions. In fact, earlier money offers to a financially strapped Santa Anna, then back in power in Mexico, in exchange for further Mexican territory included a far larger sum that would have purchased Baja California as well.[171] Strong Mexican resistance to such concessions restricted the final territorial purchase to the more modest, if still substantial, Gadsden strip.[172]

Santa Anna's concern about the stability of the new U.S.-Mexican border reflected a highly volatile state of affairs involving Americans, Mexicans, and native Americans, in which dramatic adventurers from the American South called "filibusters" made bold efforts to carve out territorial domains in Mexico and central America proper. Of these, William Walker, as earlier noted, was clearly the most brazen, capturing La Paz, Baja California, in 1853 and proclaiming a new Republic of Lower California. Moving his headquarters to Ensenada, Walker then went on to declare a larger Republic of Sonora that included Baja California.[173] However Mexican troops put an end to Walker's adventure, and after later temporarily succeeding in becoming president of Nicaragua no less, Walker's filibustering career came to an abrupt end when he was captured and executed in Honduras in 1860.[174]

Walker's ghost re-emerged in part in 1910–1911 when a Mexican Liberal junta led by anarchist Ricardo Flores Magón, after setting up insurrectionary journalistic activities during 1906–1907 in the Mexican neighborhoods of Los Angeles, initiated a revolt against the Mexican dictator Porfirio Díaz with Baja California as his base.[175] The porousness of the border was reflected in the plethora of interests converging on the Liberals' campaign.[176] Their temporary seizure of

---

171 It would have included the northern part of the Mexican states of Coahuila, Chihuahua, Sonora, "and all of Lower California." Garber [1923], 91. For "Lower California" Gadsden was instructed to offer $20 million (92). See Table 2 (after 92) for the "boundary line most desired" by U.S. President Franklin Pierce which included Baja California.
172 Senators from the new U.S. state of California opposed the Gadsden Purchase precisely because it did not include Baja California (and additional Mexican territories). Kluger [2007], 500.
173 Walker's proclamation of a Republic of Lower California in 1853 was considered unhelpful to U.S. negotiators of the Gadsden Purchase since it convinced Santa Anna that the U.S. aimed at a wider annexation of Mexican territory. Garber [1923], 97.
174 For details see May [1973] and Harrison [2004].
175 See Blaisdell [1962] and Samaniego López [2006], 133–140.
176 Samaniego López notes a number of journalistic campaigns to annex Baja California in the late nineteenth and first decade of the twentieth centuries by a variety of Southern California papers. Samaniego López [2006], 135. In 1881 the Californian John C. Frémont apparently called on the U.S. Congress to purchase Baja California from Mexico in order to round up the troublesome Arizona Apache tribe (Fireman [1982], 122). Later, politicians and firms in California and Arizona used fear of a Japanese invasion of Baja California to call for its annexation (Japanese agricultural workers lived in the areas of the Valley of Mexicali and Tijuana) (175).

Mexicali was made possible by a Californian force crossing over from Californian Calexico, while their takeover of Tijuana brought in a new generation of filibusters from California intent on establishing, as the *Los Angeles Herald* put it, "The Free and Independent State of Lower California."[177] An American performer Richard Ferris even got into the act by publicizing a scheme for American annexation of California either by purchase or by force.[178]

Díaz complained to the U.S. Congress that "American filibusters" were trying to establish a "socialist" state. In fact Díaz had previously encouraged American business interests into the area by permitting foreign purchase of land and natural resources in a Baja California that continued to function formally as an indefinitely isolated territory within the state of Mexico. These interests were opposed to the separation of Baja California from Mexico because they felt their priorities better served by the Mexican government than by U.S. annexation.[179] Flores Magón for his part strongly reiterated that his revolution was not meant to separate Baja California from Mexico but to initiate a "Social Revolution" for all Mexico. In any event the Mexican military quickly retook Mexicali and Tijuana, putting an end to this curious "web of misunderstanding that linked the two Californias in 1911."[180]

What transformed Baja California from its somewhat orphaned status within Mexico proper were important economic developments during and after World War II, although an impetus for urban development had already begun as a result of the economic crisis of 1930, the year in which the territory was divided into North and South entities (the North became a state in 1952, the South in 1974).[181] World War II intensified industrial development which received a further strong impetus after 1980 with the growth of maquiladora industries, manufacturing factories along the border which acted as tariff-free exportation centers. Such formal ties with the United States as the establishment of a Free Zone in 1939 and NAFTA in 1994 accelerated the process of interdependence, along with increas-

---

177   Cited in Blaisdell [1962], 58. Less than half the force capturing Tijuana was Mexican (139).
178   Ferris' letters to his soldiers stated: "Soldiers and Citizens of the Republic of Lower California" and he called himself "president of the republic of Lower California." Blaisdell [1962], 154, 158.
179   Blaisdell [1962], 60, 32, 67.
180   Blaisdell [1962], 130, 194. For a Baja California perspective on the episode, see Aldrete [1958].
181   Marco Antonio Samaniego López in Samaniego López [2006], 131–181. As the author points out, negotiations during 1910–1945 over use of the Colorado River were important in linking the United States and Baja California. Ironically from the perspective of Californian-Mexican relations, originally the Mexican lands under consideration were being developed by a Los Angeles syndicate which included Harry Chandler, future publisher of the *Los Angeles Times*. Finally a 1944 treaty between the U.S. and Mexico agreed to 1.5 million acre-feet to go yearly to Mexico from the Colorado River. See Hundley [2001], 208, 305.

ing flows of migration to the United States. In addition, the steady increase of tourism from neighboring California locations like San Diego to Tijuana added significantly to the fusion of California and Baja California economies.[182]

Driven by an 11% annual growth rate, Baja California has seen the increase of its population from around 78,000 in 1940 to 2,487,000 in 2000, of which 48% live in Tijuana and 30% in Mexicali, both important border cities with California. Not surprisingly then, it is understandable that even from a Baja California perspective the transformation of economic Baja California is seen as necessarily intertwined with the far more powerful California economy: "bonded with the industrial dynamics of California, United States," their convergence has generated a "circle of virtuous growth in the region." Indeed, granted that such "interdependence with the Californian economy" has been the key to the dynamics of Baja California's spurt during the second half of the twentieth century, recent estimates from the Baja California side confirm that "the growth of the economy of California" will remain "the determining factor" for future growth and development of Baja California.[183]

4.

When on the Third of May 1535 that archetypal Conquistador, Hernán Cortés de Monroy y Pizarro, Marquéz del Valle de Oaxaca, presumably baptized the land before him in the bay of La Paz as "California," he became the somewhat inadvertent Father of a process and phenomenon that this volume has traced to the present through the perhaps controversial vision of a Greater California and its civilization in the offing.

As earlier noted, what is often overlooked after recording Cortés' historic triumph over the Aztec empire and subsequent mastery in Mesoamerica is that much of that career, certainly after 1521, was driven by his relentless quest for an appropriate passage to the South Seas and thus to the "Indies", as a result of which Cortés discovered and permanently located a "California" on the global map. Thanks to his intrepidity as well as prior concrete establishment of Spanish suzerainty over middle America, Cortés should be therefore regarded as no less the archetypal Globalizer.

---

182 Alejandro Mungaray Lagarda & Samaniego López in Samaniego López [2006], 183–184, 189.
183 Alejandro Mungaray Lagarda & Samaniego López in Samaniego López [2006], 201, 202, 207, 208: "la clave del crecimiento económico de Baja California se encuentra en el crecimiento de la economía de California y su interdependencia con ella, que de esta forma se constituye en el factor determinante de la estructura regional" (202).

For notwithstanding the achievement of the Magellan mission in circumnavigating the globe in 1521, it is Cortés who manifests the larger implications of seeking the completion of a persistent global presence with all the appurtenances, benign and not so benign, of power, institutions, economy, and ideology that such presence has subsequently carried. In this more extended course of the globalization process after the sixteenth century, California was the unwitting gainer from a host of external factors, of which perhaps the most relevant is the clear decline of non-Western powers and empires in the eighteenth century, specifically including the Ottomans in the eastern Mediterranean and Middle East, the Mughals in India, the Qing in China, Mataram in the East Indies, as well as the deliberate self-isolation of Tokugawa Japan after 1639. Then in the nineteenth century California, starting with the Gold Rush of 1848–1849, took off in a series of dramatic economic and geographic pulsations which rendered it the premier economy and civilization located on the west coast of the entire western hemisphere.

Ultimate beneficiaries of Cortés the Conquistador and Cortés the Globalizer, Californians are also inheritors of the less salubrious features of such imposing legacies. Yet to the critic who would prefer that such features be expunged from world history, it can only be countered that the reality of the weight of California civilization and of Greater California cannot be ignored, if only because there are responsibilities that accrue to such weight. This volume has certainly not taken on the complex sets of issues which must necessarily follow if the account presented is to be more than an exercise in feuilletonist boosterism. Necessarily it precedes the hard work to follow. But no work of such a scale and magnitude can get very far without a prior vision.

The civilization of Greater California is the vision; the civilization of present-day California is her beholder.

Epilogue:
California and the *Paradiso*

"You wish the world to believe you are the granddaughter
of Troy, the famous, and daughter of Rome."
                    Giovanni Boccaccio (to fellow Florentines), *Life of Dante*

"quand d'apparve una montagna bruna
Per la distanza, e parvemi alta tanto,
Quando veduta non m'aveva alcuna."

"When there appeared to us a Mountain, dim with distance;
And to me it seemed the highest I have ever seen."
Ulysses to Dante
                    Dante Alighieri, *Inferno*, XXV. 133–136

Somewhere in the latter stages of his tramp through the Inferno, Florentine poet Dante Alighieri – accompanied by his cicerone, the Mantuan poet Virgil – has occasion to run into none other than Ulysses (aka Odysseus). Though doomed to an eternity in the Inferno, the pagan Ulysses is at least conceded the honor of directing Dante toward the Mountain of Purgatory, atop which the poet's spiritual journey will reach its ultimate goal by ascending directly into the celestial Paradise under the guidance of his divine intercessor Beatrice.

This interesting, some would argue ultimate, work of faith conceived by medieval Christendom has laid permanent proprietary claims over the very notion of "Paradise" – notwithstanding, as we earlier noted, the word's origins (*pairidaeza*) in pre-Christian Avestan-Pahlavi Persia and practical instantiations in Cyrus the Great's installations for his Achaemenid Empire.[1] Rather than ignoring such claims, let us call upon Dante's monumental design, in order, however, to reach some very different conclusions that favor identification of California with our "Mountain of Paradise" label.

As Dante commentators have regularly noted, Dante's account leading to his preferred Paradiso may arise from familiar medieval concerns but it also contains features original with him. In the first place, Dante's story of Ulysses' quest and

---

[1] See the basis for the Greek "paradeisos" from which West European versions of "paradise" are derived, as well as further details, in Moynihan [1979], 1–2. Giamatti [1966], 11–12, notes its use in Greek to mean "park" by citing Xenophon's *Anabasis*: "There Cyrus had a palace and a large park full of wild animals." Giamatti also traces the Herbew *pard's* from the same Persian source as the Greek.

sighting of the Mountain of Purgatory (*il dilettoso monte*) is entirely his invention.[2] Leaving the Latin town of Gaieta (named after Aeneas' nurse), Dante's Ulysses inspires his crew to embark on a journey into the unknown by timely reminders to them that they are not brutes but follow "virtue and knowledge" (*virtute a coscenza*).[3] Passing Seville ("Sibilia") and Ceuta ("Setta"), the hardy ship and crew go through the narrow pass of the Pillars of Hercules to enter for the first time the "deep open sea" (*l'alto mare aperto*) where no humans dwell. Eventually – assuming that the position of the stars they follow is an accurate guide – they even cross the equator and are in wholly unchartered waters when they joyfully espy the highest mountain they have ever seen. Unfortunately a tempest, presumably sent by a greater Power ("as pleased another"), throws them into a whirlpool which sucks the entire ship and crew down to their present Infernal address.[4]

In the second place, far from treating them as fictions and allegories, Dante regards his Eden and the terrestrial paradise atop this Mountain of Purgatory as occupying an actual geographic location on earth. If the center of the globe is Jerusalem, then Eden bears a perfect antipodal relation to it and must take up a place directly opposite Jerusalem. As Charles Singleton has pointed out, the biblical account supports Dante's assumption that Satan fell to the southern side of the globe, causing a huge displacement in the waters which produced the Mountain of Purgatory with Eden at its peak. Hence, at least according to Dante's seamanship, this Mountain must constitute an isle "somewhere, say, in our South Pacific."[5]

---

[2] Dante Alighieri [1900] *Inferno*, I.77 and the commentary on 297 (100–142). The reader should assume that Ulysses' tale, being told in Greek, would be communicated directly to Virgil, who presumably knew Greek, whereas the pilgrim Dante did not. *Inferno*, xxvi.73–75 and 297 (73–75),

[3] This particular passage from the *Divine Comedy*, fondly quoted by Primo Levi when he was an inmate at the Auschwitz death camp, acted as a trumpet-like reminder to Levi of his own humanity despite the crushing camp conditions. See "Il canto di Ulisse," in Levi [1958], 143–144; more generally 138–145.

[4] Dante Alighieri [1900], *Inferno*, XXVI.90–142. Masciandaro [1991] argues that Ulysses was also driven by "the nostalgia for Eden" (137). Given that Ulysses is a mythical character, Singleton [1977], 147, infers that the pilgrim Dante is the first *human* to spot the Mountain of Purgatory.

[5] Singleton [1977], 143–148. Singleton refers to texts by Augustine, Aquinas, and Albertus Magnus which support Dante's position of a real geographic location for Eden, noting that for Albertus Magnus the Christian paradise occupies the highest location on earth: while it does not quite reach up to the lunar sphere proper, it does participate in the properties of the Moon (142–144). Singleton adds that Adam and Eve must have been expelled from Eden to a place directly opposite Eden, which must therefore be Palestine or Mesopotamia (153). See also Dronke [1984]: "What is unusual in Dante's conception is that he sets both purgatory and Eden in the Antipodes. It is a deliberate symmetry in his image of the world: the earthly paradise, scene of the fall, must be exactly opposite Jerusalem, scene of the redemption" (390).

In the third place, Dante goes to considerable lengths to claim a certain autonomous status for his earthly paradise no less than for the celestial paradise to which his pilgrim aspires. In a previous work *De Monarchia*, Dante had already made clear that the "terrestrial paradise" and the "celestial paradise" constituted two separate goals; otherwise he would have had to concede that the "Emperor" – Dante's personal preference – who rules in the "terrestrial" sphere (*per terrestrem paradisum*) was subordinate to the "Pope," ruler of the "celestial" (*per paradisum celestem*).[6] This concern is not paramount in the *Divine Comedy*, but as has been noted, "more than any other medieval thinker" Dante does his best to see the strictly human domain as valid in its own right: the pilgrim must "celebrate" the earthly paradise before going on to the "celestial paradise," even though "in a certain sense" (*quodam modo*) human felicity is "ordered" to "immortal felicity."[7] As a result, "the pivotal landscape of the poem remains ... the terrestrial paradise."[8]

And, finally,[9] this "pivotal" landscape is embodied in the appearance of one of Dante's most memorable inventions. A lovely young woman – later identified as "Matelda" – "plays a central role" for Dante's pilgrimage by introducing him into the pure garden of the earthly paradise.[10] She rounds up all the characteristics and gestures of that landscape through her dancing, singing, gathering of flowers, and general joyfulness and gaiety, for she is a young virgin fully in the state of love. In her person are united the earthly and the heavenly, the active as well as the contemplative, the natural and the divine: she is human nature before sin, the crowning manifestation of that *paradisus voluptatis*, the original Eden.[11] Commentators liken Dante's Matelda to the genre of the *pastorella* whose Arcadian features highlighted the poets' favored love-object of the "shepherdess"; yet, as has been equally noted, Dante's own evocation of his Matelda, however much it may be indebted to such precedents, is more about the traits of an aristocrat, a

---

6   Singleton [1977], 266; Dante Alighieri [1998], 312–325 (3.15).
7   Following in detail the analysis by Dronke [1984], 395–396. Although Dante's position does not seem completely coherent, Dronke's emphasis that Dante at least did his best to give full validity to the earthly or human paradise is shared by other commentators.
8   Giamatti [1966], 118.
9   A fifth facet of Dante's originality that we will not consider is his derivation of the stream in his Eden from a divine source (Heaven) to produce the double stream *Lethe* (forgetfulness) and *Eunoia* (well-remembrance). Dronke [1984], 402; Dante Alighieri [1901], *Purgatorio*, XXVIII.121.
10 Giamatti [1966], 110.
11 Singleton [1977], 211, Dronke [1984], 405. For further clarification of this passage I am indebted to Olivia Wise.

queen, indeed a "pagan goddess," than a mere rustic shepherdess.[12] Being both Proserpine and Venus proper, gentle and mockingly provocative, she immediately fires Dante into falling in love with her and craving to possess her in blissful, sensuous union.[13]

It is exactly at this crossroads that one may part ways with Dante's own path toward Beatrice and the "celestial paradise" that she confers. Matelda grants Dante a taste of what lies beyond her, but for Dante's own trajectory she is ultimately no more than a handmaiden to Beatrice's promise of a fully Catholic Christian arrival. Once Matelda takes him across the stream to the more formidable Beatrice, Dante instantly loses his interest in the former and plunges into the elaborate liturgical, processional and ideological symbology of the final cantos of the *Purgatorio*.[14]

Dante may prefer to move beyond his own stirring version of an "earthly paradise" to the particulars of his medieval commitment to Christian faith, but this need not be the only option. Instead one may choose to embrace Matelda and the "terrestrial paradise" in order to commit to the ramifications of the myth of a pagan golden age that had once also motivated the young author of the *Vita Nuova*: "Those who in antiquity poetized/ about the age of gold and its felicitous state,/ perhaps, *on Parnassus*, they dreamt of this spot."[15] As Dante himself must concede, seen in a non-Christian context the Mountain of Purgatory is akin to the ancients' Parnassus where Virgilian Reason and the Justice of the philosophers and poets once ruled.[16]

Indeed Dante's own reading of the "terrestrial paradise" belongs to a broader body of prior pagan as well as Christian ideals converging images of late-classical Bowers of Venus with the Christian Garden topping a luminous mountain.[17]

---

12 Dronke [1984], 397–398, 404. Dronke describes her as "this innocent yet deeply sensual girl, who for him [Dante] evokes a pagan paradise" (398) and "a woman of spellbinding physical seductiveness, under whose spell Dante falls" (400). Of course, as in the case of Elizabeth I of England, one can be both "shepherdess" and "queen." See Yates [1975], 60–64.

13 Dante Alighieri [1901], *Purgatorio*, XXVIII.49–51, 64–66, XXIX.1. Dronke [1984], 404, on Matelda's "gaily provocative" manner. As Singleton [1977], 211, puts it, even Venus is not more in love than Matelda. See also Giamatti [1966]. 110, 119.

14 See in general Masciandaro [1991, Lansing [1994], and Singleton [1977], 218.

15 Dante Alighieri [1901], *Purgatorio*, XXVIII.139–141 (emphasis added).

16 Singleton [1977], 574. Characteristically, Dante admirers write patronizingly that "at best" the pagans held to a myth of the golden age which however lacked the "sanctifying" grace of Dantean Christianity, a condescension that merely exposes their impoverished understanding of Ancient sensibilities. Singleton [1977], 261. Notwithstanding, the "celestial Athens" continues to serve as a Dantean model: "the celestial Athens, the utopian harmony of the three pagan schools." Masciandaro [1991], 62.

17 Lansing [1994], 102. Significantly Dante's entry into the terrestrial paradise is announced by the dawn appearance of the star Venus or "Cytherea" ("Citerea"). Dante [1901], *Purgatorio*,

Early Renaissance poets like Petrarch conceded that such a grove or enclosure was sacred in its dedication to the goddess Venus – so long as the Christian "Truth" was not yet known. Increasingly, however, subsequent Renaissance poets began to regard the Garden as potentially dangerous: "Venus has begun to acquire some of the traits of Circe, her isle of Cyprus those of Circe's island of Aeaea."[18] Inheriting a great deal of such mythological allusions, Dante, it seems clear, manages to make colorful use of them while keeping to the purity of Matelda's sensuality as the very quintessence of an innocent "springtime" (*primavera*),[19] but far from frightening off potential votaries, the more dangerous elements contained in such references may have served to lure future generations of adventurers and explorers to follow in effect Dante's cartographic hints of a Mountain of Paradise located somewhere in the fabled South Seas: the discovery of the New World came to form a more palpable "record of the quest for happiness and innocence in the great unspoiled garden."[20] And as we have already claimed on several occasions, "California" is at the core of the web of allusions and imaginative geographies driving these quests.

*

"Know that to the right hand of the Indies was an island called California, very near to the region of the Terrestrial Paradise" (*a la parte del Paraiso terrenal*)[21] – according to its original mythical identification, California may not have been touted as the original terrestrial paradise itself, but it was certainly placed in the closest intimacy with it. If Dante's Ulysses embarks on his epochal voyage by leaving Circe, his historical successors end up "reaching" and "naming" an island of "Circe."[22] "Described as an enchantress – Circe, or one of the Sirens or the Lorelei," California marks the European imaginal's landfall on the most

---

XXVII, 94–96. For the larger aesthetic-political significance of the "cytherean" motif in cultural history, see Chytry [2005] and [2009].
18   Following Giamatti [1966], 82–85, 126, 126–128, 126 (note 2).
19   "…here/spring is everlasting, and every kind of fruit; this is the nectar of which each one speaks." Dante Alighieri [1901], *Purgatorio*, XXVIII.142–144. Dronke [1984], 397. Dronke argues that this *primavera* is "forever" but also that it is a "paradise lost" (405).
20   Giamatti [1966], 6.
21   Montalvo [2003], 727.
22   Dante Alighieri [1900], *Inferno*, XXVI.91. The Siren ("Sirene") is also mentioned for luring Ulysses away from "his wandering way." Dante Alighieri [1901], *Purgatorio*, XIX,22. For Giamatti [1966], 6, Dante's Matelda belongs to the line of Eve while the later Renaissance enchanted gardens "are lineal descendants of Homer's Circe." Still, it is often overlooked that although Homer's Circe is indeed a sorceress who performs debilitating spells on Odysseus' crew, ultimately she is very helpful to him in his odyssey and is always recognized by him as a "god" (θεόν), e. g. *Odyssey*, X.573.

"dangerous" of realms: the "Land of the Great Feminie" earlier celebrated in the presumed medieval messages of Prester John.[23]

Circe, Venus, the Great Feminie – what more appropriate legacy for a future Queen of California named Calafía? Certainly what remains clear in such evocations is that from Christopher Columbus to Hernán Cortés[24] these inducements of an earthly paradise located somewhere along a long chain of islands toward the "Hesperia" of the South Seas played its role in powerfully driving these explorers to discover and baptize a concrete body of land – in almost every significant sense a proper island – as "California."

To the lament that particularly after Cortés this tradition would become fatally secularized, Kevin Starr's monumental demonstration of the persistence of the motif of a "California Dream" acts as a clear and definite riposte. Still, it may be reasonably urged that notwithstanding possible comparisons on these levels of an "earthly paradise," the ultimate thrust of Dante's pilgrimage is after all the "celestial paradise" about which nothing so far has been endorsed on behalf of California. In the *Paradiso* proper Dante's Beatrice leads him through the familiar medieval cosmology of planets, sun, fixed stars, primum mobile and empyrean (a cosmology common to Islam no less than to Christendom). What possible substitute can the discovered Mountain of Paradise as California suggest?

During the exact same 1530s decade when California was being discovered and named, Nicolaus Copernicus was embarking on the final version of his heliocentric theory of the heavens with the aid of Georg Joachim Rheticus.[25] Whatever the deeper spiritual ramifications of his theory for Copernicus himself, Copernicus' most radical spokesman Giordano Bruno soon turned heliocentricity into a cosmic evangelium directly challenging the primacy of the Church.[26] Bruno experienced the salvational-religious component of Copernicus' heliocentricity by undergoing liberation out of the narrow shell of medieval cosmology into the dazzling "open spaces and inexhaustible treasures of the ever-changing, eternal and infinite universe."[27] It is just this spirituality and religiosity inspired by Copernicus and Bruno that California can legitimately claim.

---

23   Polk [1991], 13, 38–41.
24   For Columbus' obsession with finding the earthly paradise, see the details in Polk [1991], 43–50.
25   The heliocentric theory was first developed around 1503–1513, Copernicus' manuscript was "essentially finished by 1536," and Rheticus' arrival in 1539 helped to provide the final push for publication of the *De Revolutionibus Orbium Coelestium* (1543) by 1540. See the details in Repcheck [2007],52, 80, 132, 149.
26   Details in Chytry [2005], 71–73, and Blumenberg [1987], 353–376.
27   Koyré [1957], 43.

In his captivating essay "Unto the Stars Themselves," Kevin Starr recounts the steps by which California became the world center for modern astronomical investigation and insight.[28] Historian Carey McWilliams had already noted that thanks to "the exceptional environment of California," a series of Californian entrepreneurs first thought up the idea of mountains as appropriate sites for full-scale observatories: from the James Lick Observatory in Northern California to the Mount Wilson and Mount Palomar Observatories realized by the Pasadena astronomer George Ellery Hale in Southern California, the range of mountains geophysically making up the Californian Mountain of Paradise served as concretely ideal sites for an unprecedented penetration by humankind into the depths of the cosmos.[29] What Starr's account significantly adds is the profound spirituality, indeed religiosity, driving such cosmic pioneers. There atop the Californian Mountain of Paradise known as Mount Wilson, at some 5,700 feet above the Los Angeles Basin and some 30 miles from the Pacific Ocean, astronomer Edwin Hubble was enabled to confirm for the first time in history the existence of multiple galaxies – of which our Milky Way is but one – and the overall expanding character of the cosmos – two fundamental transformations in the human reading of the celestial dimension.[30] Nothing suggested by Dante's interpretation of the heavenly spheres compares with such genuinely awe-inspiring cosmic discoveries.

It will be countered that the two visions cannot be strictly compared since the Dantean is primarily meant to be symbolic or allegorical while the modern Californian account of the heavens is simply one facet in a consistently secularizing science of nature. Yet Dante also sincerely believed that his account of the heavens, the celestial Paradiso revealed by Beatrice to Dante, offered an accurate cosmographic mapping, and for their part modern investigators atop the mountains of California were themselves driven by higher spiritual aspirations accompanied by the satisfying joy of contemplating the true immensity of the cosmos. Indeed, at least in one prominent case, they were all too aware of, and grateful for, the affinity of their vocation with Dante and the *Divine Comedy* proper. The young Italian student Giorgio Abetti recalls that on an occasion when George Ellery Hale led him up a trail to the top of Mount Wilson, Hale recited "with perfect accent" verses from the *Divine Comedy* that included the revealing line "lo sommo er'alto che vincea la vista" – "the summit was so high that it overcame sight" – referring specifically to Dante's Mountain of Purgatory.[31]

---

28 Starr [1997], 61–89.
29 See McWilliams' study "Ladder to the Stars," in McWilliams [1949], 251,252,256–257.
30 For Hubble, see in general Christianson [1995].
31 Dante Alighieri [1901], *Purgatorio*, IV.40. Recorded in Wright [1994], 232 (Wright incorrectly writes "commo" instead of "sommo"). A great admirer of Galileo, Hale later also had occasion

Hale's spiritual commitment to this "celestial paradise" and to his Egyptian, Persian, Babylonian and Hellenic predecessors is confirmed by his construction of a monastic residence on Mount Wilson with all the appurtenances of liturgy and ritual that were intended to underscore the spiritual lessons of the "new and vast conception of an ordered cosmos."[32] Accordingly, having departed from Dante's itinerary by highlighting the centrality of "Matelda" and the focality of her "earthly paradise," one may also go on to claim that California as candidate for this "*terrestrial* paradise" upholds as well the range of historic mountain sites from which modernity has succeeded in gazing into and learning about this stunningly expansive "*celestial* paradise," the scope and beauty of which neither Dante nor his Beatrice had the faintest premonition.

Yet it is perhaps permissible to argue that such an alternate "celestial paradise" first made accessible by Californian astronomers still belongs in a larger sense to the Dantean tradition. For thanks to Dante Alighieri, it has become increasingly commonplace to associate each individual's pilgrimage toward culture, salvation, and enlightenment with reverence toward the "starry heavens." In the final analysis it is by reaffirming the primacy of contemplation of these "starry heavens," as Anaxagoras and Aristotle once located the justification for human existence on this planet, that a civilization merits the status of world civilization.[33] And all three of Dante's *cantiche* end by disclosing to the seeker the luminous realm of the stars: from the *Inferno* "we issued out again to see the stars" (*quindi uscimmo a riveder le stele*), from the *Purgatorio* "I came back ... pure and ready to mount to the stars" (*io ritornai ... puro e disposto a salire alle stele*), until, in the final memorable words of the *Paradiso* – words of paramount resonance to this civilization of a Greater California in the making – the Dantean pilgrim comes face to face with the "Love that moves the sun and the other stars":

l'amor che move il sole e l'altre stele.[34]

---

     to see the heavens through Galileo's original telescope kept at Arcetri near Florence (346).

32   Hale, cited in Starr [1997], 79. As Starr emphasizes, "Hale sought to create a college of astronomy in direct succession to those of ancient Mesopotamia, Egypt, or Greece, with all that such mystic associations implied for Hale and his entire generation....Hale became especially sensitive to the linkage *between religion and astronomy* in Egyptian culture" (emphasis added).

33   For the larger connection between "Matelda" and the "star-maiden" Astraea or Virgo, see Singleton [1977], 184–203; more generally Yates [1975].

34   Dante Alighieri [1900], *Inferno*, XXXIV.39; [1901], *Purgatorio*, XXXIII.142, 145; [1899], *Paradiso*, XXXIII.145.

Bibliography

Abel, Angelika [2003]. *Thomas Mann im Exil: Zum zeitgeschichtlichen Hintergrund der Emigration* (Munich: Wilhelm Fink).
Abbott, Carl [1993], *The Metropolitan Frontier: Cities in the Modern American West* (Tucson, AZ: University of Arizona Press).
Aesthesis [2007–2010]. *International Journal of Art and Aesthetics in Management and Organizational Life* (2007–2010) (University of Essex, UK).
Aldrete, Enrique [1958]. *Baja California heroica: episodios de la invasión filibustera-magonista de 1911* (Mexico City, Mexico: Frumentum).
Allan, Robin [1999]. *Walt Disney and Europe: European Influences on the Animated Feature Films of Walt Disney* (Bloomington, IN: Indiana University Press).
Alvarado, Juan Bautista [1876]. *Historia de California* (Manuscript Banc C-D, Bancroft Library, University of California, Berkeley). 5 vols.
Anger, Kenneth [1965]. *Hollywood Babylon* (Phoeniz, AZ: Associated Professional Services).
Anger, Kenneth [1984]. *Kenneth Anger's Hollywood Babylon II* (New York, NY: Dutton).
Arrington, Leonard J. [1958]. *Great Basin Kingdom: An Economic History of the Latter-day Saints 1830–1900* (Cambridge, MA: Harvard University Press).
Austin, Rob & Lee Devin [2003]. *Artful Making: What Managers Need to Know about How Artists Work* (New York, NY: Prentice-Hall).
Avalle-Arce, Juan Bautista [1990]. *Amadís de Gaula: el primitivo y el de Montalvo* (Mexico: Fundo de Cultura Económica).
Baker, Carlos [1996]. *Emerson among the Eccentrics: A Group Portrait* (New York, NY: Viking).
Bahr, Ehrhard [2007]. *Weimar on the Pacific: German Exile Culture in Los Angeles and the Crisis of Modernism* (Berkeley, CA: University of California Press).
Bakker, Elna S. [1971]. *An Island Called California: An Ecological Introduction to its Natural Communities* (Berkeley, CA: University of California Press).
Balbus, Isaac D. [1982]. *Marxism and Domination: A Neo-Hegelian, Feminist, Psychoanalytic Theory of Sexual, Political and Technological Liberation* (Princeton, NJ: Princeton University Press).

Bardhan, Ashok Deo, Dwight M. Jaffee & Cynthia A. Kroll [2004]. *Globalization and a High-Tech Economy: California, the United States and Beyond* (Boston, MA: Kluwer).

Barron, Stephanie; Sherrie Bernstein & Ilene Susan Fort (eds.) [2000]. *Made in California: Arts, Image, and Identity, 1900–2000* (Berkeley, CA: University of California Press).

Bartl, Andrea [1996]. *Geistige Atemräume: Auswirkungen des Exils auf Heinrich Manns* Empfang bei der Welt, *Franz Werfels* Stern der Ungeborenen *und Hermann Hesses* Das Glasperlenspiel (Bonn: Bouvier Verlag).

Baudrillard, Jean [1986]. *Amérique* (Paris: Bernard Grasset).

Beard, Betty [2010]. "California on the Mind of Arizona Leaders" (July 25, 2010), *The Arizona Republic*.

Beebe, Rose Marie & Robert M. Senkewicz (eds.) [2001]. *Lands of Promise and Despair: Chronicles of Early California, 1535–1846* (Berkeley, CA: Heyday Books).

Beidleman, Richard G. [2006]. *California's Frontier Naturalists* (Berkeley, CA: University of California Press).

Bennington, Geoffrey & Jacques Derrida [1993]. *Jacques Derrida* (Chicago, IL: University of Chicago Press), transl.

Benoît de Sainte-Maure [1998]. *Le Roman de Troie* (Paris: Le Livre de Poche).

Berlin, Isaiah [1979]. "Nationalism: Past Neglect and Present Power" (1978), in *Against the Current: Essays in the History of Ideas* (Harmondsworth, UK: Penguin).

Bernbach, Udo [1994]. *Der Wahn des Gesamtkunstwerks: Richard Wagners politisch-ästhetische Utopie* (Frankfurt: Fischer).

Blaisdell, Lowell L. [1962]. *The Desert Revolution: Baja California, 1911* (Madison, WI: University of Wisconsin Press).

Blau, Evelyne [1995]. *Krishnamurti: 100 Years* (New York, NY: Stewart, Taburi and Chang).

Blumenberg, Hans [1987]. *The Genesis of the Copernican World* (Cambridge, MA: The MIT Press, 1975), transl.

Boissonnade, P. [1923]. *Du Nouveau sur la Chanson de Roland* (Paris: Librarie Ancienne Honoré Champion, 1923).

Bowers, Michael W. [2006]. *The Sagebrush State: Nevada's History, Government, and Politics* (Reno, NV: University of Nevada Press), 3rd ed.

Brands, H. W. [2002]. *The Age of Gold: The California Gold Rush and the New American Dream* (New York, NY: Doubleday).

Brecht, Bertolt [1966]. *Galileo* (New York, NY: Grove, 1952), Charles Laughton transl.

Brecht, Bertolt [1967]. *Gesammelte Werke* (Frankfurt: Suhrkamp), Vol. 10.

Brecht, Bertolt [1993]. *Journals 1934–1955* (New York, NY: Routledge, 1973), transl.
Brode, Douglas [2004]. *From Walt to Woodstock: How Disney Created the Counterculture* (Austin, TX: University of Texas Press).
Brown, Justine [2002]. *Hollywood Utopia* (Vancouver, Canada: New Star Books).
Brown, Steven E. F. [2011]. "Booming Silicon Valley GDP Growth leaves San Francisco Behind (13 September 2011)," *San Francisco Business Times*.
Bürgin, Hans & Hans-Otto Mayer [1965]. *Thomas Mann: Eine Chronik seines Lebens* (Frankfurt: S. Fischer).
Burns, John F. & Richard J. Orsi (eds.) [2003]. *Taming the Elephant: Politics, Government, and Law in Pioneer California* (Berkeley, CA: University of California Press).
Burrus, Ernest J. [1965]. *Kino and the Cartography of Northwestern New Spain* (Tucson, AZ: Arizona Historical Society).
California Budget Project [2005]. "Planning for California's Future: The State's Population is Growing, Aging, and Becoming More Diverse" (Sacramento, CA: Budget Backgrounder).
California Institute for Federal Policy Research [2003]. "California Institute Special Report: California's Balance of Payments with the Federal Treasury, Fiscal Years 1981–2002) (17 October 2003)," www.callinst.org/piubs/balrpt02.htm.
California Institute of the Arts [2005–2009]. "The Cal Arts Story Produced for the California Institute of the Arts by Walt Disney Productions" (film/video).
Canemaker, John [2009]. "Speech for Walt Disney Family Museum Newsletter."
Caputo, John D. [1997]. *The Prayers and Tears of Jacques Derrida: Religion without Religion* (Bloomington, IN: Indiana University Press).
Carnoy, A. [1922]. "Paradis d'Orient – Paradis d'Occident," *Le Muséon*, 35: 213–239.
Carroll, David (ed.) [1990]. *The States of 'Theory': History, Arts, and Critical Discourse* (New York, NY: Columbia University Press).
Casper, Drew [2007]. *Postwar Hollywood, 1946–1962* (Malden, MA: Blackwell).
Cassidy, David C. [2005]. *J. Robert Oppenheimer and the American Century* (New York, NY: Pi Press).
Castells, Manuel [2001]. *The Internet Galaxy: Reflections on the Internet, Business and Society* (Oxford: Oxford University Press).
Christianson, Gale E. [1995]. *Edwin Hubble: Marine of the Nebulae* (New York, NY: Farrar, Straus and Giroux).
Chytry, Josef [1989]. *The Aesthetic State: A Quest in Modern German Thought* (Berkeley, CA: University of California Press).
Chytry, Josef [2005]. *Cytherica: Aesthetic-Political Essays in an Aphrodisian Key* (New York, NY: Peter Lang).

Chytry, Josef [2008]. "California Civilization and European Speculative Thought: An Evolving Relationship," *California History*, 85:4, 50–69, 73–75.

Chytry, Josef [2009]. *Unis vers Cythère: Aesthetic-Political Investigations in Polis Thought and the Artful Firm* (New York, NY: Peter Lang).

Clendenning, John [1985]. *The Life and Thought of Josiah Royce* (Madison, WI: University of Wisconsin Press).

CNNMoney [2013]. "California could be the next Oil Boom State" (14 January 2013)."

Cook, Bruce [1983]. *Brecht in Exile* (New York, NY: Holt, Rinehart & Winston).

Cortés, Hernán [1986]. *Hernán Cortés: Letters from Mexico* (New Haven, CT: Yale University Press). Anthony Pagden (transl.).

Covarrubias, Miguel [1946]. *Mexico South: The Isthmus of Tehuantepec* (New York, NY: Alfred A. Knopf).

Crawford, Dorothy Lamb [2009]. *A Windfall of Musicians: Hitler's Émigrés and Exiles in Southern California* (New Haven, CT: Yale University Press).

Dante Alighieri [1899]. *The Paradiso of Dante Alighieri* (London: Dent), text and transl.

Dante Alighieri [1900]. *The Inferno of Dante Alighieri* (London: Dent), text and transl.

Dante Alighieri [1901]. *The Purgatorio of Dante Alighieri* (London: Dent), text and transl.

Dante Alighieri [1998]. *Dante's Monarchia* (Toronto, CA: Pontifical Institute of Mediaeval Studies), text and transl.

Dares the Phrygian [1873]. *De Excidio Troiae Historia* (Leipzig: Teubner).

Davis, Erik [2006]. *The Visionary State: A Journey through California's Spiritual Landscape* (San Francisco, CA: Chronicle Books).

Davis, Mike [1990]. *Ecology of Fear: Los Angeles and the Imagination of Disaster* (New York, NY: Vintage).

Davis, Ronald L. [1993]. *The Glamour Factory: Inside Hollywood's Big Studio System* (Dallas, TX: Southern Methodist University Press).

Demaray, John G. [1987]. *Dante and the Book of the Cosmos* (Philadelphia, PA: The American Philosophical Society).

Derrida, Jacques [1989]. *Of Spirit: Heidegger and the Question* (Chicago, IL: University of Chicago Press, 1987), transl.

Derrida, Jacques [1990]. "Some Statements and Truisms about Neologisms: Newisms, Postisms, Parasitisms, and other small Seismisms," in Carroll [1990], 63–94.

Derrida, Jacques [1994]. *Specters of Marx: The State of the Debt, the Work of Mourning, and the New International* (New York: Routledge, 1993), transl.

Derrida, Jacques [1995a]. *Points ... Interviews, 1974–1994* (Stanford, CA: Stanford University Press, 1992), transl.
Derrida, Jacques [1995b]. *The Gift of Death* (Chicago, IL: University of Chicago Press, 1992), transl.
Derrida, Jacques [1997]. *Politics of Friendship* (London, Verso, 1994), transl.
Derrida, Jacques [2002]. *Acts of Religion* (New York, NY: Routledge), transl.
Dewitt, Howard A. [1989]. *Readings in California Civilization: Interpretive Issues* (Dubuque, IA: Kendall/Hunt Publishing Co.), 2nd ed.
Díaz del Castillo, Bernal [1963]. *The Conquest of New Spain* (Harmondsworth, UK: Penguin), transl.
Disneyland Park (Anaheim) [2009]. http://en/wikipedia.org/wiki/Disneyland_Park_(Anaheim).
Dobson, John [1999]. *The Art of Management and the Aesthetic Manager: The Coming Way of Business* (Westport, CT: Quorum).
Drinkwater, John [1931]. *The Life and Adventures of Carl Laemmle* (New York, NY: Putnam's).
Dronke, Peter [1984]. "Dante's Earthly Paradise: Towards an Interpretation of *Purgatorio* XXVIII," in *The Medieval Poet and his World* (Rome: Edizioni di Storia e Letteratura), 388–405.
Dronke, Peter [1997]. *Dante's Second Love: The Originality and the Contexts of the Convivio* (Exeter, UK: The Society for Italian Studies).
Dunlop, Beth [1006]. *Building a Dream: The Art of Disney Architecture* (New York, NY: Henry N. Abrams).
Dyn [1943]. "Dyn: The Review of Modern Art," 4:5 (The Amerindian Number).
Dynaton Reviewed [1977]. Review of 1951 show at San Francisco Museum of Modern Art: Lee Mullican, Gordon Onslow Ford, Wolfgang Paalen (San Francisco, CA: Gallery Paule Anglim).
Emerson, Ralph Waldo [1981]. *The Portable Emerson* (New York, NY: Penguin), new ed.
Encyclopedia of California [1984]. *Encyclopedia of California* (New York, NY: Somerset).
Engelbert, Omer [1956]. *The Last of the Conquistadors: Junípero Serra (1713–1784)* (New York, NY: Harcourt, Brace), transl.
Epstein, Edward Jay [2005]. *The Big Picture: The New Logic of Money and Power in Hollywood* (New York, NY: Random House).
Eribon, Didier [1991]. *Michel Foucault* (Cambridge, MA: Harvard University Press, 1989), transl.
Fagan, Brain M [2003]. *Before California; An Archaeologist Looks at our Earliest Inhabitants* (Lanham, MD: Rowman & Littlefield).

Fireman, Bert M. [1982]. *Arizona: Historic Land* (New York, NY: Alfred A. Knopf).
Foglesong, Richard E. [2001]. *Married to the Mouse: Walt Disney World and Orlando* (New Haven, CT: Yale University Press).
Forbes, Alexander [1839]. *California: A History of Upper and Lower California* (San Francisco, CA: John Henry Nash, 1937).
Foucault, Michel [1978]. *The History of Sexuality: An Introduction* (New York, NY: Vintage, 1976), Vol. 1, transl.
Foucault, Michel [1979]. *Discipline and Punish: The Birth of the Prison* (New York, NY: Vintage, 1975), transl.
Foucault, Michel [1985]. *The Use of Pleasure* (New York, NY: Random House, 1984), transl.
Foucault, Michel [1986]. *The Care of the Self* (New York, NY: Pantheon, 1984), transl.
Foucault, Michel [1988]. Politics, *Philosophy, Culture: Interviews and other Writings 1977–1984* (New York, NY: Routledge), transl.
Foucault, Michel [1997-]. *The Essential Works of Michel Foucault 1954–1984* (New York, NY: The Free Press), Paul Rabinow, series editor. Vols 1,2,3 to date, transl.
Foucault, Michel [2003]. *The Essential Foucault: Selections from the Essential Works of Foucault 1954–1984* (New York, NY: The New Press, 1994), transl.
Francis, Jessie Davies [1936]. *An Economic and Social History of Mexican California (1822–1846)*, Vol. 1 (Ph.D. dissertation, University of California, Berkeley).
Francis, Mark & Andreas Reimann [1999]. *The California Landscape Garden: Ecology, Culture, and Design* (Berkeley, CA: University of California Press).
Frazer, R. M., Jr. [transl.] [1966]. *The Trojan War: The Chronicles of Dictys of Crete and Dares the Phrygian* (Bloomington, IN: Indiana University Press).
Friedrich, Otto [1986]. *City of Nets: A Portrait of Hollywood in the 1940s* (New York, NY: Harper & Row).
Gabler, Neal [1988]. *An Empire of their Own: How the Jews Invented Hollywood* (New York, NY: Crown).
Gabler, Neal [2006]. *Walt Disney: The Triumph of the American Imagination* (New York, NY: Alfred A. Knopf).
Garber, Paul Neff [1923]. *The Gadsden Treaty* (Philadelphia, PA: Press of the University of Pennsylvania).
Geoffrey of Monmouth [1958]. *History of the Kings of Britain* (New York, NY: Dutton). Sebastian Evans (transl.).
Giamatti, A. Bartlett [1966]. *The Earthly Paradise and the Renaissance Epic* (Princeton, NJ: Princeton University Press).

Goldsborough, James O. [1993]. "California's Foreign Policy," *Foreign Affairs* (Spring), 88–95.

Gopnik, Alison [2009]. *The Philosophical Baby: What Children's Minds Tell Us about Truth, Love, and the Meaning of Life* (New York, NY: Farrar, Straus and Giroux).

Gordon, Larry [2012]. "A Collection that Identifies California as a World Apart," *Los Angeles Times* (16 December 2012).

Greenwalt, Emmett A. [1955]. *California Utopia: Point Loma 1897–1942* (San Diego, CA: Point Loma Publications), 2nd ed.

Griswold de Castillo, Richard [1990]. *The Treaty of Guadalupe Hidalgo: A Legacy of Conflict* (Norman, OK: University of Oklahoma Press).

Gruen, Victor [1964]. *The Heart of our Cities; The Urban Crisis: Diagnosis and Cure* (New York, NY: Simon & Schuster).

Guillet de Monthoux, Pierre [2004]. *The Art Firm: Aesthetic Management and Metaphysical Marketing from Wagner to Wilson* (Stanford, CA: Stanford Business Books).

Gutiérrez, Ramón A. & Richard J. Orsi (eds.) [1998]. *Contested Eden: California Before the Gold Rush* (Berkeley, CA: University of California Press).

Hale, George Ellery [1924]. *The Depths of the Universe* (New York, NY: Charles Scribner's).

Hale, George Ellery [1926]. *Beyond the Milky Way* (New York, NY: Charles Scribner's).

Hall, Peter [1998]. *Cities in Civilization* (New York, NY: Pantheon).

Hanson, Victor Davis [2003]. *Mexifornia: A State of Becoming* (San Francisco, CA: Encounter Books).

Harrison, Brady [2004]. *Agent of Empire: William Walker and the Imperial Self in American Literature* (Athens, GA: University of Georgia Press).

Harrison, Gilbert A. [1983]. *The Enthusiast: A Life of Thornton Wilder* (New Haven, CT: Ticknor & Fields).

Hawgood, John A. [1958]. "The Pattern of Yankee Infiltration in Mexican Alta California, 1821–1846," *Pacific Historical Review*, 27 (February), 27–37.

Hayes-Bautista, David E. [2004]. *La Nueva California: Latinos in the Golden State* (Berkeley, CA: University of California Press).

Heany, Ed; Shelley Rideout & Katie Wadell [2008]. *Berkeley Bohemia: Artists and Visionaries of the Early 20th Century* (Salt Lake City, UT: Gibbs Smith).

Hegel, G. W. F. [1969]. *Hegel's Science of Logic* (New York: Humanity Books), transl.

Hench, John (with Peggy van Pelt) [2008]. *Designing Disney: Imagineering and the Art of the Show* (New York, NY: Disney Editions).

Herzog, Lawrence A. [1990]. *Where North Meets South: Cities, Space, and Politics on the U.S.-Mexico Border* (Austin, TX: University of Texas Press).

Hine, Robert V. [1992]. *Josiah Royce: From Grass Valley to Harvard* (Norman, OK: University of Oklahoma Press).

Hirsch, Foster [1981]. *The Dark Side of the Screen: Film Noir* (San Diego, CA: A. S. Barnes).

Horkheimer, Max [1974]. *Eclipse of Reason* (New York, NY: Seabury, 1947), transl.

Horkheimer, Max and Theodor W. Adorno [1969]. *Dialektik der Aufklärung: Philosophische Fragmente* (Frankfurt, Fischer, 1944).

Horkheimer, Max and Theodor W. Adorno [2002]. *Dialectic of Enlightenment* (New York, NY: Continuum, 1969), transl.

Howard, Ebenezer [1951]. *Garden Cities of Tomorrow* (London: Faber & Faber. 1945).

Hozic, Aida A. [2001]. *Hollyworld: Space, Power, and Fantasy in the American Economy* (Ithaca, NY: Cornell University Press).

Hughes, H. Stuart [1952]. *Oswald Spengler: A Critical Estimate* (New York, NY: Charles Scribners).

Hughes, H. Stuart [1975]. *The Sea Change: The Migration of Social Thought, 1930–1965* (New York, NY: Harper & Row).

Hundley, Norris, Jr. [2001]. *The Great Thirst: Californians and Water: A History* (Berkeley, CA: University of California Press).

Hunt, Rockwell D. & Nellie Van de Grift Sánchez [1929]. *A Short History of California* (New York, NY: Thomas Crowell).

Huntington, Samuel P. [1996]. *The Clash of Civilizations and the Remaking of World Order* (New York, NY: Simon & Schuster).

Huntington, Samuel P. [2004]. *Who Are We? The Challenges to America's National Identity* (New York, NY: Simon & Schuster).

Israel, Nico [1997]. "Damage Control: Adorno, Los Angeles, and the Dislocation of Culture," *The Yale Journal of Criticism*, 10:1, 85–113.

Janssens, Don Agustín [1963]. *The Life and Adventures in California of Don Agustín Janssens 1834–1856* (San Marino, CA: The Huntington Library), transl. William H. Eillison & Francis Price (eds.).

Jay, Martin [1973]. *The Dialectical Imagination: A History of the Frankfurt School and the Institute of Social Research 1923–1950* (Boston, MA: Little Brown).

Jeffers, Robinson [1956]. *Themes in My Poems* (San Francisco, CA: The Book Club of California).

Jewell, Richard B. [2007]. *The Golden Age of Cinema: Hollywood 1929–1945* (Malden, MA: Blackwell).

THEOLOGY · CHRISTIANITY

"Serious scholars of virtually any dimension of Balthasar's thought cannot afford to be ignorant of this work."
—*The New Ressourcement*

"Lett proves to be a skillful and lucid interpreter of Balthasar's challenging body of work, while remaining focused on the substantial theological issues that are at stake."
—*Theology*

How is it possible for Christ to act in the place of humanity? In *Hans Urs von Balthasar's Theology of Representation*, Jacob Lett broaches this perplexing soteriological question and offers the first book-length analysis of Balthasar's theology of representation (*Stellvertretung*). Lett's study shows how Balthasar rehabilitates the category of representation by developing it in relationship to the central mysteries of the Christian faith: concerned by the lack of metaphysical and theological foundations for understanding the question above, Balthasar ultimately grounds representation in the trinitarian life of God, making "action in the place of the other" central to divine and creaturely being. Lett not only articulates the centrality of representation to Balthasar's theological project but also demonstrates that Balthasar's theology of representation has the potential to reshape discussions in the fields of soteriology, Christology, trinitarian theology, anthropology, and ecclesiology.

This work covers a wide range of themes in Balthasar's theology, including placial and spatial metaphors, a post-Chalcedonian Christology of Christ's two wills, and theories of drama. Lett also considers Balthasar's key interlocutors (Gregory of Nyssa, Maximus, Aquinas, Przywara, Ulrich, Barth) and expands this base to include voices beyond those typically found in Balthasarian scholarship, including Dietrich Bonhoeffer and Dorothee Sölle.

JACOB LETT is a senior lecturer in theology and vice principal of academics at Nazarene Theological College and director of the Manchester Wesley Research Centre.

COVER IMAGE: Mim Friday / Alamy Stock Photo   COVER DESIGN: Bruce Gore | Gore Studio, Inc.

NOTRE DAME PRESS

UNDPRESS.ND.EDU

Johnson, David Alan [1992]. *Founding the Far West: California, Oregon, ana Nevada, 1840–1890* (Berkeley, CA: University of California Press).
Jones, Ernest [1953]. *The Life and Work of Sigmund Freud* (New York, NY: Basic Books), Vol. 1.
Jungk, Peter Stephan [1987]. *Franz Werfel: Eine Lebensgeschichte* (Frankfurt: S. Fischer).
Jungk, Robert [1958]. *Brighter than a Thousand Suns: A Personal History of the Atomic Scientists* (New York, NY: Harcourt, Brace), transl.
Karlstrom, Paul J. (ed.). *On the Edge of America: California Modernist Arts, 1900–1950* (Berkeley, CA: University of California Press).
Klarmann, Adolf D. [1946]. "Franz Werfel's Eschatology and Cosmogony," *Modern Language Quarterly*, 7: 385–410.
Karman, James [1987]. *Robinson Jeffers: Poet of California* (San Francisco, CA: Chronicle Books).
Katz, Barry [1982]. *Herbert Marcuse and the Art of Liberation: An Intellectual Biography* (London: Verso).
Kellner, Douglas [1984]. *Herbert Marcuse and the Crisis of Marxism* (Berkeley, CA: University of California Press).
Kerouac, Jack [1962]. *Big Sur* (New York, NY: Farrar, Straus).
Klingmann, Anna [2007]. *Brandscapes: Architecture in the Experience Economy* (Cambridge, MA: The MIT Press).
Kluger, Richard [2007]. *Seizing Destiny: How America Grew from Sea to Shining Sea* (New York, NY: Alfred A. Knopf).
Kniesche, Thomas W. (ed.) [1995]. *Körper/Kultur: Kalifornische Studien zur deutschen Moderne* (Würzburg: Königshausen & Neumann).
Kohner, Frederick [2001]. *Gidget* (New York, NY: Berkley Books, 1957).
Kotkin, Joel & Paul Grabowicz [1982]. *California, Inc.* (New York, NY: Avon).
Koyré, Alexandre [1957]. *From the Closed World to the Infinite Universe* (Baltimore, MD: The Johns Hopkins University Press).
Kripal, Jeffrey J. [2007]. *Esalen: America and the Religion of No Religion* (Chicago, IL: University of Chicago Press).
Kroeber, Theodora [1961]. *Ishi in Two Worlds: A Biography of the Last Wila Indian in North America* (Berkeley, CA: University of California Press).
Kuklick, Bruce [1972]. *Josiah Royce: An Intellectual Biography* (Indianapolis, IN: The Bobbs-Merrill Co.).
Kuklick, Bruce [1977]. *The Rise of American Philosophy: Cambridge, Massachusetts 1860–1930* (New Haven, CT: Yale University Press).
Kunneman, Harry & Hent de Vries (eds.) [1989]. *Die Aktuälitat der 'Dialektik der Aufklärung'* (Frankfurt: Campus).

Landauer, Susan [1996]. *The San Francisco School of Abstract Expressionism* (Berkeley, CA: University of California Press).
Langley, Lester [1988]. *MexAmerica, Two Countries, One Future* (New York, NY: Crown).
Lansing, Richard [1994]. "Narrative Design in Dante's Earthly Paradise," *Dante Studies*, 112: 101–113.
Laurel, Brenda [1993]. *Computers as Theatre* (Reading, MA: Addison-Wesley).
Leighly, John [1972]. *California as an Island: An Illustrated Essay* (San Francisco, CA: Book Club of California).
León-Portilla, Miguel [1985]. *Hernán Cortés y la Mar del Sur* (Madrid: Ediciones Cultura Hispanica, Instituto de Coopercicion Iberoamericana).
Leonard, George [1988]. *Walking on the Edge of the World: A Memoir of the Sixties* (Boston, MA: Houghton Mifflin).
Levi, Primo [1958]. *Se questo è un uomo* (Turin, Italy: Einaudi).
Little, William T. [1987]. "Spain's Fantastic Vision and the Mythic Creation of California," *The California Geographer*, 27: 1–38.
Look [1966], "California (28 June 1966)."
Lorenzo, Ramón (ed.) [1985]. *Crónica Troiana: Introdución e Texto* (Coruña, Spain: Real Academia Galega).
Los Angeles Times [2009]. "California is Free Vibrant and Diverse: Interview with Kevin Starr (28 July 2009)."
Los Angeles Times [2010]. "Native-born Californians regain Majority Status" (1 April 2010)."
Lowenthal, Abraham F. [2009]. *Global California: Rising to the Cosmopolitan Challenge* (Stanford, CA: Stanford University Press).
Lowenthal, Abraham F. & Katarine Burgess (eds.) [1993]. *The California-Mexico Connection* (Stanford, CA: Stanford University Press).
Lutyens, Mary [1975]. *Krishnamurti: The Years of Awakening* (New York, NY: Farrar, Straus & Giroux).
Lutyens, Mary [1983]. *Krishnamurti: The Years of Fulfillment* (New York, NY: Farrar, Straus & Giroux).
Lutz, E. G. [1998]. *Animated Cartoons: How They are Made, their Origin and Development* (Bedford, MA: Applewood Books, 1920).
Lyman, Edward Leo [1986]. *Political Deliverance: The Mormon Quest for Utah Statehood* (Urbana, IL: University of Illinois Press).
McClure, Michael [1963]. *Meat Science Essays* (San Francisco, CA: City Lights Books).
McClure, Michael [1991]. *Rebel Lions* (San Francisco, CA: New Directions).
McClure, Michael [1993]. *Lighting the Corners: On Art, Nature, and the Visionary – Essays and Interviews* (Albuquerque, NM: University of New Mexico Press).

McClure, Michael [1999]. *Touching the Edge: Dharma Devotions from the Hummingbird Sangha* (Boston, MA: Shambhala).

McPhee, John [1993]. *Assembling California* (New York, NY: Farrar, Straus and Giroux).

McWilliams, Cary [1949]. *California: The Great Exception* (Westport, CT: Greenwood).

McWilliams, Cary [1973]. *Southern California: An Island on the Land* (Salt Lake City, UT: Peregrin Smith, 1946).

Macey, David [1995]. *The Lives of Michel Foucault: A Biography* (New York, NY: Vintage, 1993).

Mahler-Werfel, Alma [1960]. *Mein Leben* (Frankfurt: S. Fischer Verlag).

Malloy, William M. (ed.) [1910]. *Treaties, Conventions, International Acts, Protocols and Agreements between the United States of America and Other Powers 1776–1909* (Washington, DC: Government Printing Office, 1910). Volume 1.

Mann, Thomas [1948a]. *Doktor Faustus: Das Leben des deutschen Tonsetzers Adrian Leverkühn, Erzählt von einem Freunde* (Stockholm: Bermann-Fischer).

Mann, Thomas [1948b]. *Doctor Faustus: The Life of the German Composer Adrian Leverkühn* (New York, NY: Alfred A. Knopf), H. T. Lowe-Porter (transl.).

Mann, Thomas [1961]. *The Story of a Novel: The Genesis of Doctor Faustus* (New York, NY: Alfred A. Knopf, 1949), transl.

Mann, Thomas [1992]. *Selbstkommentare: 'Doktor Faustus' und 'Die Entstehung des Doktor Faustus'* (Frankfurt: Fischer), Hans Wyling (ed.).

Mannheim, Steve [2002]. *Walt Disney and the Quest for Community* (Aldershot, UK: Ashgate).

Marcuse, Herbert [1961]. *Eros and Civilization: A Philosophical Inquiry into Freud* (New York, NY: Vintage, 1955).

Marcuse, Herbert [1964]. *One-Dimensional Man: Studies in the Ideology of Advanced Industrial Society* (Boston, MA: Beacon).

Marcuse, Herbert [1969]. *An Essay on Liberation* (Harmondsworth, UK: Penguin).

Marcuse, Herbert [1972]. *Counterrevolution and Revolt* (Boston, MA: Beacon).

Marcuse, Herbert [1978]. *The Aesthetic Dimension: Toward a Critique of Marxist Aesthetics* (Boston, MA: Beacon).

Marcuse, Herbert [2005]. *The New Left and the 1960s: Collected Papers of Herbert Marcuse* (London: Routledge), Douglas Kellner (ed.), Vol. 3.

Marcuse, Herbert [2007]. *Art and Liberation: Collected Papers of Herbert Marcuse* (London: Routledge), Douglas Kellner (ed.), Vol. 4.

Marks, Richard Lee [1993]. *Cortés: The Great Adventurer and the Fate of Aztec Mexico* (New York, NY: Afred A. Knopf).
Marling, Karal Ann (ed.) [1997]. *Designing Disney's Theme Parks: The Architecture of Reassurance* (Montreal, CA: Canadian Centre for Architecture).
Marx, Karl & Friedrich Engels [1975 -]. *Marx-Engels Gesamtausgabe* [MEGA] (Berlin: Dietz, 1975 -).
Masciandaro, Franco [1991]. *Dante as Dramatist: The Myth of the Earthly Paradise and Tragic Vision in the* Divine Comedy (Philadelphia, PA: University of Pennsylvania Press).
May, Robert E. [1973]. *The Southern Dream of a Caribbean Empire, 1854–1861* (Baton Rouge; LA: Louisiana State University Press).
Miller, Daisy Disney (as told to Pete Martin) [1957]. *The Story of Walt Disney* (New York, NY: Henry Holt & Co.).
Miller, Henry [1957]. *Big Sur and the Oranges of Hieronymous Bosch* (New York, NY: New Directions).
Miller, Henry [1965]. *The Air-Conditioned Nightmare* (London: Panther, 1945).
Miller, Hunter (ed.) [1933]. *Treaties and Other International Acts of the United States of America* (Washington, DC: United States Government Printing Office, 1933), Volume 3 (Documents 41–79: 1819–35).
Miller, James [1993]. *The Passion of Michel Foucault* (New York, NY: Simon & Schuster).
Miller, Robert Ryal [1998]. *Juan Alvarado, Governor of California, 1836–1842* (Norman, OK: University of Oklahoma Press).
Milner, Clyde A., II; Carol A. O'Connor & Martha A. Sandweiss (eds.) [1994]. *The Oxford History of the American West* (New York, NY: Oxford University Press).
Moehring, Eugene [2000]. *Resort City in the Sunbelt: Las Vegas, 1930–2000* (Reno, NV: University of Nevada Press), 2nd ed.
Montalvo, Garci Rodríquez de [1988]. *Amadís de Gaula* (Madrid: Catedra). Juan Manuel Cacho Blecua (ed.). Vol. II (Books III & IV).
Montalvo, Garci Rodríquez de [1991]. *Amadís de Gaula* (Madrid: Catedra). Juan Manuel Cacho Belcua (ed.). Vol. I (Books I & II).
Montalvo, Garci Rodríguez de [1992]. *The Labors of the Very Brave Knight Esplandián* (Binghamton, NY: State University of New York at Binghamton). William Thomas Little (transl. & commentator).
Montalvo, Garcí Rodriquez de [2003]. *Sergas de Esplandián* (Madrid: Editorial Castalia). Carlos Sainz de la Maza (ed.).
Montalvo, Garci Rodríguez de [2004]. *Amadis de Gaule* (Aldershot, UK: Ashgate), Helen Moore (ed.), transl.
Montero Garrido, Cruz [1994–1995]. *La Historia, Creación Literaria: El Ejemplo del Cuatrocientos* (Madrid: Universidad Autónoma de Madrid).

Morley, Sheridan [1983]. *Tales from the Hollywood Raj: The British Colony on Screen and Off* (London: Weidenfeld & Nicolson).
Morrden, Ethan [1988]. *The Hollywood Studios: House Style in the Golden Age of the Movies* (New York, NY: Alfred A. Knopf).
Moynihan, Elizabeth B. [1979]. *Paradise as a Garden in Persia and Mughal India* (London: Scolar Press).
Muir, John [1961]. *The Mountains of California* (Garden City, NY: Anchor Books).
Muir, John [1962]. *The Yosemite* (Garden City, NY: Anchor Books).
Mumford, Lewis [1961]. The *City in History: Its Origins, Its Transformation, and its Prospects* (Harmondsworth, UK: Penguin).
Myers, Dowell; John Pitkin & Ricardo Ramirez et al. [2009]. *The New Homegrown Majority in California: Recognizing the New Reality of Growing Commitment to the Golden State* (Los Angeles, CA: Center for the Continuing Study of the California Economy, University of Southern California).
Nash, Gerald D. [1999]. *The Federal Landscape: An Economic History of the Twentieth-Century West* (Tucson, AZ: University of Arizona Press).
Newsweek [2003]. "California (28 July 2003)."
Nietzsche, Friedrich [1966]. *Werke in drei Bänden* (Munich: Carl Haners), Karl Schlechta (ed.), 3 vols.
Osio, Antonio María [1996]. *The History of Alta California: A Memoir of Mexican California* (Madison, WI: University of Wisconsin Press), transl.
Palmier, Jean-Michel [2006]. *Weimar in Exile: The Antifascist Emigration in Europe and America* (London: Verso [1987]), transl.
Parker, Kelvin M. (ed.) [1975]. *Historia Troyana* (Santiago de Compostela, Spain: Instituto P. Sarmiento de Estudios Gallegos).
Parry, J. H. [1981]. *The Discovery of the Sea* (Berkeley, CA: University of California Press).
Peeters, Benoit [2012]. *Derrida: A Biography* (London: Polity), transl.
Pez, Felipe L. & David Runsten [2003], *Mixtecs and Zapotecs Working in California: Rural and Urban Experiences* (North American Integration and Development Center, UCLA, paper).
Phoenix, Charles [2001]. *Southern California in the '50s: Sun-Fun-Fantasy* (Santa Monica, CA: Angel City Press).
Pico, Pio [1973]. *Don Pio Pico's Historical Narrative* (Glendale, CA: A. H. Clark Co.), transl.
Pierce, Frank [1976]. *Amadís de Gaula* (Boston, MA: Twayne).
Pine, Joseph B., II & James H. Gilmore [1999]. *The Experience Economy: Work is Theatre and Every Business a Stage* (Boston, MA: Harvard Business School Press).

Pitt, Leonard [1966]. *The Decline of the Californios: A Social History of the Spanish-speaking Californians, 1846–1890* (Berkeley, CA: University of California Press).

Plamper, Jan [2010]. "The History of Emotions: An Interview with William Reddy, Barbara Rosenwein, and Peter Stearns," *History and Theory*, 49 (May), 237–265.

Polk, Dora Beale [1991]. *The Island of California: A History of the Myth* (Spokane, WA: Arthur H. Clark).

Pomeroy, Earl [1968]. *The Pacific Slope: A History of California, Oregon, Washington, Idaho, Utah, and Nevada* (New York, NY: Alfred A. Knopf).

Pomeroy, Earl [2008]. *The American Far West in the Twentieth Century* (New Haven, CT: Yale University Press).

Poole, Sarah [2004]. *The Changing Face of Mexican Migrants in California: Oaxacan Mixtecs and Zapotecs in Perspective* (Center for Latin American Studies, San Diego State University, and Trans Border Institute, University of San Diego).

Postrel, Virginia [2003]. *The Substance of Style: How the Rise of Aesthetic Value is Remaking Commerce, Culture, and Consciousness* (New York, NY: HarperCollins).

Potton, Jean-François [2007]. *Barbé-Marbois: La justice et les comptes* (Paris: Éditons Michalon).

Powdermaker, Hortense [1950]. *Hollywood, The Dream Factory: An Anthropologist Looks at the Movie Makers* (Boston, MA: Little, Brown & Co.).

Powell, Jason [2006]. *Jacques Derrida: A Biography* (London: Continuum).

Raab, L. Mark & Terry L. Jones (eds.). *Prehistoric California: Archaeology and the Myth of Paradise* (Salt Lake City, UT: University of Utah Press).

Rabinbach, Anson [1997]. *In the Shadow of Catastrophe: German Intellectuals between Apocalypse and Enlightenment* (Berkeley, CA: University of California Press).

Rawls, John J. & Richard J. Orsi (eds.). [1999]. *A Golden State: Mining and Economic Development in Gold Rush California* (Berkeley, CA: University of California Press).

Repcheck, Jack [2007]. *Copernicus' Secret: How the Scientific Revolution Began* (New York, NY: Simon & Schuster).

Richardson, Robert D., Jr. [1995]. *Emerson: The Mind on Fire: A Biography* (Berkeley, CA: University of California Press).

Rickels, Laurence A. [1991]. *The Case of California* (Baltimore, MD: The Johns Hopkins University Press).

Robinson, Forrest G. [2007]. "An Interview with Kevin Starr," *Rethinking History*, 11:1 (1 March), 11–30.

Roff, Sarah [1997]. "Review of Kniesche (ed.)," in *MLN*, 112:3, 486–491.

Ronell, Avital [2008]. *The Überreader: Selected Works of Avital Ronell* (Urbana, IL: University of Illinois Press).

Ronsard, Pierre de [2010]. *The Franciad (1572)* (New York, NY: AMS Press).

Ross, Joseph E. [1989]. *Krotona of Old Hollywood, 1866–1913* (Montecito, CA: El Montecito Oaks Press), Vol. 1.

Ross, Joseph E. [2004]. *Krotona of Old Hollywood, 1914–1920* (Ojai, CA: Ross), Vol. 2.

Rosten, Leo C. [1941]. *Hollywood: The Movie Colony, The Movie Makers* (New York, NY: Harcourt, Brace & Co.).

Rothman, Hal [2002]. *Neon Metropolis: How Las Vegas Started the Twenty-First Century* (New York, NY: Routledge).

Royce, Josiah [1887]. *The Feud of Oakfield Creek: A Novel of California Life* (Boston, MA: Houghton, Mifflin & Co.).

Royce, Josiah [1893]. *The Spirit of Modern Philosophy: An Essay in the Form of Lectures* (Boston, MA: Riverside Press).

Royce, Josiah [1908]. *Race Questions, Provincialism and Other American Problems* (New York, New York, NY: Macmillan).

Royce, Josiah [1920]. *Fugitive Essays* (Cambridge, MA: Harvard University Press).

Royce, Josiah [1958]. *The Religious Aspect of Philosophy: A Critique of the Bases of Conduct and of Faith* (New York, NY: Harper Torchbook [1885]).

Royce, Josiah [1959]. *The World and the Individual*, Second Series (New York, NY: Dover [1901]).

Royce, Josiah [1964]. *Lectures on Modern Idealism* (New Haven, CT: Yale University Press [1919]).

Royce, Josiah [1969]. *The Basic Writings of Josiah Royce* (Chicago, IL: University of Chicago Press). John J. McDermott (ed.). 2 vols.

Royce, Josiah [1970a]. *California From the Conquest of 1846 to the Second Vigilante Committee in San Francisco: A Study of American Character* (Santa Barbara, CA: Peregrine [1886]).

Royce, Josiah [1970b]. *The Letters of Josiah Royce* (Chicago, IL: University of Chicago Press), John Clendenning (ed.).

Royce, Josiah [2001]. *The Problem of Christianity* (Washington, DC: The Catholic University of America Press [1913]). Frank M. Oppenheim (ed.).

Sackman, Douglas Casaux [2007]. *Orange Empire: California and the Fruits of Eden* (Berkeley, CA: University of California Press).

Sales Dasí, Emilio J. [1998]. "California, Las Amazonas y la Tradición Troyana," *Revista de Literatura Medieval*, 10: 147–167.

Samaniego López, Marco Antonio (ed.) [2006]. *Breve Historia de Baja California* (Mexicali, Mexico: Universidad Autónoma de Baja California).
San Francisco Chronicle [2010]. "California Leads Nation in Green Tech" (7 October 2010).
San Francisco Chronicle [2012]. "Study: Sierra Nevada adds 1–2 mm Elevation a Year" (6 May 2012).
Santayana, George [1967]. *The Genteel Tradition: Nine Essays* (Cambridge, MA: Harvard University Press).
Saxenian, AnnaLee [2006]. *The New Argonauts: Regional Advantage in a Global Economy* (Cambridge, MA: Harvard University Press).
Schatz, Thomas [1988]. *The Genius of the System: Hollywood Filmmaking in the Studio Era* (New York, NY: Pantheon).
Schmitt, Bernd & Alex Simonson [1997]. *Marketing Aesthetics: The Strategic Management of Brands, Identity and Image* (New York, NY: The Free Press).
Schmitt, Bernd; David L. Rogers & Karen Vrotsos [2004]. *There's No Business That's Not Show Business: Marketing in an Experience Culture* (Upper Saddle River, NJ: Prentice Hall).
Schoenberg, Allan A. [1992]. *A Natural History of California* (Berkeley, CA: University of California Press).
Schou, Nicholas [2010]. *Orange Sunshine: The Brotherhood of Eternal Love and its Quest to Spread Peace, Love, and Acid to the World* (New York, NY: Thomas Dunne Books).
Schrage, Michael [2000]. *Serious Play: How the World's Best Companies Simulate to Innovate* (Cambridge, MA: Harvard Business School Press).
Scott, Alan J. [2005]. *On Hollywood: The Place, The Industry* (Princeton, NJ: Princeton University Press).
Sheridan, Thomas E. [1995]. *Arizona: A History* (Tucson, AZ: University of Arizona Press).
Singleton, Charles S. [1977]. *Journey to Beatrice* (Baltimore, MD: The Johns Hopkins Press, 1958).
Smith, Matthew Wilson [2007]. *The Total Work of Art: From Bayreuth to Cyberspace* (London: Routledge).
Sokol, A. E. [1949]. "California: A Possible Derivation of the Name," *California Historical Society Quarterly*, 28:1, 23–30.
Spicer, Edward H. [1962]. *Cycles of Conquest: The Impact of Spain, Mexico, and the United States on the Indians of the Southwest, 1533–1960* (Tucson, AZ: University of Arizona Press).
Starn, Orin [2004]. *Ishi's Brain: In Search of America's Last 'Wild' Indian* (New York, NY: Norton).

Starr, Kevin [1973]. *Americans and the California Dream, 1850–1915* (New York, NY: Oxford University Press).
Starr, Kevin [1985]. *Inventing the Dream: California Through the Progressive Era* (New York, NY: Oxford University Press).
Starr, Kevin [1990]. *Material Dreams: Southern California Through the 1920s* (New York, NY: Oxford University Press).
Starr, Kevin [1996]. *Endangered Dreams: The Great Depression* (New York, NY: Oxford University Press).
Starr, Kevin [1997]. *The Dream Endures: California Enters the 1940s* (New York, NY: Oxford University Press).
Starr, Kevin [2002]. *Embattled Dreams: California in War and Peace 1940–1950* (New York, NY: Oxford University Press).
Starr, Kevin [2004]. *Coast of Dreams: California on the Edge, 1990–2003* (New York, NY: Knopf).
Starr, Kevin [2005a]. *California: A History* (New York, NY: Modern Library).
Starr, Kevin [2005b]. "Schwarzenegger has his Head Examined: An Intellectual Biography of our Governor (27 March 2005)," *Los Angeles Times*.
Starr, Kevin [2009]. *Golden Dreams: California in an Age of Abundance 1950–1963* (New York, NY: Oxford University Press).
Starr, Kevin [2010]. *Golden Gate: The Life and Times of America's Greatest Bridge* (New York, NY: Bloomsbury).
State of California [2007]. *Population Projections for California and its Counties 2000–2050* (Sacramento, CA: Department of Finance), July.
Steiman, Lionel B. [1985]. *Franz Werfel, The Faith of an Exile: From Prague to Beverly Hills* (Waterloo, Canada: Wilfred Laurier University Press).
Steinhauer, Jennifer [2009]. "Pinch of Reality Threatens the California Dream (21 July 2009)," *New York Times*.
Taylor, John Russell]1093]. *Stranger in Paradise: The Hollywood Emigrés, 1933–1950* (New York, NY: Holt, Rinehart & Winston).
Tays, George [1932]. *Revolutionary California: The Political History of the Mexican Period, 1822–1846*. University of California, Berkeley, Ph. D. dissertation.
Teece, David J. [2009]. *Dynamic Capabilities and Strategic Management: Organizing for Innovation and Growth* (Oxford: Oxford University Press).
Thomas, Bob [1998]. *Building a Company: Roy O. Disney and the Creation of an Entertainment Empire* (New York, NY: Hyperion).
Thomas, Hugh [1993]. *Conquest: Montezuma, Cortés, and the Fall of Old Mexico* (New York, NY: Simon and Schuster).
Time [1969]. "California: A State of Excitement (7 November 1969)."
Time [1991]. "California: The Endangered Dream (18 November 1991)."

Time [2009]. "Why California is Still America's Future (And That's a Good Thing Too) (23 October)" (Michael Grunwald).
Torres Lanzas, Pedro [1900]. *Relación descriptiva de los mapas, planos, &, de México y Floridas existentes en el Archivo General de Indias* (Sevilla, Spain: Imp. de El Mercantil), Vol. 1.
Trapp, Kenneth R. (ed.). *The Arts and Crafts Movement in California* (Oakland, CA: The Oakland Museum).
Wagoner, Jay J. [1975]. *Early Arizona: Prehistory to Civil War* (Tucson, AZ: University of Arizona Press).
Walt Disney Family Museum [2000]. "Walt: The Man behind the Myth" (DVD).
Walt Disney Treasures [2001]. "The Disneyland Story" [1954] (film/video).
Warner, Charles Dudley [1891]. *Our Italy* (New York, NY: Harper & Bros.).
Watts, Steven [1997]. *The Magic Kingdom: Walt Disney and the American Way of Life* (Boston, MA: Houghton Mifflin).
Weber, David J. [1988]. *Myth and the History of the Hispanic Southwest: Essays by David J. Weber* (Albuquerque, NM: University of New Mexico Press).
Werfel, Alma Mahler (with E. B. Ashton) [1958]. *And the Bridge is Love* (New York, NY: Harcourt, Brace & Co.).
Werfel, Franz [1910–1944]. Franz Werfel, Papers, 1910–1944. University of California, Los Angeles, Department of Special Collections, Collection 512.
Werfel, Franz [1946a]. *Star of the Unborn* (New York, NY: Viking), transl.
Werfel, Franz [1946b]. *Stern der Ungeborenen: Ein Reiseroman* (Stockholm: Bermann-Fischer Verlag).
West, Nathaniel [1962]. *Miss Lonelyhearts & The Day of the Locust* (New York, NY: New Directions).
Whitaker, Peter [1985]. *Brecht's Poetry; A Critical Study* (Oxford: Clarendon).
White, Richard [1991]. *"It's Your Misfortune and None of My Own": A History of the American West* (Norman, OK: University of Oklahoma Press).
Whitley, David [2008]. *The Idea of Nature in Disney Animation* (Aldershot, UK: Ashgate).
Wiggershaus, Rolf [1986]. *Die Frankfurter Schule: Geschichte, Theoretische Entwicklung, Politische Bedeutung* (Munich: Carl Hanser).
Wiley, Peter & Robert Gottlieb [1982]. *Empires in the Sun: The Rise of the New American West* (New York, NY: G. P. Putnam's Sons).
Wilson, E. Dotson & Brian S. Ebbert (eds.) [2000]. *California's Legislature* (Sacramento, CA: California State Assembly).
Wright, Helen [1994]. *Explorer of the Universe: A Biography of George Ellery Hale* (Woodbury, NY: American Institute of Physics Press, 1966).
Yates, Frances A. [1975]. *Astraea: The Imperial theme in the Sixteenth Century* (London: Routledge & Kegan Paul).

Zhang, Junfu & Nikesh Patel [2005]. *The Dynamics of California's Biotechnology Industry* (San Francisco, CA: Public Policy Institute of California).

www.ingramcontent.com/pod-product-compliance
Lightning Source LLC
Chambersburg PA
CBHW061444300426
44114CB00014B/1831